THE
LANGUAGE
OF
LETTING
GO

HARPER/HAZELDEN TITLES OF RELATED INTEREST

Codependent No More, Melody Beattie

Beyond Codependency, Melody Beattie

Each Day a New Beginning: Daily Meditations for Women

Touchstones: A Book of Daily Meditations for Men

*Days of Healing, Days of Joy: Daily Meditations
for Adult Children*

Worthy of Love: Meditations on Loving Ourselves and Others

*Answers in the Heart: Daily Meditations for Men and Women
Recovering from Sex Addiction*

THE
LANGUAGE
OF
LETTING
GO

DAILY MEDITATIONS
FOR CODEPENDENTS

MELODY BEATTIE

A Hazelden Book
HarperCollins*Publishers*

THE LANGUAGE OF LETTING GO: *Daily Meditations for Codependents.*
Copyright © 1990 by the Hazelden Foundation. This edition
published by arrangement with the Hazelden Foundation. All
rights reserved. Printed in the United States of America. No part
of this book may be used or reproduced in any manner what-
soever without written permission except in the case of
brief quotations embodied in critical articles and reviews. For
information address HarperCollins Publishers, 10 East 53rd
Street, New York, NY 10022.

FIRST HARPERCOLLINS EDITION PUBLISHED IN 1990.

Library of Congress Cataloging-in-Publication Data

Beattie, Melody.
    The language of letting go: daily meditations for codependents
 / Melody Beattie and Scott Egleston.
        p.   cm.
    "A Harper/Hazelden book."
    ISBN 0-06-255389-5
    1. Codependents—Prayer-books and devotions—English.
    1. Egleston, Scott.   II. Title.
    BV4596.C57B4   1990
    616.86—dc20   89-84787
                                                    CIP

94 95 96 97 98 BANTA 23 22 21 20

This edition is printed on acid-free paper that meets the American
National Standards Institute Z39.48 Standard.

DEDICATION

For her help in writing this book, I acknowledge and thank Rebecca Post, my editor at Hazelden.

This book is dedicated to

God

The readers of *Codependent No More*

and *Beyond Codependency*

And my friend, Louie

INTRODUCTION

This is a book of meditations. It is designed to help you spend a few moments each day remembering what you know.

I have touched on principles from *Codependent No More* and *Beyond Codependency.* I've also included some new thoughts and ideas.

It is a book to help you feel good and assist you in the process of self-care and recovery.

Thanks for the support, encouragement, and success you've given me. I hope I have given you a gift in return too.

Melody

January

Make New Year's goals. Dig within, and discover what you would like to have happen in your life this year. This helps you do your part. It is an affirmation that you're interested in fully living life in the year to come.

Goals give us direction. They put a powerful force into play on a universal, conscious, and subconscious level.

Goals give our life direction.

What would you like to have happen in your life this year? What would you like to do, to accomplish? What good would you like to attract into your life? What particular areas of growth would you like to have happen to you? What blocks, or character defects, would you like to have removed?

What would you like to attain? Little things and big things? Where would you like to go? What would you like to have happen in friendship and love? What would you like to have happen in your family life?

Remember, we aren't controlling others with our goals — we are trying to give direction to *our* life.

What problems would you like to see solved? What decisions would you like to make? What would you like to happen in your career?

What would you like to see happen inside and around you?

Write it down. Take a piece of paper, a few hours of your time, and write it all down — as an affirmation of you, your life, and your ability to choose. Then let it go.

Certainly, things happen that are out of our control. Sometimes, these events are pleasant surprises; sometimes, they are of another nature. But they are all part of the chapter that will be this year in our life and will lead us forward in the story.

The new year stands before us, like a chapter in a book, waiting to be written. We can help write that story by setting goals.

Today, I will remember that there is a powerful force motivated by writing down goals. I will do that now, for the year to come, and regularly as needed. I will do it not to control but to do my part in living my life.

Healthy Limits   January 2

Boundaries are vital to recovery. Having and setting healthy limits is connected to all phases of recovery: growing in self-esteem, dealing with feelings, and learning to really love and value ourselves.

Boundaries emerge from deep within. They are connected to letting go of guilt and shame, and to changing our beliefs about what we deserve. As our thinking about this becomes clearer, so will our boundaries.

Boundaries are also connected to a Higher Timing than our own. We'll set a limit when we're ready, and not a moment before. So will others.

There's something magical about reaching that point of becoming ready to set a limit. We know we mean what we say; others take us seriously too. Things change, not because we're controlling others, but because we've changed.

Today, I will trust that I will learn, grow, and set the limits I need in my life at my own pace. This timing need only be right for me.

Nurturing Self-Care   January 3

. . .there isn't a guidebook for setting boundaries. Each of us has our own guide inside ourselves. If we continue to work at recovery, our boundaries will develop. They will get healthy

*and sensitive. Our selves will tell us what we need to know,
and we'll love ourselves enough to listen.*

— Beyond Codependency

What do we need to do to take care of ourselves?

Listen to that voice inside. What makes you angry? What have you had enough of? What don't you trust? What doesn't feel right? What can't you stand? What makes you uncomfortable? What do you want? Need? What don't you want and need? What do you like? What would feel good?

In recovery, we learn that self-care leads us on the path to God's will and plan for our life. Self-care never leads away from our highest good; it leads toward it.

Learn to nurture that voice inside. We can trust ourselves. We can take care of ourselves. We are wiser than we think. Our guide is within, ever-present. Listen to, trust, and nurture that guide.

Today, I will affirm that I am a gift to myself and the Universe. I will remember that nurturing self-care delivers that gift in its highest form.

Separating from Family Issues   January 4

We can draw a healthy line, a healthy boundary, between ourselves and our nuclear family. We can separate ourselves from their issues.

Some of us may have family members who are addicted to alcohol and other drugs and who are not in recovery from their addiction.

Some of us may have family members who have unresolved codependency issues. Family members may be addicted to misery, pain, suffering, martyrdom, and victimization.

We may have family members who have unresolved abuse issues or unresolved family of origin issues.

We may have family members who are addicted to work, eating, or sex. Our family may be completely enmeshed, or we may have a disconnected family in which the members have little contact.

We may be like our family. We may love our family. But we are separate human beings with individual rights and issues. One of our primary rights is to begin feeling better and recovering, whether or not others in the family choose to do the same.

We do not have to feel guilty about finding happiness and a life that works. And we do not have to take on our family's issues as our own to be loyal and to show we love them.

Often when we begin taking care of ourselves, family members will reverberate with overt and covert attempts to pull us back into the old system and roles. We do not have to go. Their attempts to pull us back are their issues. Taking care of ourselves and becoming healthy and happy does not mean we do not love them. It means we're addressing our issues.

We do not have to judge them because they have issues; nor do we have to allow them to do anything they would like to us just because they are family.

We are free now, free to take care of ourselves with family members. Our freedom starts when we stop denying their issues, and politely, but assertively, hand their stuff back to them — where it belongs — and deal with our own issues.

Today, I will separate myself from family members. I am a separate human being, even though I belong to a unit called a family. I have a right to my own issues and growth; my family members have a right to their issues and a right to choose where and when they will deal with these issues. I can learn to detach in love from my family members and their issues. I am willing to work through all necessary feelings in order to accomplish this.

Some of us have felt so alienated that we've forgotten we're not alone. We've come to believe that we have to do it ourselves. Some of us have been abandoned. Some have gone without love. Some of us have gotten used to people never being there for us. Some of us have struggled, had hard lessons to learn.

God's there, always ready to help. There is an ample supply of people to care about us too. We will, if we want it, receive love and support, comfort and nurturing. If we take the risk to ask for it, help is there. We can draw on the strength of our recovery group and allow ourselves to be helped and supported by our Higher Power. Friends will come, good friends.

We aren't alone. *And we don't have to do it ourselves.* We're not *doing it ourselves.* There is no shortage of love. Not anymore.

Today, God, help me let go of my need to do it alone and my belief that I am alone. Help me tap into Your Divine Power and Presence, and Your resources for love, support, and friendship. Open my eyes and heart so I can see the love, help, and support that's there for me. Help me know I am loved.

Relationships   **January 6**

If we are unhappy without a relationship, we'll probably be unhappy with one as well. A relationship doesn't begin our life; a relationship doesn't become our life. A relationship is a continuation of life.

— Beyond Codependency

Relationships are the blessing and bane of recovery. Relationships are where we take our recovery show on the road.

Each day, we are faced with the prospect of functioning in several different relationships. Sometimes, we choose these relationships; sometimes, we don't. The one choice we usually have in our relationships concerns our own behavior. In recovery from codependency, our goal is to behave in ways that demonstrate responsibility for ourselves.

We're learning to acknowledge our power to take care of ourselves in our relationships. We're learning to be intimate with people when possible.

Do we need to detach from someone who we've been trying to control? Is there someone we need to talk to, even though what we have to say may be uncomfortable? Is there someone we've been avoiding because we're afraid to take care of ourselves with that person? Do we need to make an amend? Is there someone we need to reach out to, or show love?

Recovery is not done apart from our relationships. Recovery is done by learning to own *our* power and to take care of ourselves in relationships.

Today, I will participate in my relationships to the best of my ability. I will make myself available for closeness and sharing with people I trust. I will ask for what I need and give what feels right.

Dealing with Painful Feelings   January 7

Feelings of hurt or anger can be some of the most difficult to face. We can feel so vulnerable, frightened, and powerless when these feelings appear. And these feelings may trigger memories of other, similar times when we felt powerless.

Sometimes, to gain a sense of control, we may punish the people around us, whether they are people we blame for these feelings or innocent bystanders. We may try to "get even," or we may manipulate behind people's backs to gain a sense of power over the situation.

These actions may give us a temporary feeling of satisfaction, but they only postpone facing our pain.

Feeling hurt does not have to be so frightening. We do not have to work so hard to avoid it. While hurt feelings aren't as much fun as feeling happy, they are, still, just feelings.

We can surrender to them, feel them, and go on. That does not mean we have to seek out hurt feelings or dwell unnecessarily on them. Emotional pain does not have to devastate us. We can sit still, feel the pain, figure out if there's something we need to do to take care of ourselves, and then go on with our life.

We do not have to act in haste; we do not have to punish others to get control over our feelings. We can begin sharing our hurt feelings with others. That brings relief and often healing to them and to us.

Eventually, we learn the lesson that real power comes from allowing ourselves to be vulnerable enough to feel hurt. Real power comes from knowing we can take care of ourselves, even when we feel emotional pain. Real power comes when we stop holding others responsible for our pain, and we take responsibility for all our feelings.

Today, I will surrender to my feelings, even the emotionally painful ones. Instead of acting in haste, or attempting to punish someone, I will be vulnerable enough to feel my feelings.

Vulnerability   **January 8**

Some of us may have made a decision that no one was ever going to hurt us again. We may automatically go on "feelings freeze mode" when faced with emotional pain. Or, we may terminate a relationship the first time we feel hurt.

Hurt feelings are a part of life, relationships, and recovery.

It is understandable that we don't want to feel any more pain. Many of us have had more than our share. In fact, at some time in our life, we may have been overwhelmed, crushed, or stopped in our tracks by the amount of pain we felt. We may not have had the resources to cope with our pain or take care of ourselves.

That was yesterday. Today, we don't have to be so frightened of pain. It does not have to overwhelm us. We are becoming strong enough to deal with hurt feelings. And we don't have to become martyrs, claiming that hurt feelings and suffering are all there is to life.

We need only allow ourselves to feel vulnerable enough to feel hurt, when that's appropriate, and take responsibility for our feelings, behaviors, and what we need to do to take care of ourselves. We don't have to analyze or justify our feelings. We need to feel them, and try not to let them control our behavior.

Maybe our pain is showing us we need to set a boundary; maybe it's showing us we're going in a wrong direction; maybe it's triggering a deep healing process.

It's okay to feel hurt; it's okay to cry; it's okay to heal; it's okay to move on to the next feeling, when it's time. Our willingness and capacity to feel hurt will eventually be matched by our willingness and capacity to feel joy.

Being in recovery does not mean immunity from pain; it means learning to take loving care of ourselves when we are in pain.

Today, I will not strike out at those who cause me pain. I will feel my emotions and take responsibility for them. I will accept hurt feelings as part of being in relationships. I am willing to surrender to the pain as well as the joy in life.

We have been doing the wrong things for the right reasons.
                                        — Codependent No More

Caretaking: the act of taking responsibility for other people while neglecting responsibility for ourselves. When we instinctively feel responsible for the feelings, thoughts, choices, problems, comfort, and destiny of others, we are caretakers. We may believe, at an unconscious level, that others are responsible for our happiness, just as we're responsible for theirs.

It's a worthy goal to be a considerate, loving, nurturing person. But caretaking is neglecting ourselves to the point of feeling victimized. Caretaking involves caring for others in ways that hamper them in learning to take responsibility for themselves.

Caretaking doesn't work. It hurts other people; it hurts us. People get angry. They feel hurt, used, and victimized. So do we.

The kindest and most generous behavior we can choose is taking responsibility for ourselves — for what we think, feel, want, and need. The most beneficial act we can perform is to be true to ourselves, and let others take responsibility for themselves.

Today, I will pay attention to my actual responsibilities to myself. I will let others do the same. If I am in doubt about what my actual responsibilities are, I will take an inventory.

Fear   **January 10**

Do not be too timid and squeamish about your actions. All life is an experiment. The more experiments you make the better. What if they are a little coarse, and you may get your

10

*coat soiled or torn? What if you do fail, and get fairly rolled
in the dirt once or twice? Up again; you shall never be so
afraid of a tumble.*

— *Ralph Waldo Emerson*

Fear can be a big stopper for many of us: fear of fragility,
fear of failure, fear of making a mistake, fear of what others
might think, *fear of success.* We may second-guess our next
action or word until we talk ourselves out of participating
in life.

"But I failed before!" "I can't do it good enough!" "Look
at what happened last time!" "What if...?" These statements
may disguise fear. Sometimes the fear is disguising shame.

After I finished the first two chapters of a book I was writing, I read them and grimaced. "No good," I thought. "Can't
do it." I was ready to pitch the chapters, and my writing
career, out the window. A writer friend called, and I told
her about my problem. She listened and told me: "Those
chapters are fine. Stop being afraid. Stop criticizing yourself. And keep on writing."

I followed her advice. The book I almost threw away became a *New York Times* best-seller.

Relax. Our best is good enough. It may be better than we
think. Even our failures may turn out to be important learning experiences that lead directly to — and are necessary for
— an upcoming success.

Feel the fear, then let it go. Jump in and do it — whatever
it is. If our instincts and path have led us there, it's where
we need to be.

*Today, I will participate in life to the best of my ability. Regardless
of the outcome, that makes me a winner.*

"There's a good trick that people in dysfunctional relation-ships use," said one recovering woman. "The other person does something inappropriate or wrong, then stands there until you feel guilty and end up apologizing."

It's imperative that we stop feeling so guilty.

Much of the time, the things we feel guilty about are not our issues. Another person behaves inappropriately or in some way violates our boundaries. We challenge the behavior, and the person gets angry and defensive. Then *we* feel guilty.

Guilt can prevent us from setting the boundaries that would be in our best interests, and in other people's best interests. Guilt can stop us from taking healthy care of ourselves.

We don't have to let others count on the fact that we'll always feel guilty. We don't have to allow ourselves to be con-trolled by guilt — earned or unearned! We can break through the barrier of guilt that holds us back from self-care. Push. Push harder. We are not at fault, crazy, or wrong. We have a right to set boundaries and to insist on appropriate treat-ment. We can separate another's issues from our issues, and let the person experience the consequences of his or her own behavior, including guilt. We can trust ourselves to know when our boundaries are being violated.

Today, I will let go of my big and little guilty feelings. Light and love are on my side.

Finding Balance   January 12

The goal of recovery is balance — that precious middle ground.

Many of us have gone from one extreme to another: years of taking care of everyone but ourselves, followed by a time of refusing to focus on anyone's needs but our own.

We may have spent years refusing to identify, feel, and deal with our feelings, followed by a period of absolute obsession with every trace of emotional energy that passes through our body.

We may succumb to powerlessness, helplessness, and victimization, then we swing to the other extreme by aggressively wielding power over those around us.

We can learn to give to others while taking responsibility for ourselves. We can learn to take care of our feelings, as well as our physical, mental, and spiritual needs. We can nurture the quiet confidence of owning our power as equals in our relationships with others.

The goal of recovery *is* balance, but sometimes we get there by going to extremes.

Today, I will be gentle with myself, understanding that sometimes to reach the middle ground of balance, I need to explore the peaks and valleys. Sometimes, the only way I can extricate myself from a valley is to jump high enough to land on a peak, and then slowly ease myself down.

Good Feelings   **January 13**

When we talk about feelings in recovery, we often focus on the troublesome trio — pain, fear, and anger. But there are other feelings available in the emotional realm — happiness, joy, peace, contentment, love, closeness, excitement.

It's okay to let ourselves feel pleasurable feelings too.

We don't have to worry when we experience good feelings; we don't have to scare ourselves out of them; we don't have to sabotage our happiness. We do that, sometimes, to get to the more familiar, less-joyous terrain.

It's okay to feel good. We don't have to analyze, judge, or justify. We don't have to bring ourselves down, or let others bring us down, by injecting negativity.

We can let ourselves feel good.

Today, I will remind myself that it is my right to feel as good as I can. I can have many moments of feeling good; I can find a balanced place of feeling content, peaceful, and good.

Accepting Anger   January 14

Anger is one of the many profound effects life has on us. It's one of our emotions. And we're going to feel it when it comes our way — or else repress it.
                                                — Codependent No More

If I was working a good program, I wouldn't get angry.... If I was a good Christian, I wouldn't feel angry.... If I was really using my affirmations about how happy I am, I wouldn't be angry.... Those are old messages that seduce us into not feeling again. Anger is part of life. We need not dwell in it or seek it out, but we can't afford to ignore it.

In recovery, we learn we can shamelessly feel all our feelings, including anger, and still take responsibility for what we do when we feel angry. We don't have to let anger control us, but it surely will if we prevent ourselves from feeling it.

Being grateful, being positive, being healthy, does not mean we never feel angry. Being grateful, positive, and healthy means we feel angry when we need to.

Today, I will let myself be angry, if I need to. I can feel and release my emotions, including anger, constructively. I will be grateful for my anger and the things it is trying to show me. I can feel and accept all my emotions without shame, and I can take responsibility for my actions.

We learn some behaviors have self-defeating consequences, while others have beneficial consequences. We learn we have choices.

— Beyond Codependency

It is so easy to come to the defense of others. How clear it is when others are being used, controlled, manipulated, or abused. It is so easy to fight their battles, become right-eously indignant, rally to their aid, and spur them on to victory.

"You have rights," we tell them. "And those rights are being violated. Stand up for yourself, without guilt."

Why is it so hard, then, for us to rally to our own behalf? Why can't we see when we are being used, victimized, lied to, manipulated, or otherwise violated? Why is it so difficult for us to stand up for ourselves?

There are times in life when we can walk a gentle, loving path. There are times, however, when we need to stand up for ourselves — when walking the gentle, loving path puts us deeper into the hands of those who could mistreat us.

Some days, the lesson we're to be learning and practicing is one of setting boundaries. Some days, the lesson we're learning is that of fighting for ourselves and our own rights.

Sometimes, the lesson won't stop until we do.

Today, I will rally to my own cause. I will remember that it is okay to stand up for myself when that action is appropriate. Help me, God, to let go of my need to be victimized. Help me appropriately, and with confidence, stand up for myself.

As a matter of fact, prayer is the only real action in the full sense of the word, because prayer is the only thing that changes one's character. A change in character, or a change in soul, is a real change.
                    — *Emmet Fox*, The Sermon on the Mount

Erica Jong has said that we are spiritual beings who are human. Praying and meditating are ways we take care of our spirit. Prayer and meditation are disciplines suggested by the Eleventh Step of Twelve Step recovery programs: Al-Anon, CoDa, Adult Children of Alcoholics, and others.

Prayer and meditation are not necessarily connected to organized religion. Prayer and meditation are ways to improve our personal relationship with a Higher Power to benefit ourselves, our life, and our growth. Praying is how we connect with God. We don't pray because we have to; we pray because we want to. It is how we link our soul to our Source.

We're learning to take care of our emotions, our mind, and our physical needs. We're learning to change our behaviors. But we're also learning to take care of our spirit, *our soul,* because that is where all true change begins.

Each time we talk to God, we are transformed. Each time we connect with our Higher Power, we are heard, touched, and changed for the best.

Today, I will practice prayer and meditation. Whether I feel desperate, uneasy, or peaceful, I will make the effort to connect with my Higher Power, at least for a moment today.

Acting As If   **January 17**

The behavior we call "acting as if" can be a powerful recovery tool. Acting as if is a way to practice the positive. It's a positive form of pretending. It's a tool we use to get ourselves unstuck. It's a tool we make a conscious decision to use.

Acting as if can be helpful when a feeling begins to control us. We make a conscious decision to act as if we feel fine and are going to be fine.

When a problem plagues us, acting as if can help us get unstuck. We act as if the problem will be or *already* is solved, so we can go on with our life.

Often, acting as if we are detached will set the stage for detachment to come in and take over.

There are many areas where acting as if — combined with our other recovery principles — will set the stage for the reality we desire. We can act as if we love ourselves, until we actually do begin to care for ourselves. We can act as if we have a right to say no, until we believe we do.

We don't pretend we have enough money to cover a check. We don't pretend an alcoholic is not drinking. We use acting as if as part of our recovery, to set the stage for our new behaviors. We force ourselves through positive recovery behaviors, disregarding our doubts and fears, until our feelings have time to catch up with reality.

Acting as if is a positive way to overcome fears, doubts, and low self-esteem. We do not have to lie; we do not have to be dishonest with ourselves. We open up to the positive possibilities of the future, instead of limiting the future by today's feelings and circumstances.

Acting as if helps us get past shaky ground and into solid territory.

God, show me the areas where acting as if could help set the stage for the reality I desire. Guide me as I use this powerful recovery tool to help create a better life and healthier relationships.

Sometimes in life, things happen too fast. We barely solve one problem when two new problems surface. We're feeling great in the morning, but we're submerged in misery by nightfall.

Every day we face interruptions, delays, changes, and challenges. We face personality conflicts and disappointments. Often when we're feeling overwhelmed, we can't see the lessons in these experiences.

One simple concept can get us through the most stressful of times. It's called *gratitude*. We learn to say, *thank you*, for these problems and feelings. *Thank you* for the way things are. I don't like this experience, but *thank you* anyway.

Force gratitude until it becomes habitual. Gratitude helps us stop trying to control outcomes. It is the key that unlocks positive energy in our life. It is the alchemy that turns problems into blessings, and the unexpected into gifts.

Today, I will be grateful. I will start the process of turning today's pain into tomorrow's joy.

Owning Our Power   January 19

There is one feeling we need to pay particular attention to in recovery: feeling victimized. We do not need to become comfortable with that feeling.

How do we feel when we've been victimized? Helpless. Rageful. Powerless. Frustrated.

Feeling victimized is dangerous. Often, it can prompt us into addictive or other compulsive behaviors.

In recovery, we're learning to identify when we're feeling victimized, *when we are actually being victimized*, and *why* we're feeling victimized. We're learning to own our power, to take care of ourselves, and to remove ourselves as victims.

Sometimes, owning our power means we realize we are victimizing ourselves — and others are not doing anything to hurt us. They are living their lives, as they have a right to, and we are feeling victimized because we're attempting to control their process, or we're unreasonably expecting them to take care of us. We may feel victimized if we get stuck in a codependent belief, such as, *Other people make me feel. . . . Others hold the key to my happiness and destiny. . . .* or, *I can't be happy unless another behaves in a particular way, or a certain event takes place. . . .*

Other times, owning our power means we realize that we are being victimized by another's behavior. Our boundaries are being invaded. In that case, we figure out what we need to do to take care of ourselves to stop the victimization; we need to set boundaries.

Sometimes, a change of attitude is all that's required. *We are not victims.*

We strive to have compassion for the person who victimized us, but understand that compassion often comes later, after we've removed ourselves as victims in body, mind, and spirit. We also understand that too much compassion can put us right back into the victim slot. Too much pity for a person who is victimizing us may set up a situation where the person can victimize us again.

We try not to force consequences or crises upon another person, but we also do not rescue that person from logical consequences of his or her behavior. If there is a part that is our responsibility to play in delivering those consequences, we do our part — not to control or punish, but to be responsible for ourselves and to others.

We try to figure out what we may be doing that is causing us to feel victimized, or what part we are playing in the system, and we stop doing that too. We are powerless over others and their behavior, but we can own our power to remove ourselves as victims.

Today, I will take responsibility for myself and show it to others by not allowing myself to be victimized. I cannot control outcomes, but I can control my attitude toward being victimized. I am not a victim; I do not deserve to be victimized.

New Beginnings   January 20

Resentments are the blocks that hold us back from loving ourselves and others. Resentments do not punish the other person; they punish us. They become barriers to feeling good and enjoying life. They prevent us from being in harmony with the world. Resentments are hardened chunks of anger. They loosen up and dissolve with forgiveness and letting go.

Letting go of resentments does not mean we allow the other person to do anything to us that he or she wants. It means we accept what happened in the past, and we set boundaries for the future. We can let go of resentments and still have boundaries!

We try to see the good in the person, or the good that ultimately evolved from whatever incident we feel resentful about. We try to see our part.

Then we put the incident to rest.

Praying for those we resent helps. Asking God to take our resentments from us helps too.

What better way to begin a new year than by cleaning the slate of the past, and entering this one free of resentments.

Higher Power, help me become ready to let go of my resentments. Bring any resentments that are hidden within me, and blocking me, to the surface. Show me what I need to do to take care of myself by letting go of resentments, and then help me do that.

Part of taking responsibility for ourselves means taking responsibility for what we want and need, and knowing that's okay to do.

Learning to tune-in to ourselves, learning to listen to ourselves, is an art. It takes practice. We can use our ability to guess what others want and need, and apply that skill to ourselves.

What does it sound like we might want and need? What would we guess would help us feel better? What are our feelings telling us? Our body? Our mind? Our intuition?

If we ask, then listen closely; we'll hear the answer.

We are wiser than we think, and we can be trusted.

What we want and need counts. It's important, and it's valid. It's okay to learn to participate in meeting our own needs.

We can learn to identify what we want and need and be patient with ourselves while we're learning.

Today, I will pay attention to what I want and need. I will not discount myself.

Appreciating Our Past   **January 22**

It is easy to be negative about past mistakes and unhappiness. But it is much more healing to look at ourselves and our past in the light of experience, acceptance, and growth. Our past is a series of lessons that advance us to higher levels of living and loving.

The relationships we entered, stayed in, or ended taught us necessary lessons. Some of us have emerged from the most painful circumstances with strong insights about who we are and what we want.

Our mistakes? Necessary. Our frustrations, failures, and sometimes stumbling attempts at growth and progress? Necessary too.

Each step of the way, we learned. We went through exactly the experiences we needed to, to become who we are today. Each step of the way, we progressed.

Is our past a mistake? No. The only mistake we can make is mistaking that for the truth.

Today, God, help me let go of negative thoughts I may be harboring about my past circumstances or relationships. I can accept, with gratitude, all that has brought me to today.

New Energy Coming   January 23

Fun becomes fun, love becomes love, life becomes worth living. And we become grateful.
                                    — Beyond Codependency

There is a new energy, a new feeling coming into our life. *We cannot base our expectations about how we will feel tomorrow, or even a few hours from now, on how we feel at this moment.*

There are no two moments in time alike. We are recovering. We are changing. Our life is changing. At times, things haven't worked out the way we wanted. *We had lessons to learn*. The future shall not be like the past.

The truly difficult times are almost over. The confusion, the most challenging learning experiences, the difficult feelings are about to pass.

Do not limit the future by the past!

Reflect on the beginning of your recovery. Haven't there been many changes that have brought you to where you are now? Reflect on one year ago. Haven't you and your circumstances changed since then?

Sometimes, problems and feelings linger for a while. These times are temporary. Times of confusion, uncertainty, times of living with a particular unsolved problem do not last forever.

We make these times doubly hard by comparing them to our past. Each situation and circumstance has had its particular influence in shaping who we are. We do not have to scare ourselves by comparing our present and future to a painful past, especially our past before we began recovering or before we learned through a particular experience.

Know that the discomfort will not be permanent. Do not try to figure out how you shall feel or when you shall feel differently. Instead, trust. Accept today, but do not be limited by it.

A new energy is coming. A new feeling is on the way. We cannot predict how it will be by looking at how it was or how it is, because it shall be entirely different. We have not worked and struggled in vain. It has been for and toward something.

Times are changing for the better. Continue on the path of trust and obedience. Be open to the new.

Today, God, help me not judge or limit my future by my past. Help me be open to all the exciting possibilities for change, both within and around me.

Clearing the Slate   January 24

One of the greatest gifts we can give is an open, loving heart. And holding on to negative feelings from past relationships is our greatest barrier to that gift.

Most of us have had relationships that have ended. When we examine these relationships, we need to clear the emotional slate. Are we holding on to anger or resentments? Are we still feeling victimized? Are we living with the self-defeating beliefs that may be attached to these relationships — *Women can't be trusted.... Bosses use people.... There is no such thing as a good relationship....*

Let go of all that may be blocking your relationships today. With great certainty, we can know that old feelings and self-defeating beliefs will block us today from giving and getting the love we desire. We can clear the slate of the past. It begins with awareness, honesty, and openness. The process is complete when we reach a state of acceptance and peace toward all from our past.

Today, I will begin the process of letting go of all self-defeating feelings and beliefs connected to past relationships. I will clear my slate so I am free to love and be loved.

Step One   January 25

We admitted we were powerless over alcohol — that our lives had become unmanageable.
                                              — Step One of Al-Anon

There are many different versions of the First Step for recovering codependents. Some of us admit powerlessness over alcohol or another's alcoholism. Some of us admit powerlessness over people; some over the impact of growing up in an alcoholic family.

One of the most significant words in the First Step is the word *we*. We come together because of a common problem, and, in the coming together, we find a common solution.

Through the fellowship of Twelve Step programs, many of us discover that although we may have felt alone in our pain, others have experienced a similar suffering. And now many are joining hands in a similar recovery.

We. A significant part of recovery. A shared experience. A shared strength, stronger for the sharing. A shared hope — for better lives and relationships.

Today, I will be grateful for the many people across the world who call themselves ''recovering codependents.'' Help me know that each time one of us takes a step forward, we pull the entire group forward.

Off The Hook January 26

We can learn not to get hooked into unhealthy, self-defeating behaviors in relationships — behaviors such as caretaking, controlling, discounting ourselves, and believing lies.

We can learn to watch for and identify hooks, and choose not to allow ourselves to be hooked.

Often, people do things consciously or without thinking that pull us into a series of our self-defeating behaviors we call codependency. More often than not, these hooks can be almost deliberate, and the results predictable.

Someone may stand before us and hint or sigh about a problem, *knowing* or *hoping* that hint or sigh will hook us into taking care of him or her. That is *manipulation.*

When people stand around us and hint and sigh about something, then coyly say, "Oh, never mind, that's not for you to worry about," that's a *game.* We need to recognize it. We're about to get sucked in, if we allow that to happen.

We can learn to insist that people ask us directly for what they want and need.

What are the words, the signs, the looks, the hints, the cues that hook us into a predictable, and often self-defeating behavior?

What makes you feel sympathy? Guilt? Responsible for another?

Our strong point is that we care so much. Our weak point is that we often underestimate the people with whom we're dealing. *They* know what they're doing. It is time we give up our naive assumption that people don't follow agendas of their own in their best interest, and not necessarily in ours.

We also want to check ourselves out. Do we give out hooks, looks, hints, hoping to hook another? We need to insist that we behave in a direct and honest manner with others, instead of expecting them to rescue us.

If someone wants something from us, insist that the person ask us directly for it. Require the same from ourselves. If someone baits the hook, we don't have to bite it.

Today, I will be aware of the hooks that snag me into the caretaking acts that leave me feeling victimized. I will ignore the hints, looks, and words that hook me, and wait for the directness and honesty I, and others, deserve.

Needing People   January 27

We can find the balance between needing people too much and not letting ourselves need anyone at all.

Many of us have unmet dependency needs lingering from the past. While we want others to fulfill our desire to be loved unconditionally, we may have chosen people who cannot, or will not, be there for us. Some of us are so needy from not being loved that we drive people away by needing them too much.

Some of us go to the other extreme. We may have become used to people not being there for us, so we push them away. We fight off our feelings of neediness by becoming overly independent, not allowing ourselves to need anyone. Some of us *won't let people be there for us.*

Either way, we are living out unfinished business. We deserve better. When we change, our circumstances will change.

If we are too needy, we respond to that by accepting the needy part of us. We let ourselves heal from the pain of past needs going unmet. We stop telling ourselves we're unlovable because we haven't been loved the way we wanted and needed.

If we have shut off the part of us that needs people, we become willing to open up, be vulnerable, and let ourselves be loved. We let ourselves have needs.

We will get the love we need and desire when we begin to believe we're lovable, and when we allow that to happen.

Today, I will strive for the balance between being too needy and not allowing myself to need people. I will let myself receive the love that is there for me.

Staying in the Present Moment   January 28

Often, one of our biggest questions is "What's going to happen?" We may ask this about our relationships, our career, our recovery, our life. It is easy to tangle ourselves up in worrisome thoughts.

Worrying about what's going to happen blocks us from functioning effectively today. It keeps us from doing our best now. It blocks us from learning and mastering today's lessons. Staying in the now, doing our best, and participating fully today are all we need to do to assure ourselves that what's going to happen tomorrow will be for the best.

Worrying about what's going to happen is a negative contribution to our future. Living in the here and now is ultimately the best thing we can do, not only for today, but for tomorrow. It helps our relationships, our career, our recovery, and our life.

Things will work out, if we let them. If we must focus on the future other than to plan, all we need to do is affirm that it will be good.

I pray for faith that my future will be good if I live today well, and in peace. I will remember that staying in the present is the best thing I can do for my future. I will focus on what's happening now instead of what's going to happen tomorrow.

Going to Meetings   January 29

I am still amazed, after years of recovering, at how easily I can begin to talk myself out of attending meetings. I am also still amazed at how good I feel when I go.

— Anonymous

We don't have to stay stuck in our misery and discomfort. An immediate option is available that will help us feel better: go to a meeting, a Twelve Step support group.

Why resist what can help us feel better? Why sit in our obsession or depression when attending a meeting — even if that means an extra meeting — would help us feel better?

Too busy?

There are 168 hours in each week. Taking 1 or 2 hours a week for a meeting can maximize the potential of the remaining 166 hours. If we get into our "codependent stuff," we can easily spend a majority of our waking hours obsessing, sitting and doing nothing, laying in bed and feeling depressed, or chasing after other people's needs. Not taking those 2 hours for a meeting can cause us to waste the remaining hours.

Too tired?

There is nothing as invigorating as getting back on track. Going to a meeting can accomplish that.

Today, I will remember that going to meetings helps.

Religious Freedom   January 30

". . .a Power greater than ourselves. . . ." *"God as we understood Him."* These words introduce spirituality in the Twelve Steps. They are the first two references to God, and they are worded that way for a reason.

We each have the freedom to define, and understand, our Higher Power — God — as we choose.

That means we do not bring our religious affiliation into our recovery groups. It means that we do not try to impose our religious beliefs, or our understanding of God, on anyone else. We do not use our groups or meetings as a soap box to gain religious converts. We do not try to force the *particulars* of our religious beliefs on others.

We give ourselves, and each person, the right to a personal understanding of a Higher Power.

Today, I will respect other people's understanding of God, as well as my own. I will not allow others' judgment of my beliefs to cause me anxiety and distress. I will seek to grow spiritually in recovery, with or without the assistance of a particular religion or denomination.

Asking for What We Need   January 31

One evening, I was alone, weary, and exhausted. I was in the midst of extensive traveling, disconnected from friends and family. I had flown home for the evening, but it seemed like nobody noticed. People were used to me being gone.

It was late at night, and I began arguing with God.

"I'm out there working hard. I'm lonely. I need to know someone cares. You've told me to tell You what I need, and tonight, God, I particularly need the presence of male energy. I need a friend, someone I can trust to care about me in a nonsexual, nonexploitive way. I need to be held. Now, where are you?"

I laid down on the couch and closed my eyes. I was too tired to do anything but let go.

The telephone rang minutes later. It was a former colleague who had since become my friend. "Hey, kid," he said. "You sound really tired and needy. Stay right where you are. I'm going to drive out and give you a foot-rub. It sounds exactly like what you need."

Half an hour later, he knocked on my door. He brought a small bottle of oil with him, and gently massaged my feet, gave me a hug, told me how much he cared about me, then left.

I smiled. I had received exactly what I asked for.

It is safe to trust God.

Today, I will remember God cares about what I need, especially if I do.

February

Came to believe that a Power greater than ourselves could restore us to sanity.

— *Step Two of Al-Anon*

We come to believe in a better life through the powerful gift of other people — hearing them, seeing them, watching the gift of recovery at work in their lives.

There is a Power greater than ourselves. There is real hope now that things can and will be different and better for us and our life.

We are not in a "do it ourselves" program. We do not have to exert willpower to change. We do not have to force our recovery to happen. We do not have to pull ourselves up by our bootstraps just so we believe that there is a Power greater than ourselves — one who will get the job done in our life. This Power will do for us what your greatest and most diligent efforts could not accomplish.

Our Higher Power will restore us to a sane and beneficial life. All we do is believe.

Look. Watch. See the people around you. See the healing they have found. Then discover your own faith, your own belief, your own healing.

Today, regardless of my circumstances, I will believe to the best of my ability that a Power greater than myself can and will restore me to a peaceful, sane way of living. Then I will relax and let Him do that.

Made a decision to turn our will and our lives over to the care of God as we understood him.

— *Step Three of Al-Anon*

So much talk about a Higher Power, God as we understand God. So much joy as we come to understand Him.

Spirituality and spiritual growth are the foundations of change. Recovery from codependency is not a do-it-yourself task.

Is God a relentless taskmaster? A hard-hearted, shaming wizard with tricks up the sleeve? Is God deaf? Uncaring? Haphazard? Unforgiving?

No.

A loving God, a caring God. That is the God of our recovery. No more pain than is necessary for usefulness, healing, and cleansing. As much goodness and joy as our heart can hold, as soon as our heart is healed, open, and ready to receive. God: approving, accepting, instantly forgiving.

God has planned little gifts along the way to brighten our day, and sometimes big, delightful surprises — perfectly timed, perfect for us.

A Master Artist, God will weave together all our joy, sadness, and experience to create a portrait of our life with depth, beauty, sensitivity, color, humor, and feeling.

God as we understand Him: A loving God. The God of our recovery.

Today, I will open myself to the care of a loving God. Then, I will let God show me love.

33

Shame can be a powerful force in our life. It is the trademark of dysfunctional families.

Authentic, legitimate *guilt* is the feeling or thought that what we did is not okay. It indicates that our behavior needs to be corrected or altered, or an amend needs to be made.

Shame is an overwhelming negative sense that who we are isn't okay. Shame is a no-win situation. We can change our behaviors, but we can't change who we are. Shame can propel us deeper into self-defeating and sometimes self-destructive behaviors.

What are the things that can cause us to feel shame? We may feel ashamed when we have a problem or someone we love has a problem. We may feel ashamed for making mistakes or for succeeding. We may feel ashamed about certain feelings or thoughts. We may feel ashamed when we have fun, feel good, or are vulnerable enough to show ourselves to others. Some of us feel ashamed just for being.

Shame is a spell others put on us to control us, to keep us playing our part in dysfunctional systems. It is a spell many of us have learned to put on ourselves.

Learning to reject shame can change the quality of our life. It's okay to be who we are. We are good enough. Our feelings are okay. Our past is okay. It's okay to have problems, make mistakes, and struggle to find our path. It's okay to be human and cherish our humanness.

Accepting ourselves is the first step toward recovery. Letting go of shame about who we are is the next important step.

Today, I will watch for signs that I have fallen into shame's trap. If I get hooked into shame, I will get myself out by accepting myself and affirming that it's okay to be who I am.

What a journey!

This process of growth and change takes us along an ever-changing road. Sometimes the way is hard and craggy. Sometimes we climb mountains. Sometimes we slide down the other side on a toboggan.

Sometimes we rest.

Sometimes we grope through the darkness. Sometimes we're blinded by sunlight.

At times many may walk with us on the road; sometimes we feel nearly alone.

Ever changing, always interesting, always leading someplace better, someplace good.

What a journey!

Today, God, help me relax and enjoy the scenery. Help me know I'm right where I need to be on my journey.

Financial Responsibility February 5

We are responsible for ourselves financially.

What a frightening, grown-up thought that is for many of us — taking responsibility for money and our financial affairs. For many of us, handing over responsibility for our financial affairs has been part of a codependent trade-off in our relationships.

Some of our emotional dependency on others, on this tight tie that binds us to others, not in love, but in need and desperation, is directly related to financial dependency. Our fears and reluctance to take responsibility for our financial affairs can be a barrier to the freedom we're seeking in recovery.

Financial responsibility is an attitude. Money goes out to pay for necessities and luxuries. Money must come in, in order to go out. How much needs to come in to equal that which is going out?

Taxes...savings plans...appropriate spending habits that demonstrate an attitude of financial responsibility.... Part of being alive means learning to handle money. Even if we have a healthy contract with someone that allows us to depend on him or her for money, we still need to understand how money works. We still need to adopt an attitude of financial responsibility for ourselves. Even if we have a contract with someone else to provide for our financial needs, we need to understand the workings of the money earned and spent in our life.

Self-esteem will increase when we increase our sense of being financially responsible for ourselves. We can start where we are, with what we have today.

God, help me become willing to let go of my fears and reluctance to face the necessary parts of handling money responsibly in my life. Show me the lessons I need to learn about money.

Stopping Victimization   February 6

Before recovery, many of us lacked a frame of reference with which to name the *victimization* and *abuse* in our life. We may have thought it was normal that people mistreated us. We may have believed we deserved mistreatment; we may have been attracted to people who mistreated us.

We need to let go, on a deep level, of our need to be victimized and to be victims. We need to let go of our need to be in dysfunctional relationships and systems at work, in love, in family relationships, in friendships. We deserve better. We deserve much better. It is our right. When we believe in our right to happiness, we will have happiness.

We will fight for that right, and the fight will emerge from our souls. Break free from oppression and victimization.

Today, I will liberate myself by letting go of my need to be a victim, and I'll explore my freedom to take care of myself. That liberation will not take me further away from people I love. It will bring me closer to people and more in harmony with God's plan for my life.

Owning Our Power   February 7

We need to make a distinction between powerlessness and owning our power.

The first step in recovery is accepting powerlessness. There are some things we can't do, no matter how long or hard we try. These things include changing other people, solving their problems, and controlling their behavior. Sometimes, we feel powerless over ourselves — what we feel or believe, or the effects of a particular situation or person on us.

It's important to surrender to powerlessness, but it's equally important to own our power. We aren't trapped. We aren't helpless. Sometimes it may feel like we are, but we aren't. We each have the God-given power, and the right, to take care of ourselves in any circumstance, and with any person. The middle ground of self-care lies between the two extremes of controlling others and allowing them to control us. We can walk that ground gently or assertively, but in confidence that it is our right and responsibility.

Let the power come to walk that path.

Today, I will remember that I can take care of myself. I have choices, and I can exercise the options I choose without guilt.

Letting Go of Guilt February 8

Feeling good about ourselves is a choice. So is feeling guilty. When guilt is legitimate, it acts as a warning light, signaling that we're off course. Then its purpose is finished.

Wallowing in guilt allows others to control us. It makes us feel not good enough. It prevents us from setting boundaries and taking other healthy action to care for ourselves.

We may have learned to habitually feel guilty as an instinctive reaction to life. Now we know that we don't have to feel guilty. Even if we've done something that violates a value, extended guilt does not solve the problem; it prolongs the problem. So make an amend. Change a behavior. Then let guilt go.

Today, God, help me to become entirely ready to let go of guilt. Please take it from me, and replace it with self-love.

Letting Go in Love February 9

When people with a compulsive disorder do whatever it is they are compelled to do, they are not saying they don't love you — they are saying they don't love themselves.
— Codependent No More

Gentle people, gentle souls, go in love.

Yes, at times we need to be firm, assertive: those times when we change, when we acquire a new behavior, when we need to convince others and ourselves we have rights.

Those times are not permanent. We may need to get angry to make a decision or set a boundary, but we can't afford to stay resentful. It is difficult to have compassion for one who is victimizing us, but once we've removed ourselves as victims, we can find compassion.

Our path, our way, is a gentle one, walked in love — love for self, love for others. Set boundaries. Detach. Take care of ourselves. And as quickly as possible, do those things in love.

Today, and whenever possible, God, let me be gentle with myself and others. Help me find the balance between assertive action taken in my own best interests, and love for others. Help me understand that at times those two ideas are one. Help me find the right path for me.

Letting Go of Sadness   February 10

A block to joy and love can be unresolved sadness from the past.

In the past, we told ourselves many things to deny the pain: It doesn't hurt that much.... Maybe if I just wait, things will change.... It's no big deal. I can get through this.... Maybe if I try to change the other person, I won't have to change myself.

We denied that it hurt because we didn't want to feel the pain.

Unfinished business doesn't go away. It keeps repeating itself, until it gets our attention, until we feel it, deal with it, and heal. That's one lesson we are learning in recovery from codependency and adult children issues.

Many of us didn't have the tools, support, or safety we needed to acknowledge and accept pain in our past. It's okay. We're safe now. Slowly, carefully, we can begin to open ourselves up to our feelings. We can begin the process of feeling what we have denied so long — not to blame, not to shame, but to heal ourselves in preparation for a better life.

It's okay to cry when we need to cry and feel the sadness many of us have stored within for so long. We can feel and release these feelings.

Grief is a cleansing process. It's an acceptance process. It moves us from our past, into today, and into a better future — a future free of sabotaging behaviors, a future that holds more options than our past.

God, as I move through this day, let me be open to my feelings. Today, help me know that I don't have to either force or repress the healing available to me in recovery. Help me trust that if I am open and available, the healing will happen naturally, in a manageable way.

Divinely Led

Send me the right thought, word, or action. Show me what my next step should be. In times of doubt and indecision, please send Your inspiration and guidance.
— Alcoholics Anonymous

The good news of surrendering ourselves and our life to a Power greater than ourselves is that we come into harmony with a Grand Plan, one greater than we can imagine.

We are promised Divine Guidance if we ask for it, if we work the Twelve Steps. What greater gift could we receive than knowing our thoughts, words, and actions are being directed?

We aren't a mistake. And we don't have to control or repress ourselves or others for life to work out. Even the strange, the unplanned, the painful, and those things we call errors can evolve into harmony.

We will be guided into understanding what we need to do to take care of ourselves. We will begin to trust our instincts, our feelings, our thoughts. We will know when to go, to stop, to wait. We will learn a great truth: the plan will happen in spite of us, not because of us.

I pray today and each day that my thoughts, words, and actions may be Divinely led. I pray that I can move forward in confidence, knowing my steps are guided.

Letting Go of Those Not in Recovery   February 12

We can go forward with our life and recoveries, even though someone we love is not yet recovering.

Picture a bridge. On one side of the bridge it is cold and dark. We stood there with others in the cold and darkness, doubled over in pain. Some of us developed an eating disorder to cope with the pain. Some drank; some used other drugs. Some of us lost control of our sexual behavior. Some of us obsessively focused on addicted people's pain to distract us from our own pain. Many of us did both: we developed an addictive behavior, and distracted ourselves by focusing on other addicted people. We did not know there was a bridge. We thought we were trapped on a cliff.

Then, some of us got lucky. Our eyes opened, by the Grace of God, because it was time. We saw the bridge. People told us what was on the other side: warmth, light, and healing from our pain. We could barely glimpse or imagine this, but we decided to start the trek across the bridge anyway.

We tried to convince the people around us on the cliff that there was a bridge to a better place, but they wouldn't listen. They couldn't see it; they couldn't believe. They were not ready for the journey. We decided to go alone, because we believed, and because people on the other side were cheering us onward. The closer we got to the other side, the more we could see, and feel, that what we had been promised was real. There was light, warmth, healing, and love. The other side was a better place.

But now, there is a bridge between us and those on the other side. Sometimes, we may be tempted to go back and drag them over with us, but it cannot be done. No one can be dragged or forced across this bridge. Each person must go at his or her own choice, when the time is right. Some will come; some will stay on the other side. The choice is not ours.

We can love them. We can wave to them. We can holler back and forth. We can cheer them on, as others have cheered and encouraged us. But we cannot make them come over with us.

If our time has come to cross the bridge, or if we have already crossed and are standing in the light and warmth, we do not have to feel guilty. It is where we are meant to be. We do not have to go back to the dark cliff because another's time has not yet come.

The best thing we can do is stay in the light, because it reassures others that there is a better place. And if others ever do decide to cross the bridge, we will be there to cheer them on.

Today, I will move forward with my life, despite what others are doing or not doing. I will know it is my right to cross the bridge to a better life, even if I must leave others behind to do that. I will not feel guilty, I will not feel ashamed. I know that where I am now is a better place and where I'm meant to be.

Trusting Ourselves   February 13

What a great gift we've been given — ourselves. To listen to ourselves, to trust instinct and intuition, is to pay tribute to that gift.

What a disservice not to heed the leadings and leanings that so naturally arise from within. When will we learn that these leadings and leanings draw us into God's rich plan for us?

We will learn. We will learn by listening, trusting, and following through. What is it time to do?... What do I need to do to take care of myself?... What am I being led to do?... What do I know?

Listen, and we will know. Listen to the voice within.

Today, I will listen and trust. I will be helped to take action when that is needed. I can trust myself and God.

Valentine's Day   February 14

For children, Valentine's Day means candy hearts, silly cards, and excitement in the air.

How different Valentine's Day can be for us as adults. The Love Day can be a symbol that we have not yet gotten love to work for us as we would like.

Or it can be a symbol of something different, something better. We are in recovery now. We have begun the healing process. Our most painful relationships, we have learned, have assisted us on the journey to healing, even if they did little more than point out our own issues or show us what we don't want in our life.

We have started the journey of learning to love ourselves. We have started the process of opening our heart to love, real love that flows from us, to others, and back again. Do something loving for yourself. Do something loving and fun for your friends, for your children, or for anyone you choose.

It is the Love Day. Wherever we are in our healing process, we can have as much fun with it as we choose. Whatever our circumstances, we can be grateful that our heart is opening to love.

I will open myself to the love available to me from people, the Universe, and my Higher Power today. I will allow myself to give and receive the love I want today. I am grateful that my heart is healing, that I am learning to love.

Control   February 15

Sometimes, the gray days scare us. Those are the days when the old feelings come rushing back. We may feel needy, scared, ashamed, unable to care for ourselves.

When this happens, it's hard to trust ourselves, others, the goodness of life, and the good intentions of our Higher Power. Problems seem overwhelming. The past seems senseless; the future, bleak. We feel certain the things we want in life will never happen.

In those moments, we may become convinced that things and people outside of ourselves hold the key to our happiness. That's when we may try to control people and situations to mask our pain. When these "codependent crazies" strike, others often begin to react negatively to our controlling.

When we're in a frenzied state, searching for happiness outside ourselves and looking to others to provide our peace and stability, remember this: *Even if we could control things and people, even if we got what we wanted, we would still be ourselves. Our emotional state would still be in turmoil.*

People and things don't stop our pain or heal us. In recovery, we learn that this is our job, and we can do it by using our resources: ourselves, our Higher Power, our support systems, and our recovery program.

Often, after we've become peaceful, trusting, and accepting, what we want comes to us — with ease and naturalness.

The sun begins to shine again. Isn't it funny, and isn't it true, how all change really does begin with us?

I can let go of things and people and my need to control today. I can deal with my feelings. I can get peaceful. I can get calm. I can get back on track and find the true key to happiness — myself. I will remember that a gray day is just that — one gray day.

Detachment   February 16

The concept of letting go can be confusing to many of us. When are we doing too much or trying too hard to control people and outcomes? When are we doing too little? When is what we're doing an appropriate part of taking care of ourselves? What is our responsibility, and what isn't?

These issues can challenge us whether we've been in recovery ten days or ten years. Sometimes, we may let go so much that we neglect responsibility to ourselves or others. Other times, we may cross the line from taking care of ourselves to controlling others and outcomes.

There is no rule book. But we don't have to make ourselves crazy; we don't have to be so afraid. We don't have to do recovery perfectly. If it feels like we need to do a particular action, we can do it. If no action feels timely or inspired, don't act on it.

Having and setting healthy limits — healthy boundaries — isn't a tidy process. We can give ourselves permission to experiment, to make mistakes, to learn, to grow.

We can talk to people, ask questions, and question ourselves. If there's something we need to do or learn, it will become apparent. Lessons don't go away. If we're not taking care of ourselves enough, we'll see that. If we are being too controlling, we'll grow to understand that too.

Things will work out. The way will become clear.

Today, I will take actions that appear appropriate. I will let go of the rest. I will strive for the balance between self-responsibility, responsibility to others, and letting go.

Acceptance   February 17

Our basic recovery concept that never loses its power to work miracles is the concept called *acceptance.*

We do not achieve acceptance in a moment. We often have to work through a mirage of feelings — sometimes anger, outrage, shame, self-pity, or sadness. But if acceptance is our goal, we will achieve it.

What is more freeing than to laugh at our weaknesses and to be grateful for our strengths? To know the entire package called "us" — with all our feelings, thoughts, tendencies, and history — is worthy of acceptance and brings healing feelings.

To accept our circumstances is another miraculous cure. For anything to change or anyone to change, we must first accept ourselves, others, and the circumstance exactly as they are. Then, we need to take it one step further. We need to become *grateful* for ourselves or our circumstances. We add a touch of faith by saying, "I know this is exactly the way it's supposed to be for the moment."

No matter how complicated we get, the basics never lose their power to restore us to sanity.

Today, God, help me practice the concept of acceptance in my life. Help me accept myself, others, and my circumstances. Take me one step further, and help me feel grateful.

Recovery is not about being right; it's about allowing ourselves to be who we are and accepting others as they are.

That concept can be difficult for many of us if we have lived in systems that functioned on the "right-wrong" justice scale. The person who was right was okay; the person who was wrong was shamed. All value and worth may have depended on being right; to be wrong meant annihilation of self and self-esteem.

In recovery, we are learning how to strive for love in our relationships, not superiority. Yes, we may need to make decisions about people's behavior from time to time. If someone is hurting us, we need to stand up for ourselves. We have a responsibility to set boundaries and take care of ourselves. But we do not need to justify taking care of ourselves by condemning someone else. We can avoid the trap of focusing on others instead of ourselves.

In recovery, we are learning that what we do needs to be *right* only for us. What others do is their business and needs to be right only for them. It's tempting to rest in the superiority of being right and in analyzing other people's motives and actions, but it's more rewarding to look deeper.

Today, I will remember that I don't have to hide behind being right. I don't have to justify what I want and need with saying something is "right" or "wrong." I can let myself be who I am.

Our Path   February 19

I just spent several hours with someone from my group, and I feel like I'm losing my mind. This woman insisted that the only way I would make progress in my program was to go to her church and succumb to her religious rules. She

pushed and insisted, and insisted and pushed. She's been
in the program so much longer than I have. I kept thinking
that she must know what she's talking about. But it didn't
feel right. And now I feel crazy, afraid, guilty, and ashamed.
— *Anonymous*

The spiritual path and growth promised to us by the Twelve Steps does not depend on any religious belief. They are not contingent upon any denomination or sect. They are not, as the traditions of Twelve Step programs state, affiliated with any religious denomination or organization.

We do not have to allow anyone to badger us about religion in recovery. We do not have to allow people to make us feel ashamed, afraid, or less-than because we do not subscribe to their beliefs about religion.

We do not have to let them do it to us in the name of God, love, or recovery.

The spiritual experience we will find as a result of recovery and the Twelve Steps will be our own spiritual experience. It will be a relationship with God, a Higher Power as we understand God.

Each of us must find our own spiritual path. Each of us must build our own relationship with God as we understand God. Each of us needs a Power greater than ourselves. These concepts are critical to recovery.

So is the freedom to choose how to do that.

Higher Power, help me know that I don't have to allow anyone
to shame or badger me into religious beliefs. If they confuse that
with the spirituality available in recovery, help me give their issue
back to them. Help me discover and develop my own spirituality,
a path that works for me. Guide me, with Divine Wisdom, as I
grow spiritually.

We are powerless over other people's expectations of us. We cannot control what others want, what they expect, or what they want us to do and be.

We can control how we respond to other people's expectations.

During the course of any day, people may make demands on our time, talents, energy, money, and emotions. We do not have to say yes to every request. We do not have to feel guilty if we say no. And we do not have to allow the barrage of demands to control the course of our life.

We do not have to spend our life reacting to others and to the course they would prefer we took with our life.

We can set boundaries, firm limits on how far we shall go with others. We can trust and listen to ourselves. We can set goals and direction for *our* life. We can place value on ourselves.

We can own our power with people.

Buy some time. Think about what *you* want. Consider how responding to another's needs will affect the course of your life. We live or own life by not letting other people, their expectations, and their demands control the course of our life. We can let them have their demands and expectations; we can allow them to have their feelings. We can own our power to choose the path that is right for us.

Today, God, help me own my power by detaching, and peacefully choosing the course of action that is right for me. Help me know I can detach from the expectations and wants of others. Help me stop pleasing other people and start pleasing myself.

The present moment is all we have. Yes, we have plans and goals, a vision for tomorrow. But now is the only time we possess. And it is enough.

We can clear our mind of the residue of yesterday. We can clear our mind of fears of tomorrow. We can be present, now. We can make ourselves available to this moment, this day. It is by being fully present now that we reach the fullness of tomorrow.

Have no fear, child, a voice whispers. Have no regrets. Relinquish your resentments. Let Me take your pain. All you have is the present moment. Be still. Be here. Trust.

All you have is now. It is enough.

Today, I will affirm that all is well around me, when all is well within.

I ask that You might help me work through all my problems, to Your Glory and Honor.

— Alcoholics Anonymous

Many of us lived in situations where it wasn't okay to identify, have, or talk about problems. Denial became a way of life — our way of dealing with problems.

In recovery, many of us still fear problems. We may spend more time reacting to a problem than we do to solving it. We miss the point; we miss the lesson; we miss the gift. Problems are a part of life. So are solutions.

A problem doesn't mean life is negative or horrible. Having a problem doesn't mean a person is deficient. All people have problems to work through.

In recovery, we learn to focus on solving our problems. First, we make certain the problem is our problem. If it isn't, our problem is establishing boundaries. Then we seek the best solution. This may mean setting a goal, asking for help, gathering more information, taking an action, or letting go.

Recovery does not mean immunity or exemption from problems; recovery means learning to face and solve problems, knowing they will appear regularly. We can trust our ability to solve problems, and know we're not doing it alone. Having problems does not mean our Higher Power is picking on us. Some problems are part of life; others are ours to solve, and we'll grow in necessary ways in the process.

Face and solve *today's* problems. Don't worry needlessly about tomorrow's problems, because when they appear, we'll have the resources necessary to solve them.

Facing and solving problems — working through problems with help from a Higher Power — means we're living and growing and reaping benefits.

God, help me face and solve my problems today. Help me do my part and let the rest go. I can learn to be a problem-solver.

Strength   **February 23**

We don't always have to be *strong* to be strong. Sometimes, our strength is expressed in being vulnerable. Sometimes, we need to fall apart to regroup and stay on track.

We all have days when we cannot push any harder, cannot hold back self-doubt, cannot stop focusing on fear, cannot be *strong.*

There are days when we cannot focus on being responsible. Occasionally, we don't want to get out of our pajamas. Sometimes, we cry in front of people. We expose our tiredness, irritability, or anger.

Those days are okay. They are just okay.

Part of taking care of ourselves means we give ourselves permission to "fall apart" when we need to. We do not have to be perpetual towers of strength. We are strong. We have proven that. Our strength will continue if we allow ourselves the courage to feel scared, weak, and vulnerable when we need to experience those feelings.

Today, God, help me to know that it is okay to allow myself to be human. Help me not to feel guilty or punish myself when I need to "fall apart."

Recognizing Feelings   February 24

Experiencing feelings can be a challenge if we've had no previous experience or permission to do that. Learning to identify what we're feeling is a challenge we can meet, but we will not become experts overnight. Nor do we have to deal with our feelings perfectly.

Here are some ideas that might be helpful as you learn to recognize and deal with feelings.

Take out a sheet of paper. On the top of it write, "If it was okay to feel whatever I'm feeling, and I wouldn't be judged as bad or wrong, what would I be feeling?" Then write whatever comes to mind. You can also use the favorite standby of many people in discovering their feelings: writing or journaling. You can keep a diary, write letters you don't intend to send, or just scribble thoughts onto a note pad.

Watch and listen to yourself as an objective third person might. Listen to your tone of voice and the words you use. What do you hear? Sadness, fear, anger, happiness?

What is your body telling you? Is it tense and rigid with anger? Running with fear? Heavy with sadness and grief? Dancing with joy?

Talking to people in recovery helps too. Going to meetings helps. Once we feel safe, many of us find that we open up naturally and with ease to our feelings.

We are on a continual treasure hunt in recovery. One of the treasures we're seeking is the emotional part of ourselves. We don't have to do it perfectly. We need only be honest, open, and willing to try. Our emotions are there waiting to share themselves with us.

Today, I will watch myself and listen to myself as I go through my day. I will not judge myself for what I'm feeling; I will accept myself.

Accepting Imperfection   February 25

"Why do I do this to myself?" asked a woman who wanted to lose weight. "I went to my support group feeling so guilty and ashamed because I ate half a cookie that wasn't on the diet. I found out that *everyone* cheats a little, and some people cheat a lot. I felt so ashamed before I came to the group, as though I were the only one not doing my diet perfectly. Now I know that I'm dieting as well as most, and better than some."

Why do we do this to ourselves? I'm not talking strictly about dieting; I'm talking about life. Why do we punish ourselves by thinking that we're inferior while believing that others are perfect — whether in relationships, recovery, or a specific task?

Whether we're judging ourselves or others, it's two sides of the same coin: perfection. Neither expectation is valid.

It is far more accurate and beneficial to tell ourselves that who we are is okay and what we are doing is good enough. That doesn't mean we won't make mistakes that need correcting; doesn't mean we won't get off track from time to time; doesn't mean we can't improve. It means with all our mistakes and wandering, we're basically on course. Encouraging and approving of ourselves is how we help ourselves stay on track.

Today, I will love and encourage myself. I will tell myself that what I'm doing is good enough, and I'll let myself enjoy that feeling.

Twelve Step Programs   February 26

I was furious when I found myself at my first Al-Anon meeting. It seemed so unfair that he had the problem and I had to go to a meeting. But by that time, I had nowhere left in the world to go with my pain. Now, I'm grateful for Al-Anon and my codependency recovery. Al-Anon keeps me on track; recovery has given me a life.

— *Anonymous*

There are many Twelve Step programs for codependents: Al-Anon, Adult Children of Alcoholics, CoDa, Families Anonymous, Nar-Anon, and more. We have many choices about which kind of group is right for us and which particular group in that category meets our needs. Twelve Step groups for codependents are free, anonymous, and available in most communities. If there is not one that is right for us, we can start one.

Twelve Step groups for codependents are not about how we can help the other person; they're about how we can help ourselves grow and change. They can help us accept and deal with the ways codependency has affected us. They can help us get on track and stay there.

There is magic in Twelve Step programs. There is healing power in connecting with other recovering people. We access this healing power by working the Steps and by allowing them to work on us. The Twelve Steps are a formula for healing.

How long do we have to go to meetings? We go until we "get the program." We go until the program "gets us." Then we keep on going — and growing.

Selecting a group and then attending regularly are important ways we can begin and continue to take care of ourselves. Actively participating in our recovery program by working the Steps is another.

I will be open to the healing power available to me from the Twelve Steps and a recovery program.

People-Pleasers   February 27

Have you ever been around people-pleasers? They tend to be displeasing. Being around someone who is turned inside out to please another is often irritating and anxiety-producing.

People-pleasing is a behavior we may have adapted to survive in our family. We may not have been able to get the love and attention we deserved. We may not have been given permission to please ourselves, to trust ourselves, and to choose a course of action that demonstrated self-trust.

People-pleasing can be overt or covert. We may run around fussing over others, chattering a mile-a-minute when what we are really saying is, "I hope I'm pleasing you." Or, we may be more covert, quietly going through life making important decisions based on pleasing others.

Taking other people's wants and needs into consideration is an important part of our relationships. We have responsibilities to friends and family and employers. We have a strong inner responsibility to be loving and caring. But, people-pleasing backfires. Not only do others get annoyed with us, we often get annoyed when our efforts to please do not work as we planned. The most comfortable people to be around are those who are considerate of others but ultimately please themselves.

Help me, God, work through my fears and begin to please myself.

Letting Go of Denial   February 28

> *We are slow to believe that which if believed would hurt our feelings.*
>
> — *Ovid*

Most of us in recovery have engaged in denial from time to time. Some of us relied on this tool.

We may have denied events or feelings from our past. We may have denied other people's problems; we may have denied our own problems, feelings, thoughts, wants, or needs.

We denied the truth.

Denial means we didn't let ourselves face reality, usually because facing that particular reality would hurt. It would be a loss of something: trust, love, family, perhaps a marriage, a friendship, or a dream. And it hurts to lose something, or someone.

Denial is a protective device, a shock absorber for the soul. It prevents us from acknowledging reality *until* we feel prepared to cope with that particular reality. People can shout and scream the truth at us, but we will not see or hear it until we are ready.

We are sturdy yet fragile beings. Sometimes, we need time to get prepared, time to ready ourselves to cope. We do not let go of our need to deny by beating ourselves into acceptance; we let go of our need to deny by allowing ourselves to become safe and strong enough to cope with the truth.

We will do this, when the time is right.

We do not need to punish ourselves for having denied reality; we need only love ourselves into safety and strength so that each day we are better equipped to face and deal with the truth. We will face and deal with reality — on our own time schedule, when we are ready, and in our Higher Power's timing. We do not have to accept chastisement from anyone, including ourselves, for this schedule.

We will know what we need to know, when it's time to know it.

Today, I will concentrate on making myself feel safe and confident. I will let myself have my awarenesses on my own time schedule.

You Are Lovable   February 29

We go back. . .and back. . .and back. . .through the layers of fear, shame, rage, hurt, and negative incantations until we discover the exuberant, unencumbered, delightful, and lovable child that was, and still is, in us.
                                            — Beyond Codependency

You are lovable. Yes, you.

Just because people haven't been there for you, just because certain people haven't been able to show love for you in ways that worked, just because relationships have failed or gone sour does not mean that you're unlovable.

You've had lessons to learn. Sometimes, those lessons have hurt.

Let go of the pain. Open your heart to love.

You are lovable.

You are loved.

Today, I will tell myself I'm lovable. I will do this until I believe it.

March

In recovery, we often discuss anger objectively. Yes, we reason, it's an emotion we're all prone to experience. Yes, the goal in recovery is to be free of resentment and anger. Yes, it's okay to feel angry, we agree. Well, maybe. . . .

Anger is a powerful and sometimes frightening emotion. It's also a beneficial one if it's not allowed to harden into resentment or used as a battering ram to punish or abuse people.

Anger is a warning signal. It points to problems. Sometimes, it signals problems we need to solve. Sometimes, it points to boundaries we need to set. Sometimes, it's the final burst of energy before letting go, or acceptance, settles in.

And, sometimes, anger just is. It doesn't have to be justified. It usually can't be confined to a tidy package. And it need not cause us to stifle ourselves or our energy.

We don't have to feel guilty whenever we experience anger. We don't have to feel guilty.

Breathe deeply. We can shamelessly feel all our feelings, including anger, and still take responsibility for our behaviors.

I will feel and release any angry feelings I have today. I can do that appropriately and safely.

Feelings on the Job   March 2

I'm furious about my job. Another man got a promotion that I believe I deserve. I'm so mad I feel like quitting. Now my wife says I should deal with my feelings. What good will that do? He still got the promotion.

— *Anonymous*

Our feelings at work are as important as our feelings in any other area of our life. Feelings are feelings — and wherever we incur them, dealing with them is what helps us move forward and grow.

Not acknowledging our feelings is what keeps us stuck and gives us stomachaches, headaches, and heartburn.

Yes, it can be a challenge to deal with feelings on the job. Sometimes, things can appear useless. One of our favorite tricks to avoid dealing with feelings is telling ourselves it's useless.

We want to give careful consideration to how we deal with our feelings on our job. It may be appropriate to take our intense feelings to someone not connected to our workplace and sort through them in a safe way.

Once we've experienced the intensity of the feelings, we can figure out what we need to do to take care of ourselves on the job.

Sometimes, as in any area of our life, feelings are to be felt and accepted. Sometimes, they are pointing to a problem in us, or a problem we need to resolve with someone else.

Sometimes, our feelings are helping to point us in a direction. Sometimes, they're connected to a message, or a fear: I'll never be successful. . . . I'll never get what I want. . . . I'm not good enough. . . .

Sometimes, the solution is a spiritual approach or remedy. Remember, whenever we bring a spiritual approach to any area of our life, *we* get the benefit.

We won't know what the lesson is until we summon the courage to stand still and deal with our feelings.

Today, I will consider my feelings at work as important as my feelings at home or anywhere else. I will find an appropriate way to deal with them.

While driving one day, a woman's attention focused on the license plate of the car ahead. The license read: "B-WHO-UR." How can I? she thought. I don't know who I am!

Some of us may have felt confused when people encouraged us to be ourselves. How could we know ourselves, or be who we are, when, for years, many of us submerged ourselves in the needs of others?

We do have a self. We're discovering more about ourselves daily. We're learning we're deserving of love.

We're learning to accept ourselves, as we are for the present moment — to accept our feelings, thoughts, flaws, wants, needs, and desires. If our thoughts or feelings are confused, we accept that too.

To be who we are means we accept our past — our history — exactly as is.

To be ourselves means we are entitled to our opinions and beliefs — for the present moment and subject to change. We accept our limitations and our strengths.

To be who we are means we accept our physical selves, as well as our mental, emotional, and spiritual selves, for now. Being who we are in recovery means we take that acceptance one step further. We can appreciate ourselves and our history.

Being who we are, loving and accepting ourselves, is not a limiting attitude. Accepting and loving ourselves is how we enable growth and change.

Today, I will be who I am. If I'm not yet certain who I am, I will affirm that I have a right to that exciting discovery.

I've learned I can take care of myself, and what I can't do, God will do for me.

— Al-Anon member

God, a Higher Power as we understand Him, is our source of guidance and positive change. This doesn't mean we're not responsible for ourselves. We are. But we aren't in this alone.

Recovery is not a do-it-yourself project. We don't have to become overly concerned about changing ourselves. We can do our part, relax, and trust that the changes we'll experience will be right for us.

Recovery means we don't have to look to other people as our source to meet our needs. They can help us, but they are not the source.

As we learn to trust the recovery process, we start to understand that a relationship with our Higher Power is no substitute for relationships with people. We don't need to hide behind religious beliefs or use our relationship with a Higher Power as an excuse to stop taking responsibility for ourselves and taking care of ourselves in relationships. But we can tap into and trust a Power greater than ourselves for the energy, wisdom, and guidance to do that.

Today, I will look to my Higher Power as the source for all my needs, including the changes I want to make in my recovery.

When I meet people or get in a new relationship, I start putting all these repressive restrictions on myself. I can't have my feelings. Can't have my wants and needs. Can't have my history. Can't do the things I want, feel the feelings I'm feeling, or say what I need to say. I turn into this repressed, perfectionistic robot, instead of being who I am: Me.

— *Anonymous*

Sometimes, our instinctive reaction to being in a new situation is: Don't be yourself.

Who else can we be? Who else would you want to be? We don't *need* to be anyone else.

The greatest gift we can bring to any relationship wherever we go is being who we are.

We may think others won't like us. We may be afraid that if we just relax and be ourselves, the other person will go away or shame us. We may worry about what the other person will think.

But, when we relax and accept ourselves, people often feel much better being around us than when we are rigid and repressed. We're fun to be around.

If others don't appreciate us, do we really want to be around them? Do we need to let the opinions of others control us and our behavior?

Giving ourselves permission to be who we are can have a healing influence on our relationships. The tone relaxes. We relax. The other person relaxes. Then everybody feels a little less shame, because they have learned the truth. Who we are is all we can be, all we're meant to be, and it's enough. It's fine.

Our opinion of ourselves is truly all that matters. And we can give ourselves all the approval we want and need.

Today, I will relax and be who I am in my relationships. I will do this not in a demeaning or inappropriate way, but in a way that shows I accept myself and value who I am. Help me, God, let go of my fears about being myself.

Peace   March 6

Anxiety is often our first reaction to conflict, problems, or even our own fears. In those moments, detaching and getting peaceful may seem disloyal or apathetic. We think: If I really care, I'll worry; if this is really important to me, I must stay upset. We convince ourselves that outcomes will be positively affected by the amount of time we spend worrying.

Our best problem-solving resource is peace. Solutions arise easily and naturally out of a peaceful state. Often, fear and anxiety block solutions. Anxiety gives power to the problem, not the solution. It does not help to harbor turmoil. *It does not help.*

Peace is available if we choose it. In spite of chaos and unsolved problems around us, all is well. Things will work out. We can surround ourselves with the resources of the Universe: water, earth, a sunset, a walk, a prayer, a friend. We can relax and let ourselves feel peace.

Today, I will let go of my need to stay in turmoil. I will cultivate peace and trust that timely solutions and goodness will arise naturally and harmoniously out of the wellspring of peace. I will consciously let go and let God.

"Everything I need shall be provided today. Everything."
Say it, until you believe it. Say it at the beginning of the day.
Say it throughout the day.

Sometimes, it helps to know what we want and need. But
if we don't, we can trust that God does.

When we ask, trust, and believe that our needs will be
met, our needs will be met. Sometimes God cares about the
silliest little things, if we do.

*Today, I will affirm that my needs will be met. I will affirm that
God cares and is the Source of my supply. Then I will let go and
see that what I have risked to believe is the truth.*

*Made a decision to turn our will and our lives over to the
care of God as we understood Him.*
                                                — *Step Three of Al-Anon*

Surrendering to a Power greater than ourselves is how we
become empowered.

We become empowered in a new, better, more effective way
than we believed possible.

Doors open. Windows open. Possibilities occur. Our
energy becomes channeled, at last, in areas and ways that
work for us. We become in tune with the Plan for our life
and our place in the Universe.

And there is a Plan and Place for us. We shall see that.
We shall know that. The Universe will open up and make
a special place for us, with all that we need provided.

It will be good. Understand that it is good, now.

Learning to own our power will come, if we are open to
it. We do not need to stop at powerlessness and helplessness.

That is a temporary place where we re-evaluate where we have been trying to have power when we have none.

Once we surrender, it is time to become empowered.

Let the power come, naturally. It is there. It is ours.

Today, I will be open to understanding what it means to own my power. I will accept powerlessness where I have no power; I will also accept the power that is mine to receive.

Taking Care of Ourselves   March 9

We cannot simultaneously set a boundary and take care of another person's feelings. It's impossible; the two acts contradict.

What a tremendous asset to have compassion for others! How difficult that same quality can make it to set boundaries!

It's good to care about other people and their feelings; it's essential to care about ourselves too. Sometimes, to take good care of ourselves, we need to make a choice.

Some of us live with a deeply ingrained message from our family, or from church, about *never* hurting other people's feelings. We can replace that message with a new one, one that says it's not okay to hurt ourselves. Sometimes, when we take care of ourselves, others will react with hurt feelings.

That's okay. We will learn, grow, and benefit by the experience; they will too. The most powerful and positive impact we can have on other people is accomplished by taking responsibility for ourselves, and allowing others to be responsible for themselves.

Caring works. Caretaking doesn't. We can learn to walk the line between the two.

Today, I will set the limits I need to set. I will let go of my need to take care of other people's feelings and instead take care of my own. I will give myself permission to take care of myself, knowing it's the best thing I can do for myself and others.

Living with Families March 10

I was forty-six years old before I finally admitted to myself and someone else that my grandmother always managed to make me feel guilty, angry, and controlled.

— Anonymous

We may love and care about our family very much. Family members may love and care about us. But interacting with some members may be a real trigger to our codependency — sometimes to a deep abyss of shame, rage, anger, guilt, and helplessness.

It can be difficult to achieve detachment, on an emotional level, with certain family members. It can be difficult to separate their issues from ours. It can be difficult to own our power.

Difficult, but not impossible.

The first step is awareness and acceptance — simple acknowledgment, without guilt, of our feelings and thoughts. We do not have to blame our family members. We do not have to blame or shame ourselves. Acceptance is the goal — acceptance and freedom to choose what we want and need to do to take of ourselves with that person. We can become free of the patterns of the past. We are recovering. Progress is the goal.

Today, Higher Power, help me be patient with myself as I learn how to apply recovery behaviors with family members. Help me strive today for awareness and acceptance.

Sometimes, the way is not clear.

Our minds get clouded, confused. We aren't certain what our next step should be, what it will look like, what direction we are headed.

That is the time to stop, ask for guidance, and rest. That is the time to let go of fear. Wait. Feel the confusion and chaos, then let it go. The path will show itself. The next step shall be revealed. We don't have to know *now*. We will know in time. Trust that. Let go and trust.

Today, I will wait if the way is not clear. I will trust that out of the chaos will come clarity.

Timing   **March 12**

If we could untangle the mysteries of life and unravel the energies which run through the world; if we could evaluate correctly the significance of passing events; if we could measure the struggles, dilemmas, and aspirations of mankind, we could find that nothing is born out of time. Everything comes at its appointed moment.

— *Joseph R. Sizoo*

Timing can be frustrating. We can wait and wait for something to happen, and it seems to be forever until it comes to pass. Or, suddenly, an event or circumstance is thrust upon us, catching us by surprise. Believing that things happen too slowly or too quickly is an illusion. *Timing is perfect.*

Today, I will trust and work with Divine Order. I will accept the timing in my life today and in my past as being perfect.

In spite of our best efforts to work our programs and lean on God's guidance, we sometimes don't understand what's going on in our life. We trust, wait, pray, listen to people, listen to ourselves, and the answer still does not come.

During those times, we need to understand that we are right where we need to be, even though that place may feel awkward and uncomfortable. Our life does have purpose and direction.

We are being changed, healed, and transformed at levels deeper than we can imagine. Good things, beyond our capacity to imagine, are being prepared and brought to us. We are being led and guided.

We can become peaceful. We do not have to act in haste or urgency just to relieve our discomfort, just to get an answer. We can wait until our mind is peaceful. We can wait for clear direction. Clarity will come.

The answer will come, and it will be good for us and those around us.

Today, God, help me know I am being guided into what's good about life, especially when I feel confused and without direction. Help me trust enough to wait until my mind and vision are clear and consistent. Help me know that clarity will come.

Trusting Ourselves   March 14

Trust can be one of the most confusing concepts in recovery. Who do we trust? For what?

The most important trust issue we face is learning to trust ourselves. The most detrimental thing that's happened to us is that we came to believe we couldn't trust ourselves.

There will be some who tell us we cannot trust ourselves, we are off base and out of whack. There are those who would benefit by our mistrusting ourselves.

Fear and doubt are our enemies. Panic is our enemy. Confusion is our opposition.

Self-trust is a healing gift we can give ourselves. How do we acquire it? We learn it. What do we do about our mistakes, about those times we thought we could trust ourselves but were wrong? We accept them, and trust ourselves anyway.

We know what is best for us. We know what is right for us. If we are wrong, if we need to change our mind, we will be guided into that — but only by trusting where we are today.

We can look to others for support and reinforcement, but trust in ourselves is essential.

Do not trust fear. Do not trust panic. We can trust ourselves, stand in our own truth, stand in our own light. We have it now. Already. We have all the light we need for today. And tomorrow's light shall be given to us then.

Trust ourselves, and we will know whom to trust. Trust ourselves, and we will know what to do. When we feel we absolutely cannot trust ourselves, trust that God will guide us into truth.

God, help me let go of fear, doubt, and confusion — the enemies of self-trust. Help me go forward in peace and confidence. Help me grow in trust for myself and You, one day at a time, one experience at a time.

Removing the Victim   March 15

"Don't others see how much I'm hurting?" "Can't they see I need help?" "Don't they care?"

The issue is not whether *others* see or care. The issue is whether we see and care about ourselves. Often, when we are pointing a finger at others, waiting for them to have compassion for us, it's because we have not fully accepted our pain. We have not yet reached that point of caring about ourselves. We are hoping for an awareness in another that we have not yet had.

It is our job to have compassion for ourselves. When we do, we have taken the first step toward removing ourselves as victims. We are on the way to self-responsibility, self-care, and change.

Today, I will not wait for others to see and care; I will take responsibility for being aware of my pain and problems, and caring about myself.

Positive Energy   March 16

It's so easy to look around and notice what's wrong.
It takes practice to see what's right.
Many of us have lived around negativity for years. We've become skilled at labeling what's wrong with other people, our life, our work, our day, our relationships, ourselves, our conduct, our recovery.

We want to be realistic, and our goal is to identify and accept reality. However, this is often not our intent when we practice negativity. The purpose of negativity is usually annihilation.

Negative thinking empowers the problem. It takes us out of harmony. Negative energy sabotages and destroys. It has a powerful life of its own.

So does positive energy. Each day, we can ask what's right, what's good — about other people, our life, our work, our day, our relationships, ourselves, our conduct, our recovery.

Positive energy heals, conducts love, and transforms. Choose positive energy.

Today, God help me let go of negativity. Transform my beliefs and thinking, at the core, from negative to positive. Put me in harmony with the good.

Empowering   March 17

You can think. You can feel. You can solve your problems. You can take care of yourself.

Those words have often benefited me more than the most profound and elaborate advice.

How easy it is to fall into the trap of doubting ourselves and others.

When someone tells us about a problem, what is our reaction? Do we believe we need to solve it for the person? Do we believe that that person's future rests on our ability to advise him or her? That's standing on shaky ground — not the stuff of which recovery is made.

When someone is struggling through a feeling, or a morass of feelings, what is our reaction? That the person will never survive that experience? That it's not okay for someone to feel? That he or she will never get through this intact?

When a person is faced with the task of assuming responsibility for their life and behaviors, what is our response? That the person can't do that? I must do it myself to save him or her from dissipating into ashes? From crumbling? From failing?

What is our reaction to ourselves when we encounter a problem, a feeling, or when we face the prospect of assuming responsibility for ourselves?

Do we believe in ourselves and others? Do we give power to people — including ourselves — and their abilities? Or do we give the power to the problem, the feeling, or the irresponsibility?

We can learn to check ourselves out. We can learn to think, and consider our response, before we respond. "I'm sorry you're having that problem. I know you can figure out a solution. Sounds like you've got some feelings going on. I know you'll work through them and come out on the other side."

Each of us is responsible for *ourselves*. That does not mean we don't care. It does not mean a cold, calculated withdrawal of our support from others. It means we learn to love and support people in ways that work. It means we learn to love and support ourselves in ways that work. It means that we connect with friends who love and support us in ways that work.

To believe in people, to believe in each person's inherent ability to think, feel, solve problems, and take care of themselves is a great gift we can give and receive from others.

Today, I will strive to give and receive support that is pure and empowering. I will work at believing in myself and others — and our mutual abilities to be competent at dealing with feelings, solving problems, and taking responsibility for ourselves.

Safety   March 18

One of the long-term effects of living in a dysfunctional family — as children or adults — is that we don't feel safe.

Much of what we call codependency happens because we don't feel safe in relationships. This can cause us to control, obsess, or focus on the other person, while neglecting ourselves or shutting down our feelings.

We can learn to make ourselves feel safe and comfortable, as part of a nurturing, loving attitude toward ourselves.

Often, we get a feeling of safety and comfort when we attend Twelve Step meetings or support groups. Being with a friend or doing something nice for ourselves helps us feel protected and loved. Sometimes, reaching out to another person helps us feel safe. Prayer and meditation help us affirm that our Higher Power cares for us.

We are safe now. We can relax. Perhaps others haven't been there for us in a consistent, trustworthy way, but we are learning to be there for ourselves.

Today, I will concentrate on making myself feel safe and comfortable.

Staying Out of the Middle   March 19

"I don't want to get in the middle, but. . ." is a sign that we may have just stepped into the middle.

We do not have to get caught in the middle of other people's issues, problems, or communication. We can let others take responsibility for themselves in their relationships. We can let them work out their issues with each other.

Being a peacemaker does not mean we get in the middle. We are bearers of peace by staying peaceful ourselves and not harboring turmoil. We are peacemakers by not causing the extra chaos created when we get in the middle of other people's affairs and relationships.

Don't get in the middle unless you want to be there.

Today, I will refuse to accept any invitations to jump in the middle of others' affairs, issues, and relationships. I will trust others to work out their own affairs, including the ideas and feelings they want to communicate to each other.

Let fears slip away.

Release any negative, limiting, or self-defeating beliefs buried in your subconscious too. These beliefs may be about life, love, or yourself. Beliefs create reality.

Let go. From as deep within as your fears, resentments, and negative beliefs are stored, let them all go. Let the belief or feeling surface. Accept it; surrender to it. Feel the discomfort or unrest. Then let it go. Let new beliefs replace the old. Let peace and joy and love replace fear.

Give yourself and your body permission to let go of fears, resentments, and negative beliefs. Release that which is no longer useful. Trust that you are being healed and prepared for receiving what is good.

Today, God, help me become willing to let go of old beliefs and feelings that may be hurting me. Gently take them from me and replace them with new beliefs and feelings. I do deserve the best life and love have to offer. Help me believe that.

Considering Commitment   March 21

Pay attention to your commitments.

While many of us fear committing, it's good to weigh the cost of any commitment we are considering. We need to feel consistently positive that it's an appropriate commitment for us.

Many of us have a history of jumping — leaping headfirst — into commitments without weighing the cost and the possible consequences of that particular commitment. When we get in, we find that we do not really want to commit, and feel trapped.

Some of us may become afraid of losing out on a particular opportunity if we don't commit. It is true that we will lose out on certain opportunities if we are unwilling to commit. We still need to weigh the commitment. We still need to become clear about whether that commitment seems right for us. If it isn't, we need to be direct and honest with others and ourselves.

Be patient. Do some soul searching. Wait for a clear answer. We need to make our commitments not in urgency or panic but in quiet confidence that what we are committing to is right for us.

If something within says no, find the courage to trust that voice.

This is not our last chance. It is not the only opportunity we'll ever have. Don't panic. We don't have to commit to what isn't right for us, even if we try to tell ourselves it *should* be right for us and we *should* commit.

Often, we can trust our intuitive sense more than we can trust our intellect about commitments.

In the excitement of making a commitment and beginning, we may overlook the realities of the middle. That is what we need to consider.

We don't have to commit out of urgency, impulsivity, or fear. We are entitled to ask, Will this be *good* for me? We are entitled to ask if this commitment feels right.

Today, God, guide me in making my commitments. Help me say yes to what is in my highest good, and no to what isn't. I will give serious consideration before I commit myself to any activity or person. I will take the time to consider if the commitment is really what I want.

Letting Go of Being a Victim   March 22

It's okay to have a good day. Really.

It's okay to be doing okay and to feel like our life is manageable and on track.

Many of us have learned, as part of our survival behaviors, that the way to get the attention and approval we want is to be victims. If life is awful, too difficult, unmanageable, too hard, unfair, then others will accept, like, and approve of us, we think.

We may have learned this from living and associating with people who also learned to survive by being a victim.

We are not victims. We do not need to be victimized. We do not need to be helpless and out of control to get the attention and love we desire. In fact, the kind of love we are seeking cannot be obtained that way.

We can get the love we really want and need by only owning our power. We learn that we can stand on our own two feet, even though it sometimes feels good to lean a little. We learn that the people we are leaning on are not holding us up. They are standing next to us.

We all have bad days — days when things are not going the way we'd like, days when we have feelings of sadness and fear. But we can deal with our bad days and darker feelings in ways that reflect self-responsibility rather than victimization.

It's okay to have a good day too. We might not have as much to talk about, but we'll have more to enjoy.

God, help me let go of my need to be a victim. Help me let go of my belief that to be loved and get attention I need to be a victim. Surround me with people who love me when I own my power. Help me start having good days and enjoying them.

We need to know how far we'll go, and how far we'll allow others to go with us. Once we understand this, we can go anywhere.

— Beyond Codependency

When we own our power to take care of ourselves — set a boundary, say no, change an old pattern — we may get flack from some people. That's okay. We don't have to let their reactions control us, stop us, or influence our decision to take care of ourselves.

We don't have to control their reactions to our process of self-care. That is not our responsibility. We don't have to expect them not to react either.

People will react when we do things differently or take assertive action to nurture ourselves, particularly if our decision in some way affects them. Let them have their feelings. Let them have their reactions. But continue on your course anyway.

If people are used to us behaving in a certain way, they'll attempt to convince us to stay that way to avoid changing the system. If people are used to us saying yes all the time, they may start mumbling and murmuring when we say no. If people are used to us taking care of their responsibilities, feelings, and problems, they may give us some flack when we stop. That's normal. We can learn to live with a little flack in the name of healthy self-care. Not abuse, mind you. Flack.

If people are used to controlling us through guilt, bullying, and badgering, they may intensify their efforts when we change and refuse to be controlled. That's okay. That's flack too.

We don't have to let flack pull us back into old ways if we've decided we want and need to change. We don't have to react to flack or give it much attention. It doesn't deserve it. It will die down.

Today, I will disregard any flack I receive for changing my behaviors or making other efforts to be myself.

Appreciating Ourselves   March 24

We are the greatest thing that will ever happen to us. Believe it. It makes life much easier.
                                        — Codependent No More

It is time to stop this nonsense of running around picking on ourselves.

We may have walked through much of our life apologizing for ourselves either directly or indirectly — feeling less valuable than others, believing that they know better than we do, and believing that somehow others are meant to be here and we are not.

We have a right to be here.

We have a right to be ourselves.

We are here. There is a purpose, a reason, and an intention for our life. We do not have to apologize for being here or being who we are.

We are good enough, and deserving.

Others do not have our magic. We have our magic. It is in us.

It doesn't matter what we've done in our past. We all have a past, woven with mistakes, successes, and learning experiences. We have a right to our past. It is ours. It has worked to shape and form us. As we progress on this journey, we shall see how each of our experiences will be turned around and used for good.

We have already spent too much time being ashamed, being apologetic, and doubting the beauty of ourselves. Be done with it. Let it go. It is an unnecessary burden. Others have rights, but so do we. We are neither less than nor more than. We are equal. We are who we are. That is who we were created and intended to be.

That, my friend, is a wonderful gift.

God, help me own my power to love and appreciate myself. Help me give myself validity instead of looking to others to do that.

Letting Go of Worry   March 25

What if we knew for certain that everything we're worried about today will work out fine?

What if. . .we had a guarantee that the problem bothering us would be worked out in the most perfect way, and at the best possible time? Furthermore, what if we knew that three years from now we'd be grateful for that problem, and its solution?

What if. . .we knew that even our worst fear would work out for the best?

What if. . .we had a guarantee that everything that's happening, and has happened, in our life was meant to be, planned just for us, and in our best interest?

What if. . .we had a guarantee that the people we love are experiencing exactly what they need in order to become who they're intended to become? Further, what if we had a guarantee that others can be responsible for themselves, and we don't have to control or take responsibility for them?

What if. . .we knew the future was going to be good, and we would have an abundance of resources and guidance to handle whatever comes our way?

What if. . .we knew everything was okay, and we didn't have to worry about a thing? What would we do then?

We'd be free to let go and enjoy life.

Today, I will know that I don't have to worry about anything. If I do worry, I will do it with the understanding that I am choosing to worry, and it is not necessary.

Gifts, Not Burdens March 26

Children are gifts, if we accept them.
— Kathleen Turner Crilly

Children are gifts. Our children, if we have children, are a gift to us. We, as children, were gifts to our parents.

Sadly, many of us did not receive the message from our parents that we were gifts to them and to the Universe. Maybe our parents were in pain themselves; maybe our parents were looking to us to be their caretakers; maybe we came at a difficult time in their lives; maybe they had their own issues and simply were not able to enjoy, accept, and appreciate us for the gifts we are.

Many of us have a deep, sometimes subconscious, belief that we were, and are, a burden to the world and the people around us. This belief can block our ability to enjoy life and our relationships with others. This belief can even impair our relationship with a Higher Power: we may feel we are a burden to God.

If we have that belief, it is time to let it go.

We are not a burden. We never were. If we received that message from our parents, it is time to recognize that issue as theirs to resolve.

We have a right to treat ourselves as a gift — to ourselves, to others, and to the Universe.

We are here, and we have a right to be here.

Today, I will treat myself, and any children I have, as though we are a gift. I will let go of any beliefs I have about being a burden — to my Higher Power, my friends, my family, and myself.

After-Burn   March 27

"How could I do it? How could I say it? Even though I meant it, I still feel ashamed, guilty, and afraid."

This is common reaction to new, exciting recovery behaviors. Anything to do with owning our power and taking care of ourselves can trigger feelings of shame, guilt, and fear.

We do not have to allow these feelings to control us. They're a backlash. They're after-burn. Let them burn out.

When we start confronting and attacking feelings and messages, we will experience some after-burn. The after-burn is what we allowed to control us all our life — shame and guilt.

Many of us grew up with shame-based messages that it wasn't okay to take care of ourselves, be honest, be direct, and own our power with people. Many of us grew up with messages that it wasn't okay to be who we were and resolve problems in relationships. Many of us grew up with the message that what we want and need isn't okay.

Let it all burn off. We don't have to take after-burn so seriously. We don't let the after-burn convince us that we are wrong and don't have a right to take care of ourselves and set boundaries.

Do we really have the right to take care of ourselves? Do we really have the right to set boundaries? Do we really have the right to be direct and say what we need to say?

You bet we do.

Today, I will let any after-burn which sets in after I practice a new recovery behavior, burn off. I will not take it so seriously. God, help me let go of my shame and needless fears about what will happen to me if I really start caring for and loving myself.

Balance   **March 28**

Seek balance.
Balance emotions with reason.
Combine detachment with doing our part.
Balance giving with receiving.
Alternate work with play, business with personal activities.
Balance tending to our spiritual needs with tending to our other needs.
Juggle responsibilities to others with responsibilities to ourselves.
Balance caring about others with caring about ourselves.
Whenever possible, let's be good to others, but be good to ourselves too.
Some of us have to make up for lost time.

Today, I will strive for balance.

Getting Needs Met   **March 29**

Picture yourself walking through a meadow. There is a path opening before you. As you walk, you feel hungry. Look to your left. There's a fruit tree in full bloom. Pick what you need.

Steps later, you notice you're thirsty. On your right, there's a fresh water spring.

When you are tired, a resting place emerges. When you are lonely, a friend appears to walk with you. When you get lost, a teacher with a map appears.

Before long, you notice the flow: need and supply; desire and fulfillment. Maybe, you wonder, Someone gave me the need because Someone planned to fulfill it. Maybe I had to feel the need, so I would notice and accept the gift. Maybe closing my eyes to the desire closes my arms to its fulfillment.

Demand and supply, desire and fulfillment — a continuous cycle, unless we break it. All the necessary supplies have already been planned and provided for this journey.

Today, everything I need shall be supplied to me.

Experiment   March 30

Experiment. Try something new. Try stepping out.

We have been held back too long. We have held ourselves back too long.

As children, many of us were deprived of the right to experiment. Many of us are depriving ourselves of the right to experiment and learn as adults.

Now is the time to experiment. It is an important part of recovery. Let yourself try things. Let yourself try something new. Yes, you will make mistakes. But from those mistakes, you can learn what your values are.

Some things we just won't like. That's good. Then we'll know a little more about who we are and what we don't like.

Some things we will like. They will work with our values. They will work with who we are, and we will discover something important and life-enriching.

There is a quiet time in recovery, a time to stand still and heal, a time to give ourselves a cooling-off time. This is a time of introspection and healing. It is an important time. We deal with our issues.

There also comes a time when it is equally important to experiment, to begin to "test the water."

Recovery does not equal abstention from life. Recovery means learning to live and learning to live fully. Recovery means exploration, investigation, experimentation.

Recovery means being done with the rigid, shame-based rules from the past, and formulating healthy values based on self-love, love for others, and living in harmony with this world.

Experiment. Try something new. Maybe you won't like it. Maybe you'll make a mistake. But maybe you will like it, and maybe you'll discover something you love.

Today, I will give myself permission to experiment in life. I will stop rigidly holding myself back, and I will jump in when jumping in feels right. God, help me let go of my need to deprive myself of being alive.

Finances   March 31

Taking financial responsibility for ourselves is part of recovery. Some of us may find ourselves in hard financial times for a variety of reasons.

Our recovery concepts, including the Steps, work on money issues and restoring manageability to that area of our life. Make appropriate amends — even if that means tackling a $5,000 debt by sending in $5 a month.

Start where you are, with what you've got. As with other issues, acceptance and gratitude turn what we have into more.

Money issues are not a good place to act as if. Don't write checks until the money is in the bank. Don't spend money until you've got it in your hand.

If there is too little money to survive, use the appropriate resources available *without shame.*

Set goals.

Believe you deserve the best, financially.

Believe God cares about your finances.

Let go of your fear, and trust.

Today, I will focus on taking responsibility for my present financial circumstances, no matter how overwhelming that area of my life may feel and be.

April

Go easy. You may have to push forward, but you don't have to push so hard. Go in gentleness, go in peace.

Do not be in so much of a hurry. At no day, no hour, no time are you required to do more than you can do in peace.

Frantic behaviors and urgency are not the foundation for our new way of life.

Do not be in too much of a hurry to begin. Begin, but do not force the beginning if it is not time. Beginnings will arrive soon enough.

Enjoy and relish middles, the heart of the matter.

Do not be in too much of a hurry to finish. You may be almost done, but enjoy the final moments. Give yourself fully to those moments so that you may give and get all there is.

Let the pace flow naturally. Move forward. Start. Keep moving forward. Do it gently, though. Do it in peace. Cherish each moment.

Today, God, help me focus on a peaceful pace rather than a harried one. I will keep moving forward gently, not frantically. Help me let go of my need to be anxious, upset, and harried. Help me replace it with a need to be at peace and in harmony.

Facing Our Darker Side   **April 2**

Made a searching and fearless moral inventory of ourselves.
— Step Four of Al-Anon

By the time we get to the Fourth of the Twelve Steps, we are ready to face our darker side, the side that prevents us from loving ourselves and others, from letting others love us, and from enjoying life. The purpose of Step Four is not to make ourselves feel worse; our purpose is to begin to remove our blocks to joy and love.

We look for fears, anger, hurt, and shame from past events — buried feelings that may be affecting our life today. We search for subconscious beliefs about ourselves and others that may be interfering with the quality of our relationships. These beliefs say: *I'm not lovable.... I'm a burden to those around me.... People can't be trusted.... I can't be trusted.... I don't deserve to be happy and successful.... Life isn't worth living.* We look at our behaviors and patterns with an eye toward discerning the self-defeating ones. With love and compassion for ourselves, we try to unearth all our guilt — earned and unearned — and expose it to the light.

We perform this examination without fear of what we shall find, because this soul-searching can cleanse us and help us feel better about ourselves than we ever dreamt possible.

God, help me search out the blocks and barriers within myself. Bring what I need to know into my conscious mind, so I can be free of it. Show me what I need to know about myself.

Acceptance   April 3

Surrender to the moment. Ride it out and through, for all it's worth. Throw yourself into it.

Stop resisting.

So much of our anguish is created when we are in resistance. So much relief, release, and change are possible when we accept, simply accept.

We waste our time, expend our energy, and make things harder by resisting, repressing, and denying. Repressing our thoughts will not make them disappear. Repressing a thought already formed will not make us a better person. Think it. Let it come into reality. Then release it. A thought is not forever. If we don't like it, we can think another one or change it. But to do that, we must accept and release the first thought.

Resistance and repression will not change a thing. They will put us at war with our thoughts.

We make life harder by resisting and repressing our feelings. No matter how dark, how uncomfortable, how unjustified, how surprising, how "inappropriate" we might deem our feelings, resisting and repressing them will not free us from them. Doing that will make them worse. They will swirl inside us, torment us, make us sick, make our body ache, compel us to do compulsive things, keep us awake, or put us to sleep.

In the final analysis, all that we're really called on to do is accept our feelings by feeling them, and saying, "Yes, this is what I feel."

Feelings are for the present moment. The more quickly we can accept a feeling, the more quickly we will move on to the next.

Resisting or repressing thoughts and feelings does not change us or turn us into the person we want to be or think we should be. It puts us in resistance to reality. It makes us repressed. Eventually, it makes us depressed.

Resisting events or circumstances in our life does not change things, no matter how undesirable the events or circumstances may be.

Acceptance turns us into the person we are and want to be. Acceptance empowers the events and circumstances to turn around for the better.

What do we do if we're in resistance, in a tug-of-war with some reality in our life? *Accepting our resistance* can help us get through that too.

Acceptance does not mean we're giving our approval. It does not mean surrendering to the will and plans of another. It does not mean commitment. It is not forever. It is for the present moment. Acceptance does not make things harder; it makes things easier. Acceptance does not mean we accept abuse or mistreatment; it does not mean we forego ourselves, our boundaries, hopes, dreams, desires, or wants. It means we accept what is, so we know what to do to take care of ourselves and what boundaries we need to set. It means we accept what is and who we are at the moment, so we are free to change and grow.

Acceptance and surrender move us forward on this journey. Force does not work.

Acceptance and surrender — two concepts that hurt the most before we do them.

Today, I will practice accepting myself and my present circumstances. I will begin to watch and trust the magic that acceptance can bring into my life and recovery.

Negotiating Conflicts   April 4

> *Recovery is about more than walking away. Sometimes it means learning to stay and deal. It's about building and maintaining relationships that work.*
> — Beyond Codependency

Problems and conflicts are part of life and relationships — with friends, family, loved ones, and at work. Problem solving and conflict negotiation are skills we can acquire and improve with time.

Not being willing to tackle and solve problems in relationships leads to unresolved feelings of anger and victimization, terminated relationships, unresolved problems, and power plays that intensify the problem and waste time and energy.

Not being willing to face and solve problems means we may run into that problem again.

Some problems with people cannot be worked out in mutually satisfactory ways. Sometimes the problem is a boundary issue we have, and there is not room to negotiate.

In that case, we need to clearly understand what we want and need and what our bottom line is.

Some problems with people, though, can be worked out, worked through, and satisfactorily negotiated. Often, there are workable options for solving problems that we will not even see until we become open to the concept of working through problems in relationships, rather than running from the problems.

To negotiate problems, we must be willing to identify the problem, let go of blame and shame, and focus on possible creative solutions. To successfully negotiate and solve problems in relationships, we must have a sense of our bottom line and our boundary issues, so we don't waste time trying to negotiate non-negotiable issues.

We need to learn to identify what both people really want and need and the different possibilities for working that out. We can learn to be flexible without being too flexible. Committed, intimate relationships mean two people are learning to work together through their problems and conflicts in ways that work in both people's best interest.

Today, I will be open to negotiating conflicts I have with people. I will strive for balance without being too submissive or too demanding. I will strive for appropriate flexibility in my problem-solving efforts.

Detaching in Love   April 5

Detachment is a key to recovery from codependency. It strengthens our healthy relationships — the ones that we want to grow and flourish. It benefits our difficult relationships — the ones that are teaching us to cope. It helps us!

Detachment is not something we do once. It's a daily behavior in recovery. We learn it when we're beginning our recovery from codependency and adult children issues. And we continue to practice it along the way as we grow and change, and as our relationships grow and change.

We learn to let go of people we love, people we like, and those we don't particularly care for. We separate ourselves, and our process, from others and their process.

We relinquish our tight hold and our need to control in our relationships. We take responsibility for ourselves; we allow others to do the same. We detach with the understanding that life is unfolding exactly as it needs to, for others and ourselves. The way life unfolds is good, even when it hurts. And ultimately, we can benefit from even the most difficult situations. We do this with the understanding that a Power greater than ourselves is in charge, and all is well.

Today, I will apply the concept of detachment, to the best of my ability, in my relationships. If I can't let go completely, I'll try to "hang on loose."

Patience   April 6

How sick and tired we may become of people telling us to be patient or to learn patience. How frustrating it can be to want to finally have something, or to move forward, and then not have that happen. How irritating to have someone tell us to wait while our needs have not been met and we're in the midst of anxiety, frustration, and inaction.

Do not confuse the suggestion to be patient with the old rule about not having feelings.

Being patient does not mean we go through the sometimes grueling process of life and recovery without having feelings! Feel the frustration. Feel the impatience. Get as angry as you need to about not having your needs met. Feel your fear.

Controlling our feelings will not control the process!

We find patience by surrendering to our feelings. Patience

cannot be forced. It is a gift, one that closely follows acceptance and gratitude. When we work through our feelings to fully accept who we are and what we have, we will be ready to be and have more.

Today, I will let myself have my feelings while I practice patience.

Those Old-Time Feelings   April 7

I still have bad days. But that's okay. I used to have bad years.
— *Anonymous*

Sometimes, the old feelings creep back in. We may feel fearful, ashamed, and hopeless. We may feel not good enough, unlovable, victimized, helpless, and resentful about it all. This is codependency, a condition some describe as "soul-sickness."

Many of us felt this way when we began recovery. Sometimes, we slip back into these feelings after we've begun recovery. Sometimes there's a reason. An event may trigger these reactions, such as ending a relationship, stress, problems on the job, at home, or in friendships. Times of change can trigger these reactions. So can physical illness.

Sometimes, these feelings return for no reason.

A return to the old feelings doesn't mean we're back to square one in our recovery. They do not mean we've failed at recovery. They do not mean we're in for a long, painful session of feeling badly. They just are there.

The solution is the same: practicing the basics. Some of the basics are loving and trusting our self, detachment, dealing with feelings, giving and receiving support in the recovery community, using our affirmations, and having fun.

Another basic is working the Steps. Often, working the Steps is how we become enabled and empowered to practice the other basics, such as detachment and self-love.

If the old feelings come back, know for certain there is a way out that will work.

Today, if I find myself in the dark pit of codependency, I will work a Step to help myself climb out.

Self-Care   April 8

> *I don't precisely know what you need to do to take care of yourself. But I know you can figure it out.*
> — Beyond Codependency

Rest when you're tired.
Take a drink of cold water when you're thirsty.
Call a friend when you're lonely.
Ask God to help when you feel overwhelmed.
Many of us have learned how to deprive and neglect ourselves. Many of us have learned to push ourselves hard, when the problem is that we're already pushed too hard.

Many of us are afraid the work won't get done if we rest when we're tired. The work will get done; it will be done better than work that emerges from tiredness of soul and spirit. Nurtured, nourished people, who love themselves and care for themselves, are the delight of the Universe.

They are well-timed, efficient, and Divinely led.

Today, I will practice loving self-care.

Giving   April 9

Learning to be a healthy giver can be a challenge. Many of us got caught up in compulsive giving — charitable acts motivated by uncharitable feelings of guilt, shame, obligation, pity, and moral superiority.

We now understand that caretaking and compulsive giving don't work. They backfire.

Caretaking keeps us feeling victimized.

Many of us gave too much, thinking we were doing things right; then we became confused because our life and relationships weren't working. Many of us gave so much for so long, thinking we were doing God's will; then in recovery, we refused to give, care, or love for a time.

That's okay. Perhaps we needed a rest. But healthy giving is part of healthy living. The goal in recovery is balance — caring that is motivated by a true desire to give, with an underlying attitude of respect for ourselves and others.

The goal in recovery is to choose what we want to give, to whom, when, and how much. The goal in recovery is to give, and not feel victimized by our giving.

Are we giving because we want to, because it's our responsibility? Or are we giving because we feel obligated, guilty, ashamed, or superior? Are we giving because we feel afraid to say no?

Are the ways we try to assist people helpful, or do they prevent others from facing their true responsibilities?

Are we giving so that people will like us or feel obligated to us? Are we giving to prove we're worthy? Or are we giving because we want to give and it feels right?

Recovery includes a cycle of giving and receiving. It keeps healthy energy flowing among us, our Higher Power, and others. It takes time to learn how to give in healthy ways. It takes time to learn to receive. Be patient. Balance will come.

God, please guide my giving and my motives today.

Our happiness is not a present someone else holds in his or her hands. Our well-being is not held by another to be given or withheld at whim. If we reach out and try to force someone to give us what we believe he or she holds, we will be disappointed. We will discover that it is an illusion. The person didn't hold it. He or she never shall. That beautifully wrapped box with the ribbon on it that we believed contained our happiness that someone was holding — it's an illusion!

In those moments when we are trying to reach out and force someone to stop our pain and create our joy, if we can find the courage to stop flailing about and instead stand still and deal with our issues, we will find our happiness.

Yes, it is true that if someone steps on our foot, he or she is hurting us and therefore holds the power to stop our pain by removing his or her foot. But the pain is still ours. And so is the responsibility to tell someone to stop stepping on our feet.

Healing will come when we're aware of how we attempt to use others to stop our pain and create our happiness. We will heal from the past. We will receive insights that can change the course of our relationships.

We will see that, all along, our happiness and our well-being have been in our hands. We have held that box. The contents are ours for the opening.

God, help me remember that I hold the key to my own happiness. Give me the courage to stand still and deal with my own feelings. Give me the insights I need to improve my relationships. Help me stop doing the codependent dance and start doing the dance of recovery.

Taking responsibility for our financial affairs will improve our self-esteem and lessen anxiety.

Each of us, today, has a *present set of financial circumstances.* We have a certain amount of money in hand, and money due to us. We have a pile of bills that we owe. We have taxes to pay. Those are our present financial circumstances. No matter what the details are, acceptance, gratitude, and self-responsibility will lessen the stress.

Each of us, today, has a *financial future.* There are few future aspects of our life we can control, but one part we can play to assist our future is setting goals.

We don't have to obsess about our goals. We don't have to constantly watch and mark our progress toward them. But it is beneficial to think about our goals and write them down. What do we want to happen in our financial future? What financial problems would we like to solve? What bills would we like to be rid of? What would we like to be earning at the end of this year? The end of next year? Five years from now?

Are we willing to work for our goals and trust our Higher Power to guide us?

Pay bills on time. Contact creditors. Make arrangements. Do your best, today, to take responsibility for your finances. Set goals for the future. Then, let go of money and concentrate on living. Taking responsibility for our financial affairs does not mean making money our focus. Taking responsibility for our finances enables us to take our focus off money. It frees us to do our work and live the life we want.

We deserve to have the self-esteem and peace that accompanies financial responsibility.

Today, I will take the time necessary to be responsible for myself financially. If it is time to pay bills or talk to creditors, I will do that. If it is time to set goals, I will do that. Once I have done my part, I will let the rest go.

Letting Go of Fear   April 12

Picture yourself swimming — floating — peacefully down a gentle stream. All you need to do is breathe, relax, and go with the flow.

Suddenly, you become conscious of your situation. Frightened, overwhelmed with "what if's?" your body tenses. You begin to thrash around, frantically looking for something to grab on to.

You panic so hard you start to go under. Then you remember — you're working too hard at this. You don't need to panic. All you need to do is breathe, relax, and go with the flow. You won't drown.

Panic is our great enemy.

We don't need to become desperate. If overwhelming problems appear in our life, we need to stop struggling. We can tread water for a bit, until our equilibrium returns. Then we can go back to floating peacefully down the gentle stream. It is our stream. It is a safe stream. Our course has been charted. All is well.

Today, I will relax, breathe, and go with the flow.

Enjoyment   April 13

One of the prohibitions many of us learned in childhood is the unspoken rule *Don't have fun and enjoy life.* This rule creates martyrs — people who will not let themselves embrace the pleasures of day-to-day living.

Many of us associated suffering with some sort of sainthood. Now, we associate it with codependency. We can go through the day making ourselves feel anxious, guilty, miserable, and deprived. Or we can allow ourselves to go through that same day feeling good. In recovery, we eventually learn the choice is ours.

There is much to be enjoyed each day, and it is okay to feel good. We can let ourselves enjoy our tasks. We can learn to relax without guilt. We can even learn to have fun.

Work at learning to have fun. Apply yourself with dedication to learning enjoyment. Work as hard at learning to have fun as you did at feeling miserable.

Our work will pay off. Fun will become fun. Life will become worth living. And each day, we'll find many pleasures to be enjoyed.

Today, I will let myself enjoy life as I go through my day.

Perfectionism   April 14

Recovery from codependency is an individual process that necessitates making mistakes, struggling through problems, and facing tough issues.

Expecting ourselves to be perfect slows this process; it puts us in a guilty and anxious state. Expecting others to be perfect is equally destructive; it makes others feel ashamed and may interfere with their growth.

People are human and vulnerable, and that is wonderful. We can accept and cherish that idea. Expecting others to be perfect puts us in that codependent state of moral superiority. Expecting ourselves to be perfect makes us feel rigid and inferior.

We can let go of both ideas.

We do not need to go to the other extreme, tolerating anything people throw our way. We can still expect appropriate, responsible behavior from ourselves. But most of us can afford to loosen up a bit. And when we stop expecting others to be perfect, we may discover that they're doing much better than we thought. When we stop expecting ourselves to be perfect, we'll discover the beauty in ourselves.

Today, I will practice tolerance, acceptance, and love of others as they are, and myself as I am. I will strive for that balance between expecting too much and expecting too little from others and myself.

Communication   April 15

Part of owning our power is learning to communicate clearly, directly, and assertively. We don't have to beat around the bush in our conversations to control the reactions of others. Guilt-producing comments only produce guilt. We don't have to fix or take care of people with our words; we can't expect others to take care of us with words either. We can settle for being heard and accepted. And we can respectfully listen to what others have to say.

Hinting at what we need doesn't work. Others can't read our mind, and they're likely to resent our indirectness. The best way to take responsibility for what we want is to ask for it directly. And, we can insist on directness from others. If we need to say no to a particular request, we can. If someone is trying to control us through a conversation, we can refuse to participate.

Acknowledging feelings such as disappointment or anger directly, instead of making others guess at our feelings or having our feelings come out in other ways, is part of responsible communication. If we don't know what we want to say, we can say that too.

We can ask for information and use words to forge a closer connection, but we don't have to take people around the block with our conversations. We don't have to listen to, or participate in, nonsense. We can say what we want and stop when we're done.

Today, I will communicate clearly and directly in my conversations with others. I will strive to avoid manipulative, indirect, or guilt-producing statements. I can be tactful and gentle whenever possible. And I can be assertive if necessary.

Letting Things Happen   April 16

We do not have to work so hard at gaining our insights. Yes, we're learning that painful and disappointing things happen, often for a reason and a higher purpose. Yes, these things often work out for good. But we don't have to spend so much time and energy figuring out the purpose and plan for each detail of our life. That's hypervigilence!

Sometimes, the car doesn't start. Sometimes, the dishwasher breaks. Sometimes, we catch a cold. Sometimes, we run out of hot water. Sometimes, we have a bad day. While it helps to achieve acceptance and gratitude for these irritating annoyances, we don't have to process everything and figure out if it's in the scheme of things.

Solve the problem. Get the car repaired. Fix the dishwasher. Nurse yourself through the cold. Wait to take the shower until there's hot water. Nurture yourself through your bad day. Tend to your responsibilities, and don't take everything so personally!

If we need to recognize a particular insight or awareness, we will be guided in that direction. Certainly, we want to watch for patterns. But often, the big insights and the significant processing happen naturally.

We don't have to question every occurrence to see how it fits into the Plan. The Plan — the awareness, the insight, the potential for personal growth — will reveal itself to us. Perhaps the lesson is to learn to solve our problems without always knowing their significance. Perhaps the lesson is to trust ourselves to live, and experience, life.

Today, I will let things happen without worrying about the significance of each event. I will trust that this will bring about my growth faster than running around with a microscope. I will trust my lessons to reveal themselves in their own time.

Taking Care of Ourselves   April 17

We often refer to recovery from codependency and adult child issues as "self-care." Self-care is not, as some may think, a spin-off of the "me generation." It isn't self-indulgence. It isn't selfishness — in the negative interpretation of that word.

We're learning to take care of ourselves, instead of obsessively focusing on another person. We're learning self-responsibility, instead of feeling excessively responsible for others. Self-care also means tending to our true responsibilities to others; we do this better when we're not feeling overly responsible.

Self-care sometimes means, "me first," but usually, "me too." It means we are responsible for ourselves and can choose to no longer be victims.

Self-care means learning to love the person we're responsible for taking care of — ourselves. We do not do this to hibernate in a cocoon of isolation and self-indulgence; we do it so we can better love others, and learn to let them love us.

Self-care isn't selfish; it's self-esteem.

Today, God, help me love myself. Help me let go of feeling exces-
sively responsible for those around me. Show me what I need to
do to take care of myself and be appropriately responsible to others.

Freedom   April 18

Many of us were oppressed and victimized as children.
As adults, we may continue to keep ourselves oppressed.

Some of us don't recognize that caretaking and not setting boundaries will leave us feeling victimized.

Some of us don't understand that thinking of ourselves
as victims will leave us feeling oppressed.

Some of us don't know that we hold the key to our own
freedom. That key is honoring ourselves, and taking care
of ourselves.

We can say what we mean, and mean what we say.

We can stop waiting for others to give us what we need
and take responsibility for ourselves. When we do, the gates
to freedom will swing wide.

Walk through.

Today, I will understand that I hold the key to my freedom. I will
stop participating in my oppression and victimization. I will take
responsibility for myself, and let others do as they may.

Accepting Change   April 19

The winds of change blow through our life, sometimes
gently, sometimes like a tropical storm. Yes, we have resting
places — time to adjust to another level of living, time to get
our balance, time to enjoy the rewards. We have time to catch
our breath.

But change is inevitable, and desirable.

Sometimes, when the winds of change begin to rustle,
we're not certain the change is for the better. We may call

it stress or a temporary condition, certain we'll be restored to normal. Sometimes, we resist. We tuck our head down and buck the wind, hoping that things will quickly calm down, get back to the way things were. Is it possible we're being prepared for a new "normal"?

Change will sweep through our life, as needed, to take us where we're going. We can trust that our Higher Power has a plan in mind, even when we don't know where the changes are leading.

We can trust that the change taking place is good. The winds will take us where we need to go.

Today, help me, God, to let go of my resistance to change. Help me be open to the process. Help me believe that the place I'll be dropped off will be better than the place where I was picked up. Help me surrender, trust, and accept, even if I don't understand.

Deadlines   April 20

I don't know whether I want in or out of this relationship. I've been struggling with it for months now. It's not appropriate to let it hang indefinitely. I will give myself two months to make a decision.

— *Anonymous*

I've had this unsolved problem hanging over my head for six months now. I'm confused. I'm not certain what to do. I'm going to give myself one month to come up with a solution.

— *Anonymous*

Sometimes, it helps to set a deadline.

This can be true when we face unsolved problems, are struggling with a tough decision, have been sitting on the fence for a while, or have been floundering in confusion about a particular issue for a time.

That does not mean a deadline is written in stone. It means that we are establishing a time frame to help ourselves not feel so helpless and to help bring a solution into focus. Setting deadlines can free our energy to set the problem or issue aside, to let go, and allow the Universe, our Higher Power, and ourselves to begin to move toward a solution.

We don't always need to tell people we've got a deadline. Sometimes, it's better to be silent, or else they may feel we are trying to control them and may rebel against our deadline. Sometimes, it is appropriate to share our deadlines with others.

Deadlines are primarily a tool to help ourselves. They need to be reasonable and appropriate to each individual situation. Used properly, deadlines can be a beneficial tool to help us get through difficult problems and situations without feeling trapped and helpless. They can help us let go of worrying and obsessing, so we can focus our energies in more constructive directions. Setting a deadline can help move us out of that uncomfortable spot of feeling victimized by a person or a problem we can't solve.

Deadlines can help us detach and move forward.

Today, I will consider whether a deadline might be helpful in some area in my life. I claim Divine Wisdom and Guidance in setting appropriate deadlines for any problems or relationship issues that may be lingering.

Waiting   April 21

Wait. If the time is not right, the way is not clear, the answer or decision not consistent, wait.

We may feel a sense of urgency. We may want to resolve the issue by doing something — *anything* now, but that action is not in our best interest.

Living with confusion or unsolved problems is difficult. It is easier to resolve things. But making a decision too soon, doing something before it's time, means we may have to go back and redo it.

If the time is not right, wait. If the way is not clear, do not plunge forward. If the answer or decision feels muddy, wait.

In this new way of life, there is a Guiding Force. We do not ever have to move too soon or move out of harmony. Waiting is an action — a positive, forceful action.

Often, waiting is a God-guided action, one with as much power as a decision, and more power than an urgent, ill-timed decision.

We do not have to pressure ourselves by insisting that we do or know something before it's time. When it is time, we will know. We will move into that time naturally and harmoniously. We will have peace and consistency. We will feel empowered in a way we do not feel today.

Deal with the panic, the urgency, the fear; do not let them control or dictate decisions.

Waiting isn't easy. It isn't fun. But waiting is often necessary to get what we want. It is *not* deadtime; it is not downtime. The answer will come. The power will come. The time will come. And it will be right.

Today, I will wait, if waiting is the action I need in order to take care of myself. I will know that I am taking a positive, forceful action by waiting until the time is right. God, help me let go of my fear, urgency, and panic. Help me learn the art of waiting until the time is right. Help me learn timing.

Coping with Stress   April 22

Inevitably, there are times of stress in our lives, no matter how long we've been in recovery.

Sometimes, the stress is outside or around us. We're feeling balanced, but our circumstances are stressful. Sometimes, the stress is within; we feel out of balance.

When the stress is external and internal, we experience our most difficult times.

During stressful times, we can rely more heavily on our support systems. Our friends and groups can help us feel more balanced and peaceful in spite of our stressful conditions.

Affirming that the events taking place are a temporarily uncomfortable part of a good, solid plan can help. We can assure ourselves that we will get through. We won't be destroyed. We won't crumple or go under.

It helps to go back to the basics — to focus on detachment, dealing with feelings, and taking life one day at a time.

Our most important focus during times of stress is taking care of ourselves. We are better able to cope with the most irregular circumstances, we are better able to be there for others, if we're caring for ourselves. We can ask ourselves regularly: What do we need to do to take care of ourselves? What might help us feel better or more comfortable?

Self-care may not come as easily during times of stress. Self-neglect may feel more comfortable. But taking care of ourselves always works.

Today, I will remember that there is no situation that can't be benefited by taking care of myself.

Opening Ourselves to Love   April 23

Allowing ourselves to receive love is one of the greatest challenges we face in recovery.

Many of us have blocked ourselves from receiving love. We may have lived with people who used love to control us. They would be there for us, but at the high price of our freedom. Love was given, or withheld, to control us and have power over us. It was not safe for us to receive love from these people. We may have gotten accustomed to not receiving love, not acknowledging our need for love, because we lived with people who had no real love to give.

At some point in recovery, we acknowledge that we, too, want and need to be loved. We may feel awkward with this need. Where do we go with it? What do we do? Who can give us love? How can we determine who is safe and who isn't? How can we let others care for us without feeling trapped, abused, frightened, and unable to care for ourselves?

We will learn. The starting point is surrender — to our desire to be loved, our need to be nurtured and loved. We will grow confident in our ability to take care of ourselves with people. We will feel safe enough to let people care for us; we will grow to trust our ability to choose people who are safe and who can give us love.

We may need to get angry first — angry that our needs have not been met. Later, we can become grateful to those people who have shown us what we don't want, the ones who have assisted us in the process of believing we deserve love, and the ones who come into our life to love us.

We are opening up like flowers. Sometimes it hurts as the petals push open. Be glad. Our heart is opening up to the love that is and will continue to be there for us.

Surrender to the love that is there for us, to the love that people, the Universe, and our Higher Power send our way.

Surrender to love, without allowing people to control us or keep us from caring for ourselves. Start by surrendering to love for yourself.

Today, I will open myself to the love that is here for me. I will let myself receive love that is safe, knowing I can take care of myself with people. I will be grateful to all the people from my past who have assisted me in my process of opening up to love. I claim, accept, and am grateful for the love that is coming to me.

Lessons on the Job   April 24

Often, the spiritual and recovery lessons we're learning at work reflect the lessons we're learning in other areas of our life.

Often, the systems we're attracted to in our working life are similar to the systems in which we find ourselves living and loving. Those are the systems that reflect our issues and can help us learn our lessons.

Are we slowly learning to trust ourselves at work? How about at home? Are we slowly learning to take care of ourselves at work? How about at home? Are we slowly learning boundaries and self-esteem, overcoming fear, and dealing with feelings?

If we search back over our work history, we will probably see that it is a mirror of our issues, our growth. It most likely is now too.

For today, we can believe that we are right where we need to be — at home and at work.

Today, I will accept my present circumstances on the job. I will reflect on how what I am learning in my life applies to what I'm learning at work. If I don't know, I will surrender to the experience until that becomes clear. God, help me accept the work I have been given to do today. Help me be open to and learn what I need to be learning. Help me trust that it can and will be good.

We must each discover our own truth.

It does not help *us* if those we love find their truth. They cannot give it to us. It does not help if someone we love knows a particular truth in our life. We must discover our truth for ourselves.

We must each discover and stand in our own light.

We often need to struggle, fail, and be confused and frustrated. That's how we break through our struggle; that's how we learn what is true and right for ourselves.

We can share information with others. Others can tell us what may predictably happen if we pursue a particular course. But it will not mean anything until we integrate the message and it becomes our truth, our discovery, our knowledge.

There is no easy way to break through and find our truth.

But we can and will, if we want to.

We may want to make it easier. We may nervously run to friends, asking them to give us their truth or make our discovery easier. They cannot. Light will shed itself in its own time.

Each of us has our own share of truth, waiting to reveal itself to us. Each of us has our own share of the light, waiting for us to stand in it, to claim it as ours.

Encouragement helps. Support helps. A firm belief that each person has truth available — appropriate to each situation — is what will help.

Each experience, each frustration, each situation, has its own truth waiting to be revealed. Don't give up until you find it — for yourself.

We shall be guided into truth, if we are seeking it. We are not alone.

Today, I will search for my own truth, and I will allow others to do the same. I will place value on my vision and the vision of others. We are each on the journey, making our own discoveries — the ones that are right for us today.

Resisting Negativity   April 26

Some people are carriers of negativity. They are store-houses of pent-up anger and volatile emotions. Some remain trapped in the victim role and act in ways that further their victimization. And others are still caught in the cycle of addictive or compulsive patterns.

Negative energy can have a powerful pull on us, especially if we're struggling to maintain positive energy and balance. It may seem that others who exude negative energy would like to pull us into the darkness with them. We do not have to go. Without judgment, we can decide it's okay to walk away, okay to protect ourselves.

We cannot change other people. It does not help others for us to get off balance. We do not lead others into the Light by stepping into the darkness with them.

Today, God, help me to know that I don't have to allow myself to be pulled into negativity, even around those I love. Help me set boundaries. Help me know it's okay to take care of myself.

The rewards from detachment are great: serenity; a deep sense of peace; the ability to give and receive love in self-enhancing, energizing ways; and the freedom to find real solutions to our problems.

— Codependent No More

Letting go of our need to control can set us and others free. It can set our Higher Power free to send the best to us.

If we weren't trying to control someone or something, what would we be doing differently?

What would we do that we're not letting ourselves do now? Where would we go? What would we say?

What decisions would we make?

What would we ask for? What boundaries would be set? When would we say no or yes?

If we weren't trying to control whether a person liked us or his or her reaction to us, what would we do differently? If we weren't trying to control the course of a relationship, what would we do differently? If we weren't trying to control another person's behavior, how would we think, feel, speak, and behave differently than we do now?

What haven't we been letting ourselves do while hoping that self-denial would influence a particular situation or person? Are there some things we've been doing that we'd stop?

How would we treat ourselves differently?

Would we let ourselves enjoy life more and feel better right now? Would we stop feeling so bad? Would we treat ourselves better?

If we weren't trying to control, what would we do differently? Make a list, then do it.

Today, I will ask myself what I would be doing differently if I weren't trying to control. When I hear the answer, I will do it. God, help me let go of my need to control. Help me set myself and others free.

Anger at Family Members   April 28

Many of us have anger toward certain members of our family. Some of us have much anger and rage — anger that seems to go on year after year.

For many of us, anger was the only way to break an unhealthy bondage or connection between a family member and ourselves. It was the force that kept us from being held captive — mentally, emotionally, and sometimes spiritually — by certain family members.

It is important to allow ourselves to feel — to accept — our anger toward family members without casting guilt or shame on ourselves. It is also important to examine our guilty feelings concerning family members as anger and guilt are often intertwined.

We can accept, even thank, our anger for protecting us. But we can also set another goal: taking our freedom.

Once we do, we will not need our anger. Once we do, we can achieve forgiveness.

Think loving thoughts, think healing thoughts toward family members. But let ourselves be as angry as we need to be.

At some point, strive to be done with the anger. But we need to be gentle with ourselves if the feelings surface from time to time.

Thank God for the feelings. Feel them. Release them. Ask God to bless and care for our families. Ask God to help us take freedom and take care of ourselves.

Let the golden light of healing shine upon all we love and upon all with whom we feel anger. Let the golden light of healing shine on us.

Trust that a healing is taking place, now.

Help me accept the potent emotions I may feel toward family members. Help me be grateful for the lesson they are teaching me. I accept the golden light of healing that is now shining on me and my family. I thank God that healing does not always come in a neat, tidy package.

Initiating Relationships   April 29

Often, we can learn much about ourselves from the people to whom we are attracted.

As we progress through recovery, we learn we can no longer form relationships *solely* on the basis of attraction. We learn to be patient, to allow ourselves to take into account important facts, and to process information about that person.

What we are striving for in recovery is a healthy attraction to people. We allow ourselves to be attracted to who people *are*, not to their potential or to what we hope they are.

The more we work through our family of origin issues, the less we will find ourselves needing to work through them with the people we're attracted to. Finishing our business from the past helps us form new and healthier relationships.

The more we overcome our need to be excessive caretakers, the less we will find ourselves attracted to people who need to be constantly taken care of.

The more we learn to love and respect ourselves, the more we will become attracted to people who will love and respect us and who we can safely love and respect.

This is a slow process. We need to be patient with ourselves. The type of people we find ourselves attracted to does not change overnight. Being attracted to dysfunctional people can linger long and well into recovery. That does not mean we need to allow it to control us. The fact is, we will initiate and maintain relationships with people we need to be with until we learn what it is we need to learn — no matter how long we've been recovering.

No matter who we find ourselves relating to, and what we discover happening in the relationship, the issue is still about us, and not about the other person. That is the heart, the hope, and the power of recovery.

We can learn to take care of ourselves during the process of initiating and forming relationships. We can learn to go slowly. We can learn to pay attention. We can allow ourselves to make mistakes, even when we *know better.*

We can stop blaming our relationships on God, and begin to take responsibility for them. We can learn to enjoy the healthy relationships, and remove ourselves more quickly from the dysfunctional ones.

We can learn to look for what's good for us, instead of what's good for the other person.

God, help me pay attention to my behaviors during the process of initiating relationships. Help me take responsibility for myself and learn what I need to learn. I will trust that the people I want and need will come into my life. I understand that if a relationship is not good for me, I have the right and ability to refuse to enter into it — even though the other person thinks it may be good for him or her. I will be open to the lessons I need to learn about me in relationships, so I am prepared for the best possible relationships with people.

The goal is balance.

We need balance between work and play. We need balance between giving and receiving. We need balance in thought and feelings. We need balance in caring for our physical self and our spiritual self.

A balanced life has harmony between a professional life and a personal life. There may be times when we need to climb mountains at work. There may be times when we put extra energy into our relationships. But the overall picture needs to balance.

Just as a balanced nutritional diet takes into account the realm of our nutritional needs to stay healthy, a balanced life takes into account all our needs: our need for friends, work, love, family, play, private time, recovery time, and spiritual time — time with God. If we get out of balance, our inner voice will tell us. We need to listen.

Today, I will examine my life to see if the scales have swung too far in any area, or not far enough in some. I will work toward achieving balance.

May

This prayer is based on a section of the Big Book of Alcoholics Anonymous:

Thank you for keeping me straight yesterday. Please help me stay straight today.

For the next twenty-four hours, I pray for knowledge of Your will for me only, and the power to carry that through.

Please free my thinking of self-will, self-seeking, dishonesty, and wrong motives.

Send me the right thought, word, or action. Show me what my next step should be. In times of doubt and indecision, please send Your inspiration and guidance.

I ask that You might help me work through all my problems, to Your glory and honor.

This prayer is a recovery prayer. It can take us through any situation. In the days ahead, we'll explore the ideas in it. If we pray this prayer, we can trust it has been answered with a yes.

Today, I will trust that God will do for me what I cannot do for myself. I will do my part — working the Twelve Steps and letting God do the rest.

Our Higher Power   **May 2**

For the next twenty-four hours...

In recovery, we live life one day at a time, an idea requiring an enormous amount of faith. We refuse to look back — unless healing from the past is part of today's work. We look ahead only to make plans. We focus on this day's activity, living it to the best of our ability. If we do that long enough, we'll have enough connected days of healthy living to make something valuable of our life.

...I pray for knowledge of Your will for me only, ...

We surrender to God's will. We stop trying to control, and we settle for a life that is manageable. We *trust* our Higher Power's will for us — that it's good, generous, and with direction.

We're learning, through trial and error, to separate our will from God's will. We're learning that God's will is not offensive. We've learned that sometimes there's a difference between what others want us to do and God's will. We're also learning that God did not intend for us to be codependent, to be martyrs, to control or caretake. We're learning to trust ourselves.

...and the power to carry that through.

Some of recovery is accepting powerlessness. An important part of recovery is claiming the power to take care of ourselves.

Sometimes, we need to do things that are frightening or painful. Sometimes, we need to step out, step back, or step forward. We need to call on the help of a Power greater than ourselves to do that.

We will never be called upon to do anything that we won't be empowered to do.

Today, I can call upon an energizing Power Source to help me. That Power is God. I will ask for what I need.

Freedom from Self-Seeking

Please free my thinking of self-will, self-seeking, dishonesty, and wrong motives.
                    — paraphrased from Alcoholics Anonymous

There is a difference between owning our power to take care of ourselves, as part of God's will for our life, and self-will. There is a difference between self-care and self-seeking. And our behaviors are not as much subject to criticism as are the motives underlying them.

There is a harmonic, gentle, timely feeling to owning our power, to self-care, and to acts with healthy motives that are not present in self-will and self-seeking. We will learn discernment. But we will not always know the difference. Sometimes, we will feel guilty and anxious with no need. We may be surprised at the loving way God wants us to treat ourselves. We can trust that self-care is always appropriate. We want to be free of self-will and self-seeking, but we are always free to take care of ourselves.

God, please guide my motives today, and keep me on Your path. Help me love myself, and others too. Help me understand that more often than not, those two ideas are connected.

Freedom from Compulsive Disorders

Thank you for keeping me straight yesterday. Please help me stay straight today.
                    — paraphrased from Alcoholics Anonymous

When I first began my recovery from codependency, I was furious about having to begin another recovery program. Seven years earlier, I had begun recovery from chemical dependency. It didn't seem fair that one person should have to address two major issues in one lifetime.

I've gotten over my anger. I've learned that my recoveries aren't isolated from one another. Many of us recovering from codependency and adult children issues are also recovering from addictions: alcoholism, other drug dependency, gambling, food, work, or sex addiction. Some of us are trying to stay free of other compulsive disorders — ranging from caretaking to compulsively feeling miserable, guilty, or ashamed.

An important part of codependency recovery is staying clean and free of our compulsive or addictive behaviors. Recovery is one big room we've entered called healthy living.

We can wave the white flag of surrender to all our addictions. We can safely turn to a Power greater than ourselves to relieve us of our compulsive behavior. We know that now. Once we begin actively working a program of recovery, God will relieve us of our addictions. Ask God each morning to help us stay free of our addictions and compulsions. Thank God for helping us the day before.

Today, God, help me pay attention to all my recovery issues. Help me know that before I can work on the finer points of my recovery, such as my relationships, I must be free of addictive behaviors.

Control   May 5

Many of us have been trying to keep the whole world in orbit with sheer and forceful application of mental energy.

What happens if we let go, if we stop trying to keep the world orbiting and just let it whirl? It'll keep right on whirling. It'll stay right on track with no help from us. And we'll be free and relaxed enough to enjoy our place on it.

Control is an illusion, especially the kind of control we've been trying to exert. In fact, controlling gives other people, events, and diseases, such as alcoholism, control over us. *Whatever we try to control does have control over us and our life.*

I have given this control to many things and people in my life. I have never gotten the results I wanted from controlling or trying to control people. What I received for my efforts is an unmanageable life, whether that unmanageability was inside me or in external events.

In recovery, we make a trade-off. We trade a life that we have tried to control, and we receive in return something better — a life that is manageable.

Today, I will exchange a controlled life for one that is manageable.

Feeling Good   May 6

Make yourself feel good.

It's our job to first make ourselves feel better and then make ourselves feel good. Recovery is not only about stopping painful feelings; it is about creating a good life for ourselves.

We don't have to deny ourselves activities that help us feel good. Going to meetings, basking in the sun, exercising, taking a walk, or spending time with a friend are activities that may help us feel good. We each have our list. If we don't, we're now free to explore, experiment, and develop that list.

When we find a behavior or activity that produces a good feeling, put it on the list. Then, do it frequently.

Let's stop denying ourselves good feelings and start doing things that make us feel good.

Today, I will do one activity or behavior that I know will create a good feeling for me. If I'm uncertain about what I like, I will experiment with one behavior today.

Fear is at the core of codependency. It can motivate us to control situations or neglect ourselves.

Many of us have been afraid for so long that we don't label our feelings *fear*. We're used to feeling upset and anxious. It feels *normal*.

Peace and serenity may be uncomfortable.

At one time, fear may have been appropriate and useful. We may have relied on fear to protect ourselves, much the way soldiers in a war rely on fear to help them survive. But now, in recovery, we're living life differently.

It's time to thank our old fears for helping us survive, then wave good-bye to them. Welcome peace, trust, acceptance, and safety. We don't need that much fear anymore. We can listen to our healthy fears, and let go of the rest.

We can create a feeling of safety for ourselves, now. We are safe, now. We've made a commitment to take care of ourselves. We can trust and love ourselves.

God, help me let go of my need to be afraid. Replace it with a need to be at peace. Help me listen to my healthy fears and relinquish the rest.

Giving Ourselves What We Deserve   May 8

I worked at a good job, making a decent salary. I had been recovering for years. Each morning, I got into my car and I thanked God for the car. The heater didn't work. And the chance of the car not starting was almost as great as the chance that it would. I just kept suffering through, and thanking God. One day, it occurred to me that there was absolutely no good reason I couldn't buy myself a new car — that moment — if I wanted one. I had been gratitude-ing myself into unnecessary deprivation and martyrdom. I bought the new car — that day.

— Anonymous

Often, our instinctive reaction to something we want or need is, "No! I can't afford it!"

The question we can learn to ask ourselves is, "But, can I?"

Many of us have learned to habitually deprive ourselves of anything we might want, and often things we need.

Sometimes, we can misuse the concept of gratitude to keep ourselves unnecessarily deprived.

Gratitude for what we have is an important recovery concept. So is believing we deserve the best and making an effort to stop depriving ourselves and start treating ourselves well.

There is nothing wrong with buying ourselves what we want when we can afford to do that. Learn to trust and listen to yourself about what you want. There's nothing wrong with buying yourself a treat, buying yourself something *new.*

There are times when it is good to wait. There are times when we legitimately cannot afford a luxury. But there are many times when we can.

Today, I will combine the principles of gratitude for what I have with the belief that I deserve the best. If there is no good reason to deprive myself, I won't.

Sometimes we'll take a few steps backward. That's okay too. Sometimes it's necessary. Sometimes it's part of going forward.

— Codependent No More

Life is a Gentle Teacher. She wants to help us learn.

The lessons she wants to teach us are the ones we need to learn. Some say they are the lessons we chose to learn before we were born. Others say they are the lessons that were chosen for us.

It's frustrating to be in the midst of learning. It is like sitting in algebra class, listening to a teacher explain a subject beyond our comprehension. We do not understand, but the teacher takes the understanding for granted.

It may feel like someone is torturing us with messages that we shall never understand. We strain and strain. We become angry. Frustrated. Confused. Finally, in despair, we turn away, deciding that that formula will never be available to our mind.

Later, while taking a quiet walk, we break through. Quietly, the gift of understanding has reached that deepest place in us. We understand. We have learned. The next day in class, it's hard for us to imagine not knowing. It is hard to remember the frustration and confusion of those who have not yet caught on. It seems so *easy*. . . now.

Life is a Gentle Teacher. She will keep repeating the lesson until we learn. It is okay to become frustrated. Confused. Angry. Sometimes it is okay to despair. Then, it is okay to walk away and allow the breakthrough to come.

It shall.

Help me remember that frustration and confusion usually precede growth. If my situation is challenging me, it is because I'm learning something new, rising to a higher level of understanding. Help me be grateful, even in my frustration, that life is an exciting progression of lessons.

Enjoying the Good Days   May 10

Good feelings can become a habitual part of our life.

There is absolutely no virtue in the unnecessary suffering, which many of us have felt for much of our life. We don't have to allow others to make us miserable, and we don't have to make ourselves miserable.

A good day does not have to be the "calm before the storm." That's an old way of thinking we learned in dysfunctional systems.

In recovery, a good day or a good feeling doesn't mean we're in denial. We don't have to wreck our good times by obsessively searching for or creating a problem.

Enjoying our good days doesn't mean we're being disloyal to loved ones who are having problems. We don't have to make ourselves feel guilty because other people aren't having a good day. We don't have to make ourselves miserable to be like them. They can have their day and their feelings; we can have ours.

A good feeling is to be enjoyed. More than we can imagine, good days are ours for the asking.

Today, I will let myself enjoy what is good. I don't have to wreck my good day or good feeling; I don't have to let others spoil it either.

Many of us picked on ourselves unmercifully before recovery. We may also have a tendency to pick on ourselves after we begin recovery.

"If I was *really* recovering, I wouldn't be doing *that* again...." "I should be further along than I am." These are statements that we indulge in when we're feeling shame. We don't need to treat ourselves that way. There is no benefit.

Remember, shame blocks us. But self-love and acceptance enable us to grow and change. If we truly have done something we feel guilty about, we can correct it with an amend and an attitude of self-acceptance and love.

Even if we slip back to our old, codependent ways of thinking, feeling, and behaving, we do not need to be ashamed. We all regress from time to time. That's how we learn and grow. Relapse, or recycling, is an important and necessary part of recovery. And the way out of recycling is not by shaming ourselves. That leads us deeper into codependency.

Much pain comes from trying to be perfect. Perfection is impossible unless we think of it in a new way: *Perfection* is being who and where we are today; it's accepting and loving ourselves just as we are. We are each right where we need to be in our recovery.

Today, I will love and accept myself for who I am and where I am in my recovery process. I am right where I need to be to get to where I'm going tomorrow.

We can let ourselves be close to people.

Many of us have deeply ingrained patterns for sabotaging relationships. Some of us may instinctively terminate a relationship once it moves to a certain level of closeness and intimacy.

When we start to feel close to someone, we may zero in on one of the person's character defects, then make it so big it's all we can see. We may withdraw, or push the person away to create distance. We may start criticizing the other person, a behavior sure to create distance.

We may start trying to control the person, a behavior that prevents intimacy.

We may tell ourselves we don't want or need another person, or smother the person with our needs.

Sometimes, we defeat ourselves by trying to be close to people who aren't available for intimacy — people with active addictions, or people who don't choose to be close to us. Sometimes, we choose people with particular faults so that when it comes time to be close, we have an escape hatch.

We're afraid, and we fear losing ourselves. We're afraid that closeness means we won't be able to own our power to take care of ourselves.

In recovery, we're learning that it's okay to let ourselves be close to people. We're choosing to relate to safe, healthy people, so closeness is a possibility. Closeness doesn't mean we have to lose ourselves, or our life. As one man said, we're learning that we can own our power with people, even when we're close, even when the other person has something we need.

Today, I will be available for closeness and intimacy with people, when that's appropriate. Whenever possible, I will let myself be who I am, let others be who they are, and enjoy the bond and good feelings between us.

A helpful tool in our recovery, especially in the behavior we call detachment, is learning to identify who owns what. Then we let each person own and possess his or her rightful property.

If another person has an addiction, a problem, a feeling, or a self-defeating behavior, that is their property, not ours. If someone is a martyr, immersed in negativity, controlling, or manipulative, that is their issue, not ours.

If someone has acted and experienced a particular consequence, both the behavior and the consequence belong to that person.

If someone is in denial or cannot think clearly on a particular issue, that confusion belongs to him or her.

If someone has a limited or impaired ability to love or care, that is his or her property, not ours. If someone has no approval or nurturing to give away, that is that person's property.

People's lies, deceptions, tricks, manipulations, abusive behaviors, inappropriate behaviors, cheating behaviors, and tacky behaviors belong to them too. Not us.

People's hopes and dreams are their property. Their guilt belongs to them too. Their happiness or misery is also theirs. So are their beliefs and messages.

If some people don't like themselves, that is their choice. Other people's choices are their property, not ours.

What people choose to say and do is their business.

What is our property? Our property includes our behaviors, problems, feelings, happiness, misery, choices, and messages; our ability to love, care, and nurture; our thoughts, our denial, our hopes and dreams for ourselves. Whether we allow ourselves to be controlled, manipulated, deceived, or mistreated is our business.

In recovery, we learn an appropriate sense of ownership. If something isn't ours, we don't take it. If we take it, we learn to give it back. Let other people have their property, and learn to own and take good care of what's ours.

Today, I will work at developing a clear sense of what belongs to me, and what doesn't. If it's not mine, I won't keep it. I will deal with myself, my issues, and my responsibilities. I will take my hands off what is not mine.

Honesty   May 14

Admitted to God, to ourselves, and to another human being the exact nature of our wrongs.
— Step Five of Al-Anon

Talking opening and honestly to another person about ourselves, in an attitude that reflects self-responsibility, is critical to recovery.

It's important to admit what we have done wrong to others and to ourselves. Verbalize our beliefs and our behaviors. Get our resentments and fears out in the open.

That's how we release our pain. That's how we release old beliefs and feelings. That's how we are set free. The more clear and specific we can be with our Higher Power, ourselves, and another person, the more quickly we will experience that freedom.

Step Five is an important part of the recovery process. For those of us who have learned to keep secrets from ourselves and others, it is not just a step — it is a leap toward becoming healthy.

Today I will remember that it's okay to talk about the issues that bother me. It is by sharing my issues that I will grow beyond them. I will also remember that it's okay to be selective about those in whom I confide. I can trust my instincts and choose someone who will not use my disclosures against me, and who will give me healthy feedback.

Take Risks   May 15

Take a risk. Take a chance.

We do not have to indulge in obviously foolhardy or self-defeating risks, but we can allow ourselves to take positive risks in recovery. We cannot afford to keep ourselves paralyzed.

We do not have to keep ourselves stymied and trapped out of fear of making a mistake or failing. Naturally, we will make mistakes and fail from time to time. That's part of being fully alive. There are no guarantees. If we are waiting for guaranteed courses of action, we may spend much of our life waiting.

We do not have to shame ourselves or accept shame from anyone else, even those in recovery, for making mistakes. The goal of recovery is not to live life perfectly. The goal of recovery is to live, learn our lessons, and make overall progress.

Take a risk. Do not always wait for a guarantee. We don't have to listen to "I told you so." Dust yourself off after a mistake, and then move on to the success.

God, help me begin to take healthy risks. Help me let go of my fear of failure, and help me let go of my fear of success. Help me let go of my fear of fully living my life, and help me start experiencing all parts of this journey.

"I woke up this morning and I had a hard time for a while," said one recovering man. "Then I realized it was because I wasn't liking myself very much." Recovering people often say: "I just don't like myself. When will I start liking myself?"

The answer is: start now. We can learn to be gentle, loving, and nurturing with ourselves. Of all the recovery behaviors we're striving to attain, loving ourselves may be the most difficult, and the most important. If we are habitually harsh and critical toward ourselves, learning to be gentle with ourselves may require dedicated effort.

But what a valuable venture!

By not liking ourselves, we may be perpetuating the discounting, neglect, or abuse we received in childhood from the important people in our life. We didn't like what happened then, but find ourselves copying those who mistreated us by treating ourselves *poorly*.

We can stop the pattern. We can begin giving ourselves the loving, respectful treatment we deserve.

Instead of criticizing ourselves, we can tell ourselves we performed well enough.

We can wake up in the morning and tell ourselves we deserve a good day.

We can make a commitment to take good care of ourselves throughout the day.

We can recognize that we're deserving of love.

We can do loving things for ourselves.

We can love other people and let them love us.

People who truly love themselves do not become destructively self-centered. They do not abuse others. They do not stop growing and changing. People who love themselves well, learn to love others well too. They continually grow into healthier people, learning that their love was appropriately placed.

136

Today, I will love myself. If I get caught in the old pattern of not liking myself, I will find a way to get out.

Boundaries   May 17

Sometimes, life and people seem to push and push. Because we are so used to pain, we may tell ourselves it doesn't hurt. Because we are so used to people controlling and manipulating us, we may tell ourselves there is something wrong with us.

There's nothing wrong with us. Life is pushing and hurting to get our attention. Sometimes, the pain and pushing are pointing toward a lesson. The lesson may be that *we've* become too controlling. Or maybe we're being pushed to own our power to take care of ourselves. The issue is boundaries.

If something or somebody is pushing us to our limits, that's exactly what's happening: we're being pushed to our limits. We can be grateful for the lesson that's here to help us explore and set our boundaries.

Today, I will give myself permission to set the limits I want and need to set in my life.

Living Our Lives   May 18

Don't stop living your life!

So often, when a problem occurs, inside or around us, we revert to thinking that if we put our life on hold we can positively contribute to the solution. If a relationship isn't working, if we face a difficult decision, if we're feeling depressed, we may put our life on hold and torment ourselves with obsessive thoughts.

Abandoning our life or routines contributes to the problem and delays us from finding the solution.

Frequently, the solution comes when we let go enough to live our life, return to our routine, and stop obsessing about the problem.

Sometimes, even if we don't *feel* like we have let go or can let go, we can "act as if" we have, and that will help bring about the letting go we desire.

You don't have to give up your power to problems. You can take your focus off your problem and direct it to your life, trusting that doing so will bring you closer to a solution.

Today, I will go on living my life and tending to my routine. I will decide, as often as I need to, to stop obsessing about whatever is bothering me. If I don't feel like letting go of a particular thing, I will "act as if" I have let go of it until my feelings match my behavior.

Solving Problems   May 19

"Shame is the first feeling that strikes me whenever I, or someone I love, has a problem," said one recovering woman.

Many of us were raised with the belief that having a problem is something to be ashamed of.

This belief can do many damaging things to us. It can stop us from identifying our problems; it can make us feel alienated and inferior when we have, or someone we love has, a problem. Shame can block us from solving a problem and finding the gift from the problem.

Problems are a part of life. So are solutions. People have problems, but we, and our self-esteem, are separate from our problems.

I've yet to meet a person who didn't have problems to solve, but I've met many who felt ashamed to talk about the problems they actually had solved!

We are more than our problems. Even if our problem is our own behavior, the problem is not who we are — it's what we did.

It's okay to have problems. It's okay to talk about problems — at appropriate times, and with safe people. It's okay to solve problems.

And we're okay, even when we have, or someone we love, has a problem. We don't have to forfeit our personal power or our self-esteem. We have solved exactly the problems we've needed to solve to become who we are.

Today, I will let go of my shame about problems.

Sadness   May 20

Ultimately, to grieve our losses means to surrender to our feelings.

So many of us have lost so much, have said so many good-byes, have been through so many changes. We may want to hold back the tides of change, not because the change isn't good, but because we have had so much change, so much loss.

Sometimes, when we are in the midst of pain and grief, we become shortsighted, like members of a tribe described in the movie *Out of Africa*.

"If you put them in prison," one character said, describing this tribe, "they die."

"Why?" asked another character.

"Because they can't grasp the idea that they'll be let out one day. They think it's permanent, so they die."

Many of us have so much grief to get through. Sometimes we begin to believe grief, or pain, is a permanent condition.

The pain will stop. Once felt and released, our feelings will bring us to a better place than where we started. Feeling our feelings, instead of denying or minimizing them, is how we heal from our past and move forward into a better future. Feeling our feelings is how we let go.

It may hurt for a moment, but peace and acceptance are on the other side. So is a new beginning.

God, help me fully embrace and finish my endings, so I may be ready for my new beginnings.

Getting Needs Met   May 21

I want to change careers.... I need a friend.... I'm ready to be in a relationship....

Regularly, we become aware of new needs. We may need to change our behavior with our children. We may need a new couch, love and nurturing, a dollar, or help.

Do not be afraid to recognize a want or need. The birth of a want or need, the temporary frustration from acknowledging a need before it's met, is the start of the cycle of receiving what we want. We follow this by letting go, then receiving that which we want and need. Identifying our needs is preparation for good things to come.

Acknowledging our needs means we are being prepared and drawn to that which will meet them. We can have faith to stand in that place in between.

Today, I will let go of my belief that my needs never get met. I will acknowledge my wants and needs, then turn them over to my Higher Power. My Higher Power cares, sometimes about the silliest little things, if I do. My wants and needs are not an accident. God created me, and all my desires.

Times of Reprogramming   May 22

Do not ask for love unless you're ready to be healed enough to give and receive love.

Do not ask for joy unless you're ready to feel and release your pain, so you can feel joy.

Do not ask for success unless you're ready to conquer the behaviors that would sabotage success.

Wouldn't it be nice if we could imagine ourselves having or becoming — and then immediately receiving — what we wanted? We can *have* and *be* the good things we want. All good things are ours for the asking. But first, groundwork — preparation work — must be done.

A gardener would not plant seeds unless the ground was adequately prepared to nurture and nourish those seeds. The planting would be wasted effort. It would be wasted effort for us to get what we wanted before we were ready.

First, we need to become aware of our need or desire. This may not be easy! Many of us have become accustomed to shutting off the inner voice of our wants, needs, and desires. Sometimes, life has to work hard to get our attention.

Next we let go of the old "programming" — the behaviors and beliefs that interfere with nurturing and nourishing the good. Many of us have strong sabotaging programs, learned from childhood, that need to be released. We may need to "act as if" for a while until the belief that we deserve the good becomes real.

We combine this process with much letting go, while we are being changed at the core.

There is a naturalness to this process, but it can be intense. Things take time.

Good things are ours for the asking, if we are willing to participate in the work of groundbreaking. Work and wait.

Today, God, give me the courage to identify the good I want in my life and to ask for it. Give me also the faith and stamina I need to go through the work that must be accomplished first.

Life is not to be endured; life is to be enjoyed and embraced.

The belief that we must square our shoulders and get through a meager, deprived existence for far-off "rewards in Heaven" is a codependent belief.

Yes, most of us still have times when life will be stressful and challenge our endurance skills. But in recovery, we're learning to live, to enjoy our life, and handle situations as they come.

Our survival skills have served us well. They have gotten us through difficult times — as children and adults. Our ability to freeze feelings, deny problems, deprive ourselves, and cope with stress has helped us get where we are today. But we're safe now. We're learning to do more than survive. We can let go of unhealthy survival behaviors. We're learning new, better ways to protect and care for ourselves. We're free to feel our feelings, identify and solve problems, and give ourselves the best. We're free to open up and come alive.

Today, I will let go of my unhealthy endurance and survival skills. I will choose a new mode of living, one that allows me to be alive and enjoy the adventure.

Letting the Cycles Flow   May 24

Life is cyclical, not static. Our relationships benefit when we allow them to follow their own natural cycles.

Like the tide ebbs and flows, so do the cycles in relationships. We have periods of closeness and periods of distance. We have times of coming together and times of separating to work on individual issues.

We have times of love and joy, and times of anger.

Sometimes, the dimensions of relationships change as we go through changes. Sometimes, life brings us new friends or a new loved one to teach us the next lesson.

That does not mean the old friend disappears forever. It means we have entered a new cycle.

We do not have to control the course of our relationships, whether these be friendships or love relationships. We do not have to satisfy our need to control by imposing a static form on relationships.

Let it flow. Be open to the cycles. Love will not disappear. The bond between friends will not sever. Things do not remain the same forever, especially when we are growing and changing at such a rapid pace.

Trust the flow. Take care of yourself, but be willing to let people go. Hanging on to them too tightly will make them disappear.

The old adage about love still holds true: "If it's meant to be, it will be. And if you love someone, let them go. If they come back to you, the love is yours."

Today, I accept the cyclical nature of life and relationships. I will strive to go with the flow. I will strive for harmony with my own needs and the needs of the other person.

Loving Ourselves Unconditionally   May 25

Love yourself into health and a good life of your own.

Love yourself into relationships that work for you and the other person. Love yourself into peace, happiness, joy, success, and contentment.

Love yourself into all that you always wanted. We can stop treating ourselves the way others treated us, if they behaved in a less than healthy, desirable way. If we have learned to see ourselves critically, conditionally, and in a diminishing and punishing way, it's time to stop. Other people treated us that way, but it's even worse to treat ourselves that way now.

Loving ourselves may seem foreign, even foolish at times. People may accuse us of being selfish. We don't have to believe them.

People who love themselves are truly able to love others and let others love them. People who love themselves and hold themselves in high esteem are those who give the most, contribute the most, love the most.

How do we love ourselves? By forcing it at first. By faking it if necessary. By "acting as if." By working as hard at loving and liking ourselves as we have at not liking ourselves.

Explore what it means to love yourself.

Do things for yourself that reflect compassionate, nurturing, self-love.

Embrace and love all of yourself — past, present, and future. Forgive yourself quickly and as often as necessary. Encourage yourself. Tell yourself good things about yourself.

If we think and believe negative ideas, get them out in the open quickly and honestly, so we can replace those beliefs with better ones.

Pat yourself on the back when necessary. Discipline yourself when necessary. Ask for help, for time; ask for what you need.

Sometimes, give yourself treats. Do not treat yourself like a pack mule, always pushing and driving harder. Learn to be good to yourself. Choose behaviors with preferable consequences — treating yourself well is one.

Learn to stop your pain, even when that means making difficult decisions. Do not unnecessarily deprive yourself. Sometimes, give yourself what you want, *just because you want it.*

Stop explaining and justifying yourself. When you make mistakes, let them go. We learn, we grow, and we learn some more. And through it all, we love ourselves.

We work at it, then work at it some more. One day we'll wake up, look in the mirror, and find that loving ourselves has become habitual. We're now living with a person who gives and receives love, because that person loves him- or herself. Self-love will take hold and become a guiding force in our life.

Today, I will work at loving myself. I will work as hard at loving myself as I have at not liking myself. Help me let go of self-hate and behaviors that reflect not liking myself. Help me replace those with behaviors that reflect self-love. Today, God, help me hold myself in high self-esteem. Help me know I'm lovable and capable of giving and receiving love.

Gossip   May 26

Intimacy is that warm gift of feeling connected to others and enjoying our connection to them.

As we grow in recovery, we find that gift in many, sometimes surprising places. We may discover we've developed intimate relationships with people at work, with friends, with people in our support groups — sometimes with family members. Many of us are discovering intimacy in a special love relationship.

Intimacy is not sex, although sex can be intimate. Intimacy means mutually honest, warm, caring, safe relationships — relationships where the other person can be who he or she is and we can be who we are — and both people are valued.

Sometimes there are conflicts. Conflict is inevitable. Sometimes there are troublesome feelings to work through. Sometimes the boundaries or parameters of relationships change. But there is a bond — one of love and trust.

There are many blocks to intimacy and intimate relationships. Addictions and abuse block intimacy. Unresolved family of origin issues prevent intimacy. Controlling blocks

145

intimacy. Off balance relationships, where there is too great a discrepancy in power, prevent intimacy. Caretaking can block intimacy. Nagging, withdrawing, and shutting down can hurt intimacy.

So can a simple behavior like gossip — for example, gossiping about another for motives of diminishing him or her in order to build up ourselves or to judge the person. To discuss another person's issues, shortcomings, or failures with someone else will have a predictable negative impact on the relationship.

We deserve to enjoy intimacy in as many of our relationships as possible. We deserve relationships that have not been sabotaged.

That does not mean we walk around with our heads in the clouds; it means we strive to keep our motives clean when it comes to discussing other people.

If we have a serious issue with someone, the best way to resolve it is to bring the issue to that person.

Direct, clean conversation clears the air and paves the way for intimacy, for good feelings about ourselves and our relationships with others.

Today, God, help me let go of my fear of intimacy. Help me strive to keep my communications with others clean and free from malicious gossip. Help me work toward intimacy in my relationships. Help me deal as directly as possible with my feelings.

Recognizing Choices   May 27

We have choices, more choices than we let ourselves see.

We may feel trapped in our relationships, our jobs, our life. We may feel locked into behaviors — such as caretaking or controlling.

Feeling trapped is a symptom of codependency. When we hear ourselves say, "I have to take care of this person. . . ."

"I have to say yes. . . ." "I have to try to control that person. . . ."
"I have to behave this way, think this way, feel this way. . . ."
we can know we are *choosing* not to see choices.

That sense of being trapped is an illusion. We are not controlled by circumstances, our past, the expectations of others,
or our unhealthy expectations for ourselves. We can choose
what feels right for us, without guilt. We have options.

Recovery is not about behaving perfectly or according to
anyone else's rules. More than anything else, recovery is
about knowing we have choices and giving ourselves the
freedom to choose.

Today, I will open my thinking and myself to the choices available
to me. I will make choices that are good for me.

Letting Go of Self-Doubt   May 28

A married woman who had recently joined Al-Anon called
me one afternoon. She worked part-time as a registered nurse,
had assumed all the responsibilities for raising her two chil-
dren, and did all the household chores, including repairs and
finances. "I want to separate from my husband," she sobbed.
"I can't stand him or his abuse any longer. But tell me, please
tell me," she said, "do you think I can take care of myself?"
                                    — Codependent No More

Not only is it okay to take care of ourselves, we can take
good care of ourselves.

Many of us, so confident about our ability to take care of
others, doubt our inherent strength to care for ourselves. We
may have come to believe, from our past or present circumstances, that we need to take care of others and we need
others to take care of us. This is the ultimate codependent
belief.

No matter where this self-defeating belief was born, we can release it and replace it with a better one, a healthier one, a more accurate one.

We can take care of ourselves — whether we are in or out of a relationship. Everything we need will be provided. We will have loved ones, friends, and our Higher Power to help.

Knowing that we can take care of ourselves doesn't mean we won't have feelings of fear, discomfort, doubt, anger, and fragility at times. It means we practice "courageous vulnerability," as Colette Dowling called it in *Cinderella Complex*. We may feel scared, but we do it anyway.

Today, God, help me know how I can take care of myself.

Powerlessness and Unmanageability   May 29

Willpower is not the key to the way of life we are seeking. Surrender is.

"I have spent much of my life trying to make people be, do, or feel something they aren't, don't want to do, and choose not to feel. I have made them, and myself, crazy in that process," said one recovering woman.

"I spent my childhood trying to make an alcoholic father who didn't love himself be a normal person who loved me. I then married an alcoholic and spent a decade trying to make him stop drinking.

"I have spent years trying to make emotionally unavailable people be emotionally present for me.

"I have spent even more years trying to make family members, who are content feeling miserable, happy. What I'm saying is this: I've spent much of my life desperately and vainly trying to do the impossible and feeling like a failure when I couldn't. It's been like planting corn and trying to make the seeds grow peas. Won't work!

"By surrendering to powerlessness, I gain the presence of mind to stop wasting my time and energy trying to change and control that which I cannot change and control. It gives me permission to stop trying to do the impossible and focus on what is possible: being who I am, loving myself, feeling what I feel, and doing what I want to do with my life."

In recovery, we learn to stop fighting lions, simply because we cannot win. We also learn that the more we are focused on controlling and changing others, the more unmanageable our life becomes. The more we focus on living our own life, the more we have a life to live, and the more manageable our life will become.

Today, I will accept powerlessness where I have no power to change things, and I'll allow my life to become manageable.

Commitment   May 30

As we walk through life, there are many things and people we may lose, or lose out on, if we are unwilling to commit. We need to make a commitment for relationships to grow beyond the dating stage, to have the home or apartment we want, the job we want, or the car we desire.

We must commit, on deep levels, to careers — to goals — to family, friends, recovery. Trying something will not enable us to succeed. Committing ourselves will.

Yet, we need never commit before we are ready.

Sometimes, our fear of commitment is telling us something. We may not want to commit to a particular relationship, purchase, or career. Other times, it is a matter of our fears working their way out. Wait, then. Wait until the issue becomes clear.

Trust yourself. Ask your Higher Power to remove your fear of commitment. Ask God to remove your blocks to commitment. Ask God for guidance.

Ask yourself if you are willing to lose what you will not commit to. Then listen, quietly. And wait until a decision seems consistently right and comfortable.

We need to be able to commit, but we need never commit until we are ready.

Trust that you will commit when you want to.

God, guide me in making my commitments. Give me the courage to make those that are right for me, the wisdom to not commit to that which does not feel right, and the patience to wait until I know.

What If?   May 31

I was talking to a friend one day about something I planned to do. Actually, I was worrying about how one particular person might react to what I intended to do.

"What if he doesn't handle it very well?" I asked.

"Then," my friend replied, "you're going to have to handle it well."

"What if's" can make us crazy. They put control over our life in someone else's hands. "What if's" are a sign that we have reverted to thinking that people have to react in a particular way for us to continue on our course.

"What if's" are also a clue that we may be wondering whether we can trust ourselves and our Higher Power to do what's best for us. These are shreds of codependent ways of thinking, feeling, and behaving, and they signal fear.

The reactions, feelings, likes or dislikes of others don't have to control our behaviors, feelings, and direction. We don't need to control how others react to our choices. We can trust ourselves, with help from a Higher Power, to handle any outcome — even the most uncomfortable. And, my friend, we can trust ourselves to handle it well.

Today, I will not worry about other people's reactions, or events outside of my control. Instead, I will focus on my reactions. I will handle my life well today and trust that, tomorrow, I can do the same.

June

Directness   June 1

We feel safe around direct, honest people. They speak their minds, and we know where we stand with them.

Indirect people, people who are afraid to say who they are, what they want, and what they're feeling, cannot be trusted. They will somehow act out their truth even though they do not speak it. And it may catch everyone by surprise.

Directness saves time and energy. It removes us as victims. It dispenses with martyrdom and games. It helps us own our power. It creates respectful relationships.

It feels safe to be around direct, honest people. Be one.

Today, I will own my power to be direct. I do not have to be passive, nor do I need to be aggressive. I will become comfortable with my own truth, so those around me can become comfortable with me.

Owning Our Power   June 2

We don't have to give others so much power and ourselves so little. We don't have to give others so much credit and ourselves so little. In recovery from codependency, we learn there's a big difference between humility and discounting ourselves.

When others act irresponsibly and attempt to blame their problems on us, we no longer feel guilty. We let them face their own consequences.

When others talk nonsense, we don't question our own thinking.

When others try to manipulate or exploit us, we know it's okay to feel anger and distrust and to say no to the plan.

When others tell us that we want something that we really don't want, or someone tells us that we don't want something that we really do want, we trust ourselves. When others tell us things we don't believe, we know it's okay to trust our instincts.

We can even change our mind later.

We don't have to give up our personal power to anyone: strangers, friends, spouses, children, authority figures, or those over whom we're in authority. People may have things to teach us. They may have more information than we have, and may appear more confident or forceful than we feel. But we are equals. Our magic is not in them. Our magic, our light, is in us. And it is as bright a light as theirs.

We are not second-class citizens. By owning our power, we don't have to become aggressive or controlling. We don't have to discount others. But we don't discount ourselves either.

Today, I will own my power with people. I will let myself know what I know, feel what I feel, believe what I believe, and see what I see. I will be open to changing and learning from others and experience, but I will trust and validate myself too. I will stand in my own truth.

Charity   June 3

We need healthy boundaries about receiving money, and we need healthy boundaries about giving money.

Some of us give money for inappropriate reasons.

We may be ashamed because we have money and don't believe we deserve it. We may belong to an organization that uses shame as a form of control to coerce us out of our money that the organization wants.

We can get hooked into giving money to our children, family members, or friends because we have earned or unearned guilt. We allow ourselves to be financially blackmailed, sometimes by the people we love.

This is not money freely given, or given in health.

Some of us give money out of a sense of caretaking. We may have exaggerated feelings of responsibility for others, including financial responsibility.

We may be giving simply because we have not learned to own our power to say no when the answer is *no*.

Some of us give because we hope or believe people will love us if we take care of them financially.

We do not *have* to give money to anyone. Giving money is our choice. We do not have to allow ourselves to be victimized, manipulated, or coerced out of our money. We are financially responsible for ourselves. Part of being healthy is allowing those around us be financially responsible for themselves.

We do not have to be ashamed about having the money that we earn; we deserve to have the money we have been given — whatever the amount, without feeling obligated to give it all away, or guilty because others want what we have.

Charity is a blessing. Giving is part of healthy living. We can learn to develop healthy boundaries around giving.

Today, I will strive to begin developing healthy boundaries about giving money. I understand that giving is my choice.

Trusting God   June 4

A married couple, friends of mine, decided to make some changes in their living situation. They had always lived in the city, and now they decided they wanted to live in the country, on a lake.

They found a small, lake home. It wasn't the house of their dreams, but when they sold their city home, they would have money to remodel it. They had saved some money, so they moved into their lake home before selling their city home.

One year passed, and the city home didn't sell. My friends went through many changes during this time. They had times of patience and impatience. Some days they trusted God; other days they couldn't figure out why God was making them wait so long, why God wouldn't let them move forward with their plan. The doors just wouldn't swing wide open.

One day, a neighbor came to visit my friends. His home on the lake was my friends' dream home — everything they wanted, plus more. The first time my friends saw this house, they admired it, wishing they could have a home just like it, but then they forgot about the idea. They didn't believe it could ever be possible.

The reason the neighbor came to visit my friends was that he and his wife had decided to move. He offered my friends the first option on purchasing his home.

My friends accepted his offer, and signed a purchase agreement. Within two months, they sold their city home and their small but adequate lake home. A short time later, they moved into the home of their dreams.

Sometimes, we experience times of frustration in our life. We believe we're on track, trusting God and ourselves, yet things don't work out. We have false starts and stops. The door refuses to swing wide open.

We may wonder if God has abandoned us, or doesn't care. We may not understand where we're going, or what our direction is.

Then one day we see: the reason we didn't get what we wanted was because God had something much better planned for us.

Today, I will practice patience. I will ask, and trust, my Higher Power to send me His best.

Shame can hold us back, hold us down, and keep us staring at our feet.

— Beyond Codependency

Watch out for shame.

Many systems and people reek of shame. They are controlled by shame and may want us to play their game with them. They may be hoping to hook us and control us through shame.

We don't have to fall into their shame. Instead, we'll take the good feelings — self-acceptance, love, and nurturing.

Compulsive behaviors, sexually addictive behaviors, overeating, chemical abuse, and addictive gambling are shame-based behaviors. If we participate in them, we will feel ashamed. It's inevitable. We need to watch out for addictive and other compulsive behaviors because those will immerse us in shame.

Our past, and the brainwashing we may have had that imposed "original shame" upon us, may try to put shame on us. This can happen when we're all alone, walking through the grocery store or just quietly going about living our life. Don't think.... Don't feel.... Don't grow or change.... Don't be alive.... Don't live life.... Be ashamed!

Be done with shame. Attack shame. Go to war with it. Learn to recognize it and avoid it like the plague.

Today, I will deliberately refuse to get caught up in the shame floating around in the world. If I cannot resist it, I will feel it, accept it, then be done with it as quickly as possible. God, help me know that it's okay to love myself and help me to refuse to submit to shame. If I get off course, help me learn to change shame into guilt, correct the behavior, and move forward with my life in immediate self-love.

> *Were entirely ready to have God remove all these defects of character.*
>
> — *Step Six of Al-Anon*

We progress to the Sixth Step by working diligently, to the best of our ability, on the first five Steps. This work readies us for a change of heart, an openness to becoming changed by a Power greater than ourselves — God.

The path to this willingness can be long and hard. Many of us have to struggle with a behavior or feeling before we become ready to let it go. We need to see, over and over again, that the coping device that once protected us is no longer useful.

The defects of character referred to in Step Six are old survival behaviors that once helped us cope with people, life, and ourselves. But now they are getting in our way, and it is time to be willing to have them removed.

Trust in this time. Trust that you are being readied to let go of that which is no longer useful. Trust that a change of heart is being worked out in you.

God, help me become ready to let go of my defects of character. Help me know, in my mind and soul, that I am ready to let go of my self-defeating behaviors, the blocks and barriers to my life.

Into Orbit   **June 7**

> *It doesn't matter if they're hurting themselves. It doesn't matter that we could help them if they'd only listen to, and cooperate with, us. IT DOESN'T MATTER, DOESN'T MATTER, DOESN'T MATTER, DOESN'T MATTER.*
>
> — Codependent No More

I think I can change him. Nobody's every really loved him and appreciated him before. I'll be the one to do that, and then he'll change.... She's never been with anybody trustworthy before. I'll prove how trustworthy I am, and then she'll be able to love.... Nobody's been able to get to her, to conquer her, before. I'll be the one to do that.... Nobody's every really given him a chance.... Nobody's every really believed in him before....

These are warning signs. Red lights. Red flags. In fact, if we're thinking these thoughts, they need to be stop signs.

If we have gotten hooked into believing that somehow *we* will be the one who will make *the* difference in someone's life, if we are trying to prove how good we can be for someone, we may be in trouble.

This is a game. A deception. It won't work. It'll make us crazy. We can trust that. We're not seeing things clearly. Something's going on with *us*.

It will be self-defeating.

We may be "the one" all right — the one to wind up victimized.

The whole thought pattern reeks of codependency, of not being responsible for oneself, and of victimization. Each person needs to do his or her own work.

Nobody in the past has really understood him.... Nobody has seen what I see in her.... It's a set-up. It sets us up to stop paying attention to ourselves while we focus too much on the other person. It takes us away from our path and often puts us in orbit.

Nobody has appreciated him enough.... Nobody has been good enough to her, or done for her what I can do.... It's a rescue. It's a game move, a game we don't have to play. We don't have to prove we're the one. If we're out to show people we're the best thing that ever happened to them, it may be time to see if they're the best thing that ever happened to us.

We have not been appointed as guardian angel, god-mother, godfather, or "the one who will."

The help, support, and encouragement that truly benefits others and ourselves emerges naturally. Let it.

God, help me let go of my need to meet dysfunctional challenges in my relationships.

Fun   June 8

Have some fun — with life, with the day.

Life is not drudgery; that is an old belief. Let go of it. We are on an adventure, a journey. Events will come to pass that we cannot now fathom.

Replace heaviness and weariness of spirit with joy. Surround yourself with people and things that bring lightness of spirit.

Become sensitive to lightness of spirit.

The journey can be an exciting adventure. Let yourself enjoy it.

Today, I will have some fun with life, with recovery, with people, and with my day.

Panic   June 9

Few situations — no matter how greatly they appear to demand it — can be bettered by us going beserk.
                                        — Codependent No More

Don't panic!

If a swimmer was crossing a great lake, then suddenly focused too heavily on the distance remaining, he might start to flounder and go under — not because he couldn't swim, but because he became overwhelmed by panic.

Panic, not the task, is the enemy.

Many of us have moments when we feel crowded and overwhelmed. We have times when we feel like we cannot possibly accomplish all that needs to be done.

We may be facing a task at work, an improvement in ourselves, or change in our family life.

For a moment, it is helpful to look forward and envision the project. It is normal, when we look ahead at what needs to be done, to have moments of panic. Feel the fear, then let it go. Take our eyes off the future and the enormity of the task. If we have envisioned the goal, it will be ours. We do not have to do everything today, or at once.

Focus on today. Focus on the belief that all is well. All we need to do to reach our goal is to focus on what presents itself naturally, and in an orderly way, to us today. We shall be empowered to accomplish, peacefully, what we need to get where we want to be tomorrow.

Panic will stop this process. Trust and guided action will further it. Breathe deeply. Get peaceful. Trust. Act as guided, today.

We can get back on track by treading water until we regain our composure. Once we feel peaceful, we can begin swimming again, with confidence. Keep the focus simple, on one stroke, one movement at a time. If we can make one movement, we have progressed. If we get tired, we can float — but only if we are relaxed. Before we know it, we shall reach the shore.

Today, I will believe that all is well. I am being led, but I shall only be led one day at a time. I will focus my energy on living this day to the best of my ability. If panic arises, I will stop all activity and deal with panic as a separate issue.

Self-care means taking responsibility for ourselves. Taking responsibility for ourselves includes assuming our true responsibilities to others.

Sometimes, when we begin recovery, we're worn down from feeling responsible for so many other people. Learning that we need only take responsibility for ourselves may be such a great relief that, for a time, we disown our responsibilities to others.

The goal in recovery is to find the balance: we take responsibility for ourselves, and we identify our true responsibilities to others.

This may take some sorting through, especially if we have functioned for years on distorted notions about our responsibilities to others. We may be responsible to one person as a friend or as an employee; to another person, we're responsible as an employer or as a spouse. With each person, we have certain responsibilities. When we tend to those true responsibilities, we'll find balance in our life.

We are also learning that while others aren't responsible for us, they are accountable to us in certain ways.

We can learn to discern our true responsibilities for ourselves, and to others. We can allow others to be responsible for themselves and expect them to be appropriately responsible *to* us.

We'll need to be gentle with ourselves while we learn.

Today, I will strive for clear thinking about my actual responsibilities to others. I will assume these responsibilities as part of taking care of myself.

Much as we would like, we cannot bring everyone with us on this journey called recovery. We are not being disloyal by allowing ourselves to move forward. We don't have to wait for those we love to decide to change as well.

Sometimes we need to give ourselves permission to grow, even though the people we love are not ready to change. We may even need to leave people behind in their dysfunction or suffering because we cannot recover for them. We don't need to suffer with them.

It doesn't help.

It doesn't help for us to stay stuck just because someone we love is stuck. The potential for helping others is far greater when we detach, work on ourselves, and stop trying to force others to change with us.

Changing ourselves, allowing ourselves to grow while others seek their own path, is how we have the most beneficial impact on people we love. We're accountable for ourselves. They're accountable for themselves. We let them go, and let ourselves grow.

Today, I will affirm that it is my right to grow and change, even though someone I love may not be growing and changing alongside me.

Spontaneity and Fun   **June 12**

Practice being spontaneous. Practice having fun.

The joy of recovery is that we finally get to experiment. We get to learn new behaviors, and we don't have to do them perfectly. We only need to find a way that works for us. We even have fun experimenting, learning what we like, and how to do what we like.

Many of us have gotten into a rut with rigidity, martyrdom, and deprivation. One of the "normal" experiences many of us have been deprived of is having fun. Another one is being spontaneous. We may not have the foggiest notion what we would like to do for fun. And we may hold ourselves in check so tightly that we wouldn't allow ourselves to try something fun, anyway.

We can let ourselves go a little now and then. We can loosen up a bit. We don't have to be so stiff and rigid, so frightened about being who we are. Take some risks. Try some new activities. What would we like to do? What might we enjoy doing? Then, take another risk. Pick out a movie we'd like to see; call a friend, and invite him or her to go along. If that person says no, try someone else, or try again another time.

Decide to try something, then go through with it. Go once. Go twice. Practice having fun until fun becomes fun.

Today, I will do something just for fun. I will practice having fun until I actually enjoy it.

Hanging on to Old Relationships   June 13

We want to travel baggage-free on this journey. It makes the trip easier.

Some of the baggage we can let go of is lingering feelings and unfinished business with past relationships: anger; resentments; feelings of victimization, hurt, or longing.

If we have not put closure on a relationship, if we cannot walk away in peace, we have not yet learned our lesson. That may mean we will have to have another go-around with that lesson before we are ready to move on.

We may want to do a Fourth Step (a written inventory of our relationships) and a Fifth Step (an admission of our wrongs). What feelings did we leave with in a particular relationship? Are we still carrying those feelings around? Do we want the heaviness and impact of that baggage on our behavior today?

Are we still feeling victimized, rejected, or bitter about something that happened two, five, ten, or even twenty years ago?

It may be time to let it go. It may be time to open ourselves to the true lesson from that experience. It may be time to put past relationships to rest, so we are free to go on to new, more rewarding experiences.

We can choose to live in the past, or we can choose to finish our old business from the past and open ourselves to the beauty of today.

Let go of your baggage from past relationships.

Today, I will open myself to the cleansing and healing process that will put closure on yesterday and open me to the best today, and tomorrow, has to offer in my relationships.

Letting Go of Timing   June 14

When the time is right, child. When the time is right. How often have we heard those words — from a friend, a sponsor, our Higher Power?

We want things so badly — that job, that check, a relationship, a possession. We want our life to change.

So we wait, sometimes patiently, sometimes anxiously, wondering all the while: When will the future bring me what I long for? Will I be happy then?

We try to predict, circling dates on the calendar, asking questions. We forget that we don't hold the answers. The answers come from God. If we listen closely, we'll hear them. *When the time is right, child. When the time is right.*

Be happy now.

Today, I will relax. I am being prepared. I can let go of timing. I can stop manipulating outcomes. Good things will happen when the time is right, and they will happen naturally.

Competition Between Martyrs   June 15

"Yes, I know your spouse is an alcoholic, but my son is an alcoholic, and that's different. That's worse!"

My pain is greater than yours!

What an easy trap that can be for us. We are out to show others how victimized we have been, how much we hurt, how unfair life is, and what a tremendous martyr we are. And we won't be happy until we do!

We don't need to prove our pain and suffering to anyone. We know we have been in pain. We know we have suffered. Most of us have been legitimately victimized. Many of us have had difficult, painful lessons to learn.

The goal in recovery is not to show others how much we hurt or have hurt. The goal is to stop our pain, and to share that solution with others.

If someone begins trying to prove to us how much he or she hurts, we can say simply, "It sounds like you've been hurt." Maybe all that person is looking for *is* validation of his or her pain.

If we find ourselves trying to prove to someone how much we've been hurt or if we try to top someone else's pain, we may want to stop and figure out what's going on. Do we need to recognize how much we've hurt or are hurting?

There is no particular award or reward for suffering, as many of us tricked ourselves into believing in the height of our codependency. The reward is learning to stop the pain and move into joy, peace, and fulfillment.

That is the gift of recovery, and it is equally available to each of us, even if our pain was greater, or less, than someone else's.

167

God, help me be grateful for all my lessons, even the ones that caused me the most pain and suffering. Help me learn what I need to learn, so I can stop the pain in my life. Help me focus on the goal of recovery, rather than the pain that motivated me into it.

Feeling Good   June 16

> *Having boundaries doesn't complicate life; boundaries simplify life.*
>
> — Beyond Codependency

There is a positive aspect to boundary setting. We learn to listen to ourselves and identify what hurts us and what we don't like. But we also learn to identify what feels good.

When we are willing to take some risks and begin actively doing so, we will enhance the quality of our life.

What do we like? What feels good? What brings us pleasure? Whose company do we enjoy? What helps us to feel good in the morning? What's a real treat in our life? What are the small, daily activities that make us feel nurtured and cared for?

What appeals to our emotional, spiritual, mental, and physical self? What actually feels good to *us*?

We have deprived ourselves too long. There is no need to do that anymore, no need. If it feels good, and the consequences are self-loving and not self-defeating, do it!

Today, I will do for myself those little things that make life more pleasurable. I will not deny myself healthy treats.

Surrender   June 17

Master the lessons of your present circumstances.
We do not move forward by resisting what is undesirable

in our life today. We move forward, we grow, we change by acceptance.

Avoidance is not the key; surrender opens the door.

Listen to this truth: We are each in our present circumstances for a reason. There is a lesson, a valuable lesson, that must be learned before we can move forward.

Something important is being worked out in us, and in those around us. We may not be able to identify it today, but we can know that it is important. We can know it is good.

Overcome not by force, overcome by surrender. The battle is fought, and won, inside ourselves. We must go through it until we learn, until we accept, until we become grateful, until we are set free.

Today, I will be open to the lessons of my present circumstances. I do not have to label, know, or understand what I'm learning; I will see clearly in time. For today, trust and gratitude are sufficient.

Being Vulnerable   June 18

Part of recovery means learning to share ourselves with other people. We learn to admit our mistakes and expose our imperfections — not so that others can fix us, rescue us, or feel sorry for us, but so we can love and accept ourselves. This sharing is a catalyst in healing and changing.

Many of us are fearful of sharing our imperfections because that makes us vulnerable. Some of us have tried being vulnerable in the past, and people tried to control, manipulate, or exploit us, or they made us feel ashamed.

Some of us in recovery have hurt ourselves by being vulnerable. We may have shared things with people who didn't respect our confidence. Or we may have told the wrong people at an inappropriate time, and scared them away.

We learn from our mistakes — and despite our mistakes, it is still a good thing to allow ourselves to be vulnerable and honest. We can learn to choose safe people with whom to share ourselves. We can learn to share appropriately, so we don't scare or push people away. We can also learn to let others be vulnerable with us.

Today, God, help me learn to be appropriately vulnerable. I will not let others exploit or shame me for being vulnerable, and I will not exploit myself.

Making Life Easier   June 19

Life doesn't have to be hard.

Yes, there are times we need to endure, struggle through, and rely on our survival skills. But we don't have to make life, growth, recovery, change, or our day-to-day affairs that hard all the time.

Having life be *that* hard is a remnant of our martyrdom, a leftover from old ways of thinking, feeling, and believing. We are worthy, even when life isn't *that* hard. Our value and worth are not determined by how hard we struggle.

If we're making it *that* hard, we may be making it harder than it needs to be, said one woman. Learn to *let* things happen easily and naturally. Learn to let events, and our participation in them, fall into place. It can be easy now. Easier than it has been. We can go with the flow, take the world off our shoulders, and let our Higher Power ease us into where we need to be.

Today, I will stop struggling so hard. I will let go of my belief that life and recovery have to be hard. I will replace it with a belief that I can walk this journey in ease and peace. And sometimes, it can actually be fun.

Many of us have gone so numb and discounted our feelings so completely that we have gotten out of touch with our needs in relationships.

We can learn to distinguish whose company we enjoy, whether we're talking about friends, business acquaintances, dates, or spouses. We all need to interact with people we might prefer to avoid, but we don't have to force ourselves through long-term or intimate relationships with these people.

We are free to choose friends, dates, spouses. We are free to choose how much time we spend with those people we can't always choose to be around, such as relatives. This is our life. This is it. We can decide how we want to spend our days and hours. We're not enslaved. We're not trapped. And not one of us is without options. We may not see our options clearly. Although we may have to struggle through shame and learn to own our power, we can learn to spend our valuable hours and days with the people we enjoy and *choose* to be with.

God, help me value my time and life. Help me place value on how I feel being around certain people. Guide me as I learn to develop healthy, intimate, sharing relationships with people. Help me give myself the freedom to experiment, explore, and learn who I am and who I can be in my relationships.

The Good Feelings   June 21

Let yourself feel the good feelings too.

Yes, sometimes good feelings can be as distracting as the painful, more difficult ones. Yes, good feelings can be anxiety producing to those of us unaccustomed to them. But go ahead and feel the good feelings anyway.

Feel and accept the joy. The love. The warmth. The excitement. The pleasure. The satisfaction. The elation. The tenderness. The comfort.

Let yourself feel the victory, the delight.

Let yourself feel cared for.

Let yourself feel respected, important, and special.

These are only feelings, but they feel good. They are full of positive, upbeat energy — and we deserve to feel that when it comes our way.

We don't have to repress. We don't have to talk ourselves out of feeling good — not for a moment.

If we feel it, it's ours for the moment. Own it. If it's good, enjoy it.

Today, God, help me be open to the joy and good feelings available to me.

Work Histories   June 22

Just as we have relationship histories, most of us have work histories.

Just as we have a present circumstance to accept and deal with in our relationship life, we have a present circumstance to deal with and accept in our work life.

Just as we develop a healthy attitude toward our relationship history — one that will help us learn and move forward — we can develop a healthy attitude toward our work history.

I have worked many jobs in my life, since I was eleven years old. Just as I have learned many things about myself through my relationships, I have learned many lessons through my work. Often, these lessons run parallel to the lessons I'm learning in other areas of my life.

I have worked at jobs I hated but was temporarily dependent on. I have gotten stuck in jobs because I was afraid to strike out on my own and find my next set of circumstances.

I have been in some jobs to develop skills. Sometimes, I didn't know I was developing those skills until later on when they became an important part of the career of my choice.

I have worked at jobs where I have felt victimized, where I felt like I gave and gave and received nothing in return. I have been in relationships where I manufactured similar feelings.

I have worked at some jobs that have taught me what I absolutely didn't want; others sparked in me an idea of what I really did want and deserve in my career.

Some of my jobs have helped me develop character; others have helped me fine-tune skills. They have all been a place to practice recovery behaviors.

Just as I have had to deal with my feelings and messages about myself in relationships, I have had to deal with my feelings and messages about myself, and what I believed I deserved at work.

Just as I have needed to clear the wreckage of feelings about past relationships, I have needed to finish my business with jobs and careers.

I have been through two major career changes in my life. I learned that neither career was a mistake and no job was wasted time. I have learned something from each job, and my work history has helped create who I am.

I learned something else: there was a Plan, and I was being led. The more I trusted my instincts, what I wanted, and what felt right, the more I felt that I was being led.

The more I refused to lose my soul to a job and worked at it because I wanted to and not for the paycheck, the less victimized I felt by any career, even those jobs that paid a meager salary. The more I set goals and took responsibility for achieving the career I wanted, the more I could decide whether a particular job fit into that scheme of things. I could understand why I was working at a particular job and how that was going to benefit me.

There are times I have panicked at work and about where I was in my employment history. Panic never helped. Trust and working my program did.

There were times I looked around and wondered why I was where I was. There were times people thought I should be someplace different. But when I looked into myself and at God, *I* knew I was in the right place, for the moment.

There were times I didn't get the promotion I wanted. There were times I refused a promotion because it didn't feel right.

There are times I have had to quit a job and walk away in order to be true to myself. Sometimes, that was frightening. Sometimes, I felt like a failure. But I learned this: If I was working my program and true to myself, I never had to fear where I was being led.

There have been times I couldn't survive on the small amount of money I was receiving. Instead of bringing that issue to a particular employer and making it his or her fault, I have had to learn to bring the issue to myself and my Higher Power. I've learned I'm responsible for setting my boundaries and establishing what I believe I deserve. I've also learned God, not a particular employer, is my source of guidance.

I've learned that I'm not stuck or trapped in a job no more than I am in a relationship. I have choices. I may not be able to see them clearly right now, but I do have choices. I've learned that if I really want to take care of myself in a particular way on a job, I will do that. And if I really want to be victimized by a job, I will allow that to happen too.

I am responsible for my choices, and I have choices.

Above all else, I've learned to accept and trust my present circumstances at work. That does not mean to submit; it does not mean to forego boundaries. It means to trust, accept, then take care of myself the best I'm able to on any given day.

God, help me bring my recovery behaviors to my career affairs.

Letting Go of Old Beliefs   June 23

Try harder. Do better. Be perfect.
These messages are tricks that people have played on us. No matter how hard we try, we think we have to do better. Perfection always eludes us and keeps us unhappy with the good we've done.

Messages of perfectionism are tricks because we can never achieve their goal. We cannot feel good about ourselves or what we have done while these messages are driving us. We will never be good enough until we change the messages and tell ourselves we are good enough now.

We can start approving of and accepting ourselves. Who we are is good enough. Our best yesterday was good enough; our best today is plenty good too.

We can be who we are, and do it the way we do it — today. That is the essence of avoiding perfection.

God, help me let go of the messages that drive me into the crazies. I will give myself permission to be who I am and let that be good enough.

Detachment   June 24

Detachment doesn't come naturally for many of us. But once we realize the value of this recovery principle, we understand how vital detachment is. The following story illustrates how a woman came to understand detachment.

"The first time I practiced detachment was when I let go of my alcoholic husband. He had been drinking for seven years — since I had married him. For that long, I had been denying his alcoholism and trying to make him stop drinking.

"I did outrageous things to make him stop drinking, to make him see the light, to make him realize how much he was hurting me. I really thought I was doing things right by trying to control him.

"One night, I saw things clearly. I realized that my attempts to control him would never solve the problem. I also saw that my life was unmanageable. I couldn't make him do anything he didn't want to do. His alcoholism was controlling me, even though I wasn't drinking.

"I set him free, to do as he chose. The truth is, he did as he pleased anyway. Things changed the night I detached. He could feel it, and so could I. When I set him free, I set myself free to live my own life.

"I've had to practice the principle of detachment many times since then. I've had to detach from unhealthy people and healthy people. It's never failed. Detachment works."

Detachment is a gift. It will be given to us when we're ready for it. When we set the other person free, we are set free.

Today, wherever possible, I will detach in love.

Withholding   June 25

Sometimes, to protect ourselves, we close ourselves off from a person we're in a relationship with. Our body may be present, but we're not. We're not available to participate in the relationship.

We shut down.

Sometimes, it is appropriate and healthy to shut down in a relationship. We may legitimately need some time out.

176

Sometimes it is self-defeating to close ourselves off in a relationship.

To stop being vulnerable, honest, and present for another person can put an end to the relationship. The other person can do nothing in the relationship when we are gone. Closing ourselves makes us unavailable to that relationship.

It is common to go through temporary periods of closing down in a relationship. But it is unhealthy to make this an ongoing practice. It may be one of our relationship sabotaging devices.

Before we close down, we need to ask ourselves what we are hoping to accomplish by shutting down. Do we need some time to deal? To heal? To grow? To sort through things? Do we need time out from this relationship? Or are we reverting to our old ways — hiding, running, and terminating relationships because we are afraid we cannot take care of ourselves in any other way?

Do we need to shut down because the other person truly isn't safe, is manipulating, lying, or acting out addictively or abusively? Are we shutting down because the other person has shut down and we no longer want to be available?

Shutting down, shutting off, closing ourselves and removing our emotional presence from a relationship is a powerful tool. We need to use it carefully and responsibly. To achieve intimacy and closeness in a relationship, we need to be present emotionally. We need to be available.

God, help me be emotionally present in the relationships I choose to be in.

Surviving Slumps   June 26

A slump can go on for days. We feel sluggish, unfocused, and sometimes overwhelmed with feelings we can't sort out. We may not understand what is going on with us. Even our attempts to practice recovery behaviors may not appear to work. We still don't feel emotionally, mentally, and spiritually as good as we would like.

In a slump, we may find ourselves reverting instinctively to old patterns of thinking, feeling, and behaving, even when we know better. We may find ourselves obsessing, even when we know that what we're doing is obsessing and that it doesn't work.

We may find ourselves looking frantically for other people to make us feel better, the whole time knowing our happiness and well-being does not lay with others.

We may begin taking things personally that are not our issues, and reacting in ways we've learned all too well do not work.

We're in a slump. It won't last forever. These periods are normal, even necessary. These are the days to get through. These are the days to focus on recovery behaviors, whether or not the rewards occur immediately. These are sometimes the days to let ourselves be and love ourselves as much as we can.

We don't have to be ashamed, no matter how long we've been recovering. We don't have to unreasonably expect "more" from ourselves. We don't ever have to expect ourselves to live life perfectly.

Get through the slump. It will end. Sometimes, a slump can go on for days and then, in the course of an hour, we see ourselves pull out of it and feel better. Sometimes it can last a little longer.

Practice one recovery behavior in one small area, and begin to climb uphill. Soon, the slump will disappear. We can never judge where we will be tomorrow by where we are today.

Today, I will focus on practicing one recovery behavior on one of my issues, trusting that this practice will move me forward. I will remember that acceptance, gratitude, and detachment are a good place to begin.

Achieving Harmony   June 27

When a pianist learns a new piece of music, he or she does not sit down and instantly play it perfectly. A pianist often needs to practice each hand's work separately to learn the feel, to learn the sound. One hand picks out a part until there is a rhythm and ease in playing what is difficult. Then, the musician practices with the other hand, picking through the notes, one by one, until that hand learns its tasks. When each hand has learned its part — the sound, the feel, the rhythm, the tones — then both hands can play together.

During the time of practice, the music may not sound like much. It may sound disconnected, not particularly beautiful. But when both hands are ready to play together, music is created — a whole piece comes together in harmony and beauty.

When we begin recovery, it may feel like we spend months, even years, practicing individual, seemingly disconnected behaviors in the separate parts of our life.

We take our new skills into our work, our career, and begin to apply them slowly, making our work relationships healthier for us. We take our skills into our relationships, sometimes one relationship at a time. We struggle through our new behaviors in our love relationships.

One part at a time, we practice our new music note by note.

We work on our relationship with our Higher Power — our spirituality. We work at loving ourselves. We work at believing we deserve the best. We work on our finances. On our recreation. Sometimes on our appearance. Sometimes on our home.

We work on feelings. On beliefs. On behaviors. Letting go of the old, acquiring the new. We work and work and work. We practice. We struggle through. We go from one extreme to the other, and sometimes back through the course again. We make a little progress, go backward, and then go forward again.

It may all seem disconnected. It may not sound like a harmonious, beautiful piece of music — just isolated notes. Then one day, something happens. We become ready to play with both hands, to put the music together.

What we have been working toward, note by note, becomes a song. That song is a whole life, a complete life, a life in harmony.

The music will come together in our life if we keep practicing the parts.

Today, I will practice my recovery behaviors through the individual parts of my life. I trust that, one day, things will come together in a full, complete song.

When Things Don't Work   June 28

Frequently, when faced with a problem, we may attempt to solve it in a particular way. When that way doesn't work, we may continue trying to solve the problem in that same way.

We may get frustrated, try harder, get more frustrated, and then exert more energy and influence into forcing the same solution that we have already tried and that didn't work.

That approach makes us crazy. It tends to get us stuck and trapped. It is the stuff that unmanageability is made of.

We can get caught in this same difficult pattern in relationships, in tasks, in any area of our life. We initiate something, it doesn't work, doesn't flow, we feel badly, then try the same approach harder, even though it's not working and flowing.

Sometimes, it's appropriate not to give up and to try harder. Sometimes, it's more appropriate to let go, detach, and stop trying so hard.

If it doesn't work, if it doesn't flow, maybe life is trying to tell us something. Life is a gentle teacher. She doesn't always send neon road signs to guide us. Sometimes, the signs are more subtle. Something not working may be a sign!

Let go. If we have become frustrated by repeated efforts that aren't producing desired results, we may be trying to force ourselves down the wrong path. Sometimes, a different solution is appropriate. Sometimes, a different path opens up. Often, the answer will emerge more clearly in the quietness of letting go than it will in the urgency, frustration, and desperation of pushing harder.

Learn to recognize when something isn't working or isn't flowing. Step back and wait for clear guidance.

Today, I will not make myself crazy by repeatedly trying solutions that have proven themselves unsuccessful. If something isn't working, I will step back and wait for guidance.

God's Will   June 29

God's will most often happens in spite of us, not because of us.

We may try to second guess what God has in mind for us, looking, searching, hypervigilant to seek God's will as though it were a buried treasure, hidden beyond our reach. If we find it, we win the prize. But if we're not careful, we miss out.

That's *not* how it works.

We may believe that we have to walk on eggshells, saying, thinking, and feeling the right thing, while forcing ourselves somehow to be in the right place at the right time to find God's will. But that's not true.

God's will for us is not hidden like a buried treasure. We do not have to control or force it. We do not have to walk on eggshells in order to have it happen.

It is right there inside and around us. It is happening, right now. Sometimes, it is quiet and uneventful and includes the daily disciplines of responsibility and learning to take care of ourselves. Sometimes, it is healing us when we're in circumstances that trigger old grieving and unfinished business.

Sometimes, it is grand.

We do have a part. We have responsibilities, including caring for ourselves. But we do not have to control God's will for us. We are being taken care of. We are protected. And the Power caring for and protecting us loves us very much.

If it is a quiet day, trust the stillness. If it is a day of action, trust the activity. If it is time to wait, trust the pause. If it is time to receive that which we have been waiting for, trust that it will happen clearly and with power, and receive the gift in joy.

Today, I will trust that God's will is happening as it needs to in my life. I will not make myself anxious and upset by searching vigorously for God's will, taking unnecessary actions to control the course of my destiny or wondering if God's will has passed me by and I have missed it.

Accepting Change   June 30

One day, my mother and I were working together in the garden. We were transplanting some plants for the third time. Grown from seed in a small container, the plants had been transferred to a larger container; then transplanted into the garden. Now, because I was moving, we were transplanting them again.

Inexperienced as a gardener, I turned to my green-thumbed mother. "Isn't this bad for them?" I asked, as we dug them up and shook the dirt from their roots. "Won't it hurt these plants, being uprooted and transplanted so many times?"

"Oh, no," my mother replied. "Transplanting doesn't hurt them. In fact, it's good for the ones that survive. That's how their roots grow strong. Their roots will grow deep, and they'll make strong plants."

Often, I've felt like those small plants — uprooted and turned upside down. Sometimes, I've endured the change willingly, sometimes reluctantly, but usually my reaction has been a combination.

Won't this be hard on me? I ask. Wouldn't it be better if things remained the same? That's when I remember my mother's words: That's how the roots grow deep and strong.

Today, God, help me remember that during times of transition, my faith and my self are being strengthened.

July

Here is an exercise:

Today, let someone give to you. Let someone do something nice for you. Let someone give you a compliment or tell you something good about yourself. Let someone help you.

Then, stand there and take it. Take it in. Feel it. Know that you are worthy and deserving. Do not apologize. Do not say, "You shouldn't have." Do not feel guilty, afraid, ashamed, and panicky. Do not immediately try to give something back.

Just say, "Thank you."

Today, I will let myself receive one thing from someone else, and I will let myself be comfortable with that.

Who Knows Best? July 2

Others do not know what's best for us.

We do not know what's best for others.

It is our job to determine what's best for ourselves.

"I know what *you* need."... "I know what you *should* do.".. "Now listen, this is what I think *you* should be working on right now."

These are audacious statements, beliefs that take us away from how we operate on a spiritual plane of life. Each of us is given the ability to be able to discern and detect our own path, on a daily basis. This is not always easy. We may have to struggle to reach that quiet, still place.

Giving advice, making decisions for others, mapping out their strategy, is not our job. Nor is it their job to direct us. Even if we have a clean contract with someone to help us — such as in a sponsorship relationship — we cannot trust that others *always* know what is best for us. We are responsible for listening to the information that comes to us. We are responsible for asking for guidance and direction. But it is our responsibility to sift and sort through information, and then listen to ourselves about what is best for us. Nobody can know that but ourselves.

A great gift we can give to others is to be able to trust in them — that they have their own source of guidance and wisdom, that they have the ability to discern what is best for them *and the right to find that path by making mistakes and learning.*

To trust ourselves to be able to discover — through that same imperfect process of struggle, trial, and error — is a great gift we can give ourselves.

Today, I will remember that we are each given the gift of being able to discover what is best for ourselves. God, help me trust that gift.

Directness   July 3

So much of our communication can reflect our need to control. We say what we think others want to hear. We try to keep others from getting angry, feeling afraid, going away, or disliking us. But our need to control traps us into feeling like victims and martyrs.

Freedom is just a few words away. Those words are our truths. We can say what we need to say. We can gently, but assertively, speak our mind.

Let go of your need to control. We do not need to be judgmental, tactless, blaming, or cruel when we speak our truths. Neither do we need to hide our light. Let go, and freely be who you are.

Today, I will be honest with myself and others, knowing that if I don't, my truth will come out some other way.

Celebrate

Take time to celebrate.

Celebrate your successes, your growth, your accomplishments. Celebrate *you* and who you are.

For too long you have been too hard on yourself. Others have spilled their negative energy — their attitudes, beliefs, pain — on you. It had nothing to do with you! All along, you have been a gift to yourself and to the Universe.

You are a child of God. Beautiful, a delight, a joy. You do not have to try harder, be better, be perfect, or be anything you are not. Your beauty is in you, just as you are each moment.

Celebrate that.

When you have a success, when you accomplish something, enjoy it. Pause, reflect, rejoice. Too long you have listened to admonitions not to feel good about what you have done, lest you travel the downward road to arrogance.

Celebration is a high form of praise, of gratitude to the Creator for the beauty of God's creation. To enjoy and celebrate the good does not mean that it will be taken from you. To celebrate is to delight in the gift, to show gratitude.

Celebrate your relationships! Celebrate the lessons from the past and the love and warmth that is there today. Enjoy the beauty of others and their connection to you.

Celebrate all that is in your life. Celebrate all that is good. Celebrate you!

Today, I will indulge in the joy of celebrating.

Survivor Guilt

We begin recovering. We begin taking care of ourselves. Our recovery program starts to work in our life, and we begin to feel good about ourselves.

Then it hits. Guilt.

Whenever we begin to experience the fullness and joy of life, we may feel guilty about those we've left behind — those not recovering, those still in pain. This survivor guilt is a symptom of codependency.

We may think about the husband we've divorced who is still drinking. We may dwell on a child, grown or adult, still in pain. We may get a phone call from a nonrecovering parent who relates his or her misery to us. And we feel pulled into their pain.

How can we feel so happy, so good, when those we love are still in misery? Can we really break away and lead satisfying lives, despite their circumstances? Yes, we can.

And yes, it hurts to leave behind those we love. But keep moving forward anyway. Be patient. Other people's recovery is not our job. We cannot make them recover. We cannot make them happy.

We may ask why *we* were chosen for a fuller life. We may never know the answer. Some may catch up in their own time, but their recovery is not our business. The only recovery we can truly claim is our own.

We can let go of others with love, and love ourselves without guilt.

Today, I am willing to work through my sadness and guilt. I will let myself be healthy and happy, even though someone I love has not chosen the same path.

Step Seven   **July 6**

Humbly asked God to remove our shortcomings.
— Step Seven of Al-Anon

In the Sixth and Seventh Steps of the program, we become willing to let go of our defects of character — issues, behaviors, old feelings, unresolved grief, and beliefs that are blocking us from the joy that is ours. Then we ask God to take them from us.

Isn't that simple? We don't have to contort ourselves to *make* ourselves change. We don't have to force change. For once, we don't have to "do it ourselves." All we have to do is strive for an attitude of willingness and humility. All we have to do is ask God for what we want and need, and then trust God to do for us that which we cannot do *and do not have to* do for ourselves.

We do not have to watch with bated breath for how and when we shall change. This is not a self-help program. In this miraculous and effective program that has brought about recovery and change for millions, we *become* changed by working the Steps.

Today, God, help me surrender to recovery and to the process by which I become changed. Help me focus on the Step I need. Help me do my part, relax, and allow the rest to happen.

Getting It All Out   July 7

Let yourself have a good gripe session.
— Woman, Sex, and Addiction
Charlotte Davis Kasl, Ph.D.

Get it out. Go ahead. Get it all out. Once we begin recovery, we may feel like it's not okay to gripe and complain. We may tell ourselves that if we were really working a good program, we wouldn't need to complain.

What does that mean? We won't have feelings? We won't feel overwhelmed? We won't need to blow off steam or work through some not-so-pleasant, not-so-perfect, and not-so-pretty parts of life?

We can let ourselves get our feelings out, take risks, and be vulnerable with others. We don't have to be all put together, all the time. That sounds more like codependency than recovery.

Getting it all out doesn't mean we need to be victims. It doesn't mean we need to revel in our misery, finding status in our martyrdom. It doesn't mean we won't go on to set boundaries. It doesn't mean we won't take care of ourselves.

Sometimes, getting it all out is an essential part of taking care of ourselves. We reach a point of surrender so we can move forward.

Self-disclosure does not mean only quietly reporting our feelings. It means we occasionally take the risk to share our human side — the side with fears, sadness, hurt, rage, unreasonable anger, weariness, or lack of faith.

We can let our humanity show. In the process, we give others permission to be human too. "Together" people have their not-so-together moments. Sometimes, falling apart — getting it all out — is how we get put back together.

Today, I will let it all out if I need a release.

Going with the Flow   July 8

Go with the flow.

Let go of fear and your need to control. Relinquish anxiety. Let it slip away, as you dive into the river of the present moment, the river of your life, your place in the universe.

Stop trying to force the direction. Try not to swim against the current, unless it is necessary for your survival. If you've been clinging to a branch at the riverside, let go.

Let yourself move forward. Let yourself *be* moved forward.

Avoid the rapids when possible. If you can't, stay relaxed. Staying relaxed can take you safely through fierce currents.

If you go under for a moment, allow yourself to surface naturally. You will.

Appreciate the beauty of the scenery, as it is. See things with freshness, with newness. You shall never pass by today's scenery again!

Don't think too hard about things. The flow is meant to be experienced. Within it, care for yourself. You are part of the flow, an important part. Work with the flow. Work within the flow. Thrashing about isn't necessary. Let the flow help you care for yourself. Let it help you set boundaries, make decisions, and get you where you need to be when it is time.

You can trust the flow, and your part in it.

Today, I will go with the flow.

Overspending and Underspending   July 9

I used to beat my husband to death with my credit card. It made me feel like I had some control, some way to get even with him.

— Anonymous

I spent ten years buying everything for myself at garage sales. I didn't even buy myself a new pair of shoes. The entire time I was depriving myself, my husband was gambling, speculating on risky business deals, and doing whatever he wanted with money. I learned that when I made a decision that I deserved to have the things I wanted, and made a decision to buy something I wanted, there was enough money to do it. It wasn't about being frugal; it was about depriving myself, and being a martyr.

— *Anonymous*

Compulsive buying or overspending may give us a temporary feeling of power or satisfaction, but like other out-of-control behaviors, it has predictable negative consequences.

Underspending can leave us feeling victimized too.

There is a difference between responsible spending and martyred deprivation. There is a difference between treating ourselves well financially and overspending. We can learn to discern that difference. We can develop responsible spending habits that reflect high self-esteem and love for ourselves.

Today, I will strive for balance in my spending habits. If I am overspending, I will stop and deal with what's going on inside me. If I am underspending or depriving myself, I will ask myself if that's necessary and what I want.

Ending Relationships   July 10

It takes courage and honesty to end a relationship — with friends, loved ones, or a work relationship.

Sometimes, it may appear easier to let the relationship die from lack of attention rather than risk ending it. Sometimes, it may appear easier to let the other person take responsibility for ending the relationship.

We may be tempted to take a passive approach. Instead of saying how we feel, what we want or don't want, or what we intend to do, we may begin sabotaging the relationship, hoping to force the other person to do the difficult work.

Those are ways to end relationships, but they are not the cleanest or the easiest ways.

As we walk this path of self-care, we learn that when it is time to end a relationship, the easiest way is one of honesty and directness. We are not being loving, gentle, or kind by avoiding the truth, if we know the truth.

We are not sparing the other person's feelings by sabotaging the relationship instead of accepting the end or the change, and doing something about it. We are prolonging and increasing the pain and discomfort — for the other person and ourselves.

If we don't know, if we are on the fence, it is more loving and honest to say that.

If we know it is time to terminate a relationship, say that.

Endings are never easy, but endings are not made easy by sabotage, indirectness, and lying about what we want and need to do.

Say what you need to say, in honesty and love, when it is time. If we are trusting and listening to ourselves, we will know what to say and when to say it.

Today, I will remember that honesty and directness will increase my self-esteem. God, help me let go of my fear about owning my power to take care of myself in all my relationships.

Bring Any Request to God   July 11

Bring any request you have to God.

No request is too large; none too small or insignificant.

How often we limit God by not bringing to God everything we want and need.

Do we need help getting our balance? Getting through the day?

Do we need help in a particular relationship? With a particular character defect? Attaining a character asset?

Do we need help making progress on a particular task that is challenging us? Do we need help with a feeling? Do we want to change a self-defeating belief that has been challeng-ing us? Do we need information, an insight? Support? A friend?

Is there something in God's Universe that would really bring us joy?

We can ask for it. We can ask God for whatever we want. Put the request in God's hands, trusting it has been heard, then let it go. Leave the decision to God.

Asking for what we want and need is taking care of our-selves. Trust that the Higher Power to whom we have turned over our life and will really does care about us and about what we want and need.

Today, I will ask my Higher Power for what I want and need. I will not demand — I will ask. Then I will let go.

Letting Go of Fear of Abandonment   July 12

"Where are you, God? Where did you go?"

So many people have gone away. We may have felt so alone so much. In the midst of our struggles and lessons, we may wonder if God has gone away too.

There are wondrous days when we feel God's protection and presence, leading and guiding each step and event. There are gray, dry days of spiritual barrenness when we wonder if anything in our life is guided or planned. Wondering if God knows or cares.

Seek quiet times on the gray days. Force discipline and obedience until the answer comes, because it will.

"I have not gone away child. I am here, always. Rest in me, in confidence. All in your life is being guided and planned, each detail. I know, and I care. Things are being worked out as quickly as possible for your highest good. Trust and be grateful. I am right here. Soon you will see, and know."

Today, I will remember that God has not abandoned me. I can trust that God is leading, guiding, directing, and planning in love each detail of my life.

God as We Understand God   July 13

God is subtle, but he is not malicious.
                                        — Albert Einstein

Recovery is an intensely spiritual process that asks us to grow in our understanding of God. Our understanding may have been shaped by early religious experiences or the beliefs of those around us. We may wonder if God is as shaming and frightening as people can be. We may feel as victimized or abandoned by God as we have by people from our past.

Trying to understand God may boggle our mind because of what we have learned and experienced so far in our life.

We can learn to trust God, anyway.

I have grown and changed in my understanding of this Power greater than myself. My understanding has not grown on an intellectual level, but because of what I have *experienced* since I turned my life and my will over to the care of God, as I understood, or rather *didn't understand*, God.

God is real. Loving. Good. Caring. God wants to give us all the good we can handle. The more we turn our mind and heart toward a positive understanding of God, the more God validates us.

The more we thank God for who God is, who we are, and the exact nature of our present circumstances, the more God acts in our behalf.

In fact, all along, God planned to act in our behalf.

God is Creator, Benefactor, and Source. God has shown me, beyond all else, that how I come to understand God is not nearly as important as knowing that God understands me.

Today, I will be open to growing in my understanding of my Higher Power. I will be open to letting go of old, limiting, negative beliefs about God. No matter how I understand God, I will be grateful that God understands me.

We Are Lovable   July 14

Even if the most important person in your world rejects you, you are still real, and you are still okay.
— Codependent No More

Do you ever find yourself thinking: How could anyone possibly love me? For many of us, this is a deeply ingrained belief that can become a self-fulfilling prophecy.

Thinking we are unlovable can sabotage our relationships with co-workers, friends, family members, and other loved ones. This belief can cause us to choose, or stay in, relationships that are less than we deserve because we don't believe we deserve better. We may become desperate and cling as if a particular person was our last chance at love. We may become defensive and push people away. We may withdraw or constantly overreact.

While growing up, many of us did not receive the unconditional love we deserved. Many of us were abandoned or neglected by important people in our life. We may have concluded that the reason we weren't loved was because we were unlovable. Blaming ourselves is an understandable reaction, but an inappropriate one. If others couldn't love us, or love us in ways that worked, that's not our fault. In recovery, we're learning to separate ourselves from the behavior of others. And we're learning to take responsibility for our healing, regardless of the people around us.

Just as we may have believed that we're unlovable, we can become skilled at practicing the belief that we are lovable. This new belief will improve the quality of our relationships.

It will improve our most important relationship: our relationship with our self. We will be able to let others love us and become open to the love and friendship we deserve.

Today, God, help me be aware of and release any self-defeating beliefs I have about being unlovable. Help me begin, today, to tell myself that I am lovable. Help me practice this belief until it gets into my core and manifests itself in my relationships.

Family Buttons   July 15

I was thirty-five years old the first time I spoke up to my mother and refused to buy into her games and manipulation. I was terribly frightened and almost couldn't believe I was doing this. I found I didn't have to be mean. I didn't have to start an argument. But I could say what I wanted and needed to say to take care of myself. I learned I could love and honor myself, and still care about my mother — the way I wanted to — not the way she wanted me to.

— *Anonymous*

Who knows better how to push our buttons than family members? Who, besides family members, do we give such power?

No matter how long we or our family members have been recovering, relationships with family members can be provocative.

One telephone conversation can put us in an emotional and psychological tailspin that lasts for hours or days.

Sometimes, it gets worse when we begin recovery because we become even more aware of our reactions and our discomfort. That's uncomfortable, but good. It is by beginning this process of awareness and acceptance that we change, grow, and heal.

The process of detaching in love from family members can take years. So can the process of learning how to react in a more effective way. We cannot control what they do or try to do, but we can gain some sense of control over how we choose to react.

Stop trying to *make* them act or treat us any differently. Unhook from their system by refusing to try to change or influence them.

Their patterns, particularly their patterns with us, are their issues. How we react, or allow these patterns to influence us, is our issue. How we take care of *ourselves* is our issue.

We can love our family and still refuse to buy into their issues. We can love our family but refuse their efforts to manipulate, control, or produce guilt in us.

We can take care of ourselves with family members without feeling guilty. We can learn to be assertive with family members without being aggressive. We can set the boundaries we need and want to set with family members without being disloyal to the family.

We can learn to love our family without forfeiting love and respect for ourselves.

Today, help me start practicing self-care with family members. Help me know that I do not have to allow their issues to control my life, my day, or my feelings. Help me know it's okay to have all my feelings about family members, without guilt or shame.

Insisting on the Best   July 16

We deserve the best life and love have to offer, but we are each faced with the challenge of learning to identify what that means in our life. We must each come to grips with our own understanding of what we believe we deserve, what we want, and whether we are receiving it.

There is only one place to start, and that is right where we are, in our current circumstances. The place we begin is with us.

What hurts? What makes us angry? What are we whining and complaining about? Are we discounting how much a particular behavior is hurting us? Are we making excuses for the other person, telling ourselves we're "too demanding"?

Are we reluctant, for a variety of reasons, especially fear, to tackle the issues in our relationships that may be hurting us? Do we know what's hurting us and do we know that we have a right to stop our pain, if we want to do that?

We can begin the journey from deprived to deserving. We can start it today. We can also be patient and gentle with ourselves, as we travel in important increments from believing we deserve second best, to knowing in our hearts that we deserve the best, and taking responsibility for that.

Today, I will pay attention to how I allow people to treat me, and how I feel about that. I will also watch how I treat others. I will not overreact by taking their issues too personally and too seriously; I will not underreact by denying that certain behaviors are inappropriate and not acceptable to me.

Love, in Words and Actions   July 17

Many of us have confused notions about what it means to be loved and cared about.

Many of us were loved and cared for by people who had discrepancies between what they said and did.

We may have had a mother or father who said, "I love you" to us, and then abandoned or neglected us, giving us confused ideas about love. Thus that pattern feels like love — the only love we knew.

Some of us may have been cared for by people who provided for our needs and said they loved us, but simultaneously abused or mistreated us. That, then, becomes our idea of love.

Some of us may have lived in emotionally sterile environments, where people said they loved us, but no feelings or nurturing were available. That may have become our idea of love.

We may learn to love others or ourselves the way we have been loved, or we may let others love us the way we have been loved, whether or not that feels good. It's time to let our needs be met in ways that actually work. Unhealthy love may meet some surface needs, but not our need to be loved.

We can come to expect congruency in behavior from others. We can diminish the impact of words alone and insist that behavior and words match.

We can find the courage, when appropriate, to confront discrepancies in words and actions — not to shame, blame, or find fault, but to help us stay in touch with reality and with our needs.

We can give and receive love where behavior matches one's words. We deserve to receive and give the best that love has to offer.

Today, I will be open to giving and receiving the healthiest love possible. I will watch for discrepancies between words and behaviors that confuse me and make me feel crazy. When that happens, I will understand that I am not crazy; I am in the midst of a discrepancy.

Time to Get Angry   July 18

It's about time you got angry — yes, *that* angry.

Anger can be such a potent, frightening emotion. It can also be a feeling that guides us to important decisions, sometimes decisions difficult to make. It can signal other people's problems, our problems, or simply problems we need to address.

We deny our anger for a variety of reasons. We don't give ourselves permission to allow it to come into our awareness — at first. Understand that it does not go away; it sits in layers under the surface, waiting for us to become ready, safe, and strong enough to deal with it.

What we may do instead of facing our anger and what it is telling us about self-care, is feel hurt, victimized, trapped, guilty, and uncertain about how to take care of ourselves. We may withdraw, deny, make excuses, and hide our heads in the sand — for a while.

We may punish, get even, whine, and wonder.

We may repeatedly forgive the other person for behaviors that hurt us. We may be afraid that someone will go away if we deal with our anger toward him or her. We may be afraid we will need to go away, if we deal with our anger.

We may simply be afraid of our anger and the potency of it. We may not know we have a right, even a *responsibility* — to ourselves — to allow ourselves to feel and learn from our anger.

God, help my hidden or repressed angry feelings to surface. Help me have the courage to face them. Help me understand how I need to take care of myself with the people I feel anger toward. Help me stop telling myself something is wrong with me when people victimize me and I feel angry about the victimization. I can trust my feelings to signal problems that need my attention.

Proving It to Ourselves   July 19

I spent a year trying to prove to my husband how much his drinking was hurting me. When I began to recover, I realized I was the one who needed to realize how much his drinking was hurting me.

— *Anonymous*

202

I spent months trying to prove to a man I was dating how responsible and healthy I was. Then I realized what I was doing. He didn't need to realize how responsible and healthy I was. I did.

— Anonymous

Trying to prove how good we are, trying to prove we're good enough, trying to show someone how much he or she has hurt us, trying to show someone we're understanding, are warning signs that we may be into our self-defeating behaviors.

They can be an indication that we are trying to control someone. They can be an indication that we are not believing how good we are, that we're good enough, that someone is hurting us

They can be a warning that we've allowed ourselves to get hooked into a dysfunctional system. They may indicate that we're stuck in that cloudy fog of denial or doing something that is not good for us.

Trying excessively to make a point with another may mean that we have not yet made that point with ourselves. Once we make that point with ourselves, once *we* understand, we will know what to do.

The issue is not about others understanding and taking us seriously. The issue is not about others believing we're good and good enough. The issue is not about others seeing and believing how responsible or loving or competent we are. The issue is not about whether others realize how deeply we are feeling a particular feeling. We are the ones that need to see the light.

Today, God, help me let go of my need to control outcomes by influencing the beliefs of others. I will concentrate on accepting myself, rather than trying to prove something about myself. If I catch

myself in the codependent trap of trying to emphasize something about myself to another, I will ask myself if I need to convince myself of that point.

Letting Go of Resistance   July 20

Do not be in such a hurry to move on.

Relax. Breathe deeply. Be. Be in harmony today.

Be open. There is beauty around and in us today. There is purpose and meaning in today.

There is importance in today — not so much in what happens to us, but in how we respond.

Let today happen. We learn our lessons, we work things out, we change in a simple fashion: by living our life fully today.

Do not worry about tomorrow's feelings, problems, or gifts. Do not worry about whether we can trust ourselves, life, or our Higher Power tomorrow.

Everything we need today shall be given to us. That is a promise — from God, from the Universe.

Feel today's feelings. Solve today's problems. Enjoy today's gifts. Trust yourself, life, and your Higher Power today.

Acquire the art of living fully today. Absorb the lessons, the healing, the beauty, the love available to us today.

Do not be in such a rush to move on. There is no hurry. We cannot escape; we only postpone. Let the feelings go; breathe in peace and healing.

Do not be in such a hurry to move on.

Today, I will not run from myself, my circumstances, or my feelings. I will be open to myself, others, my Higher Power, and life. I will trust that by facing today to the best of my ability, I will acquire the skills I need to face tomorrow.

Being Is Enough July 21

We are not always clear about what we are experiencing, or why.

In the midst of grief, transition, transformation, learning, healing, or discipline — it's difficult to have perspective.

That's because we have not learned the lesson yet. We are in the midst of it. The gift of clarity has not yet arrived.

Our need to control can manifest itself as a need to know exactly what's going on. We cannot always know. Sometimes, we need to let ourselves be and trust that clarity will come later, in retrospect.

If we are confused, that is what we are supposed to be. The confusion is temporary. We shall see. The lesson, the purpose, shall reveal itself — in time, in its own time.

It will all make perfect sense — later.

Today, I will stop straining to know what I don't know, to see what I can't see, to understand what I don't yet understand. I will trust that being is sufficient, and let go of my need to figure things out.

Learning to Trust Again July 22

Many of us have trust issues.

Some of us tried long and hard to trust untrustworthy people. Over and again, we believed lies and promises never to be kept. Some of us tried to trust people for the impossible; for instance, trusting a practicing alcoholic not to drink again.

Some of us trusted our Higher Power inappropriately. We trusted God to make other people do what we wanted, then felt betrayed when that didn't work out.

Some of us were taught that life couldn't be trusted, that we had to control and manipulate our way through.

Most of us were taught, inappropriately, that we couldn't trust ourselves.

In recovery, we're healing from our trust issues. We're learning to trust again. The first lesson in trust is this: We can learn to trust ourselves. We *can* be trusted. If others have taught us we cannot trust ourselves, they were lying. Addictions and dysfunctional systems make people lie.

We can learn to appropriately trust our Higher Power — not to make people do what we want them to, but to help us take care of ourselves, and to bring about the best possible circumstances, at the best possible times, in our life.

We can trust the process — of life and recovery. We do not have to control, obsess, or become hypervigilant. We may not always understand where we are going, or what's being worked out in us, but we can trust that something good is happening.

When we learn to do this, we are ready to learn to trust other people. When we trust our Higher Power and when we trust ourselves, we will know who to trust and what to trust that person for.

Perhaps we always did. We just didn't listen closely enough to ourselves or trust what we heard.

Today, I will affirm that I can learn to trust appropriately. I can trust myself, my Higher Power, and recovery. I can learn to appropriately trust others too.

Making It Happen   July 23

Stop trying so hard to make it happen.

Stop doing *so* much, if doing so much is wearing you out or not achieving the desired results. Stop thinking so much and so hard about it. Stop worrying so about it. Stop trying to force, to manipulate, to coerce, or to *make it happen.*

Making things happen is controlling. We can take positive action to help things happen. We can do our part. But many of us do much more than our part. We overstep the boundaries from caring and doing our part into controlling, caretaking, and coercing.

Controlling is self-defeating. It doesn't work. By over-extending ourselves to make something happen, we may actually be stopping it from happening.

Do your part in relaxed, peaceful harmony. Then let it go. Just let it go. Force yourself to let it go, if necessary. "Act as if." Put as much energy into letting go as you have into try-ing to control. You'll get much better results.

It may not happen. It may not happen the way we wanted it to and hoped it would. But our controlling wouldn't have made it happen either.

Learn to let things happen because that's what they'll do anyway. And while we're waiting to see what happens, we'll be happier and so will those around us.

Today, I will stop forcing things to happen. Instead, I will allow things to happen naturally. If I catch myself trying to force events or control people, I will stop and figure out a way to detach.

Denial   July 24

Denial is a powerful tool. Never underestimate its ability to cloud your vision.

Be aware that, for many reasons, we have become experts at using this tool to make reality more tolerable. We have learned well how to stop the pain caused by reality — not by changing our circumstances, but by pretending our cir-cumstances are something other than what they are.

Do not be too hard on yourself. While one part of you was busy creating a fantasy-reality, the other part went to work on accepting the truth.

Now, it is time to find courage. Face the truth. Let it sink gently in.

When we can do that, we will be moved forward.

God, give me the courage and strength to see clearly.

Keep at It   **July 25**

Keep practicing your recovery behaviors, even when they feel awkward, even when they haven't quite taken yet, even if you don't get it yet.

Sometimes it takes years for a recovery concept to move from our mind into our heart and soul. We need to work at recovery behaviors with the diligence, effort, and repeated practice we applied to codependent behaviors. We need to force ourselves to do things even when they don't feel natural. We need to tell ourselves we care about ourselves and can take care of ourselves even when we don't believe what we're saying.

We need to do it, and do it, and do it — day after day, year after year.

It is unreasonable to expect this new way of life to sink in overnight. We may have to "act as if" for months, years, before recovery behaviors become ingrained and natural.

Even after years, we may find ourselves, in times of stress or duress, reverting to old ways of thinking, feeling, and behaving.

We may have layers of feelings we aren't ready to acknowledge until years into our recovery. That's okay! When it's time, we will.

Do not give up! It takes time to get self-love into the core of us. It takes repeated practice. Time and experience. Lessons, lessons, and more lessons.

Then, just when we think we've arrived, we find we have *more* to learn.

That's the joy of recovery. We get to keep learning and growing all of our life!

Keep on taking care of yourself, no matter what. Keep on plugging away at recovery behaviors, one day at a time. Keep on loving yourself, even when it doesn't feel natural. Act as if for as long as necessary, even if that time period feels longer than necessary.

One day, it will happen. You will wake up, and find that what you've been struggling with and working so hard at and forcing yourself to do, finally feels comfortable. It has hit your soul.

Then, you go on to learn something new and better.

Today, I will plug away at my recovery behaviors, even if they don't feel natural. I will force myself to go through the motions even if that feels awkward. I will work at loving myself until I really do.

Owning Our Power   July 26

Don't you see? We do not have to be so victimized by life, by people, by situations, by work, by our friends, by our love relationships, by our family, by ourselves, our feelings, our thoughts, our circumstances.

We are not victims. We do not have to be victims. That is the whole point!

Yes, admitting and accepting powerlessness is important. But that is a first step, an introduction to this business of recovery. Later, comes owning our power. Changing what we can. This is as important as admitting and accepting powerlessness. And there is so much we can change.

We can own our power, wherever we are, wherever we go, whoever we are with. We do not have to stand there with our hands tied, groveling helplessly, submitting to whatever comes along. There are things we can do. We can speak up. Solve the problem. Use the problem to motivate ourselves to do something good for ourselves.

We can make ourselves feel good. We can walk away. We can come back on our terms. We can stand up for ourselves. We can refuse to let others control and manipulate us.

We can do what we need to do to take care of ourselves. That is the beauty, the reward, the crown of victory we are given in this process called recovery. It is what it is all about!

If we can't do anything about the circumstance, we can change our attitude. We can do the work within: courageously face *our* issues so we are not victimized. We have been given a miraculous key to life.

We are victims no more unless we want to be.

Freedom and joy are ours for the taking, for the feeling, for the hard work we have done.

Today, I will remind myself as often as necessary that I am not a victim, and I do not need to be victimized by whatever comes my way. I will work hard to remove myself as a victim, whether that means setting and enforcing a boundary, walking away, dealing with my feelings, or giving myself what I need. God, help me let go of my need to feel victimized.

Letting Go   July 27

Stop trying so hard to control things. It is not our job to control people, outcomes, circumstances, life. Maybe in the past we couldn't trust and let things happen. But we can now. The way life is unfolding is good. Let it unfold.

Stop trying so hard to do better, be better, be more. Who we are and the way we do things is good enough for today.

Who we were and the way we did things yesterday was good enough for that day.

Ease up on ourselves. Let go. Stop trying so hard.

Today, I will let go. I will stop trying to control everything. I will stop trying to make myself be and do better, and I will let myself be.

Fear

One day, I decided to try something new. I took my ten-year-old son out on the St. Croix River on a Waverunner. A Waverunner is a small boating vehicle resembling a motorcycle.

We donned life jackets and embarked on an experience that turned out to be both exhilarating and frightening: exhilarating when I let myself enjoy it; frightening when I thought too much about what I was doing and all the terrible things that *could* happen.

Midway through our ride, my worst fear came true. We took a spill. We were floundering in thirty feet of water. The Waverunner was bobbing on the waves in front of me, like a motorized turtle on its back.

"Don't panic," my son said calmly.

"What if we drown?" I objected.

"We can't," he said. "We have life jackets on. See! We're floating."

"The machine is upside down," I said. "How are we going to turn it over?"

"Just like the man said," my son answered. "The arrow points this way."

With an easy gesture, we turned the machine right-side up.

"What if we can't climb back on?" I asked.

"We can," my son replied. "That's what Waverunners were made for: climbing on in the water."

I relaxed and as we drove off, I wondered why I had become so frightened. I thought maybe it's because I don't trust my ability to solve problems. Maybe it's because once I almost drowned when I wasn't wearing a life jacket.

But you didn't drown then either, a small voice inside reassured me. You survived.

Don't panic.

Problems were made to be solved. Life was made to be lived. Although sometimes we may be in over our heads — yes, we may even go under for a few moments and gulp a few mouthfuls of water, we won't drown. We're wearing — and always have been wearing — a life jacket. That support jacket is called "God."

Today, I will remember to take care of myself. When I get in over my head, God is there supporting me — even when my fears try to make me forget.

Have Some Fun   July 29

Have some fun. Loosen up a bit. Enjoy life!

We do not have to be so somber and serious. We do not have to be so reflective, so critical, so bound up within ourselves and the rigid parameters others, and often ourselves, have placed around us.

This is life, not a funeral service. Have some fun with it. Enter into it. Participate. Experiment. Take a risk. Be spontaneous. Do not always be so concerned about doing it right, doing the *appropriate* thing.

Do not always be so concerned about what others will think or say. What they think and say are their issues not ours. Do not be so afraid of making a mistake. Do not be so fearful and proper. Do not inhibit yourself so much.

God did not intend us to be so inhibited, so restricted, so controlled. These repressive parameters are what other people have imposed on us, what we have allowed to be done to us.

We were created fully human. We were given emotions, desires, hopes, dreams, feelings. There is an alive, excited, fun-loving child in us somewhere! Let it come out! Let it come alive! Let it have some fun — not just for two hours on Saturday evening. Bring it with us, let it help us enjoy this gift of being alive, being fully human, and being who we are!

So many rules. So much shame we've lived with. It simply isn't necessary. We have been brainwashed. It is time now to free ourselves, let ourselves go, and enter fully human into a full life.

Don't worry. We will learn our lessons when necessary. We have learned discipline. We will not go awry. What will happen is that we will begin enjoying life. We will begin enjoying and experiencing our whole self. We can trust ourselves. We have boundaries now. We have our program for a foundation. We can afford to experiment and experience. We are in touch with ourselves and our Higher Power. We are being guided, but a frozen, inanimate object cannot be guided. It cannot even be moved.

Have some fun. Loosen up a bit. Break a few rules. We won't be punished by God. We do not have to allow people to punish us. And we can stop punishing ourselves. As long as we're here and alive, let's begin to live.

Today, I will let myself have some fun with life. I will loosen up a bit, knowing I won't crack and break. God, help me let go of my need to be so inhibited, proper, and repressed. Help me inject a big dose of life into myself by letting myself be fully alive and human.

Accepting Powerlessness   July 30

Since I've been a child, I've been in an antagonistic relationship with an important emotional part of myself: my feelings. I have consistently tried to either ignore, repress, or force my feelings away. I have tried to create unnatural feelings or force away feelings that were present.

I've denied I was angry, when in fact I was furious. I have told myself there must be something wrong with me for feeling angry, when anger was a reasonable and logical response to the situation.

I have told myself things didn't hurt, when they hurt very much. I have told myself stories such as "That person didn't mean to hurt me.". . . "He or she doesn't know any better.". . . "I need to be more understanding." The problem was that I had already been too understanding of the other person and not understanding and compassionate enough with myself.

It has not just been the large feelings I have been at war with; I have been battling the whole emotional aspect of myself. I have tried to use spiritual energy, mental energy, and even physical exertion to not feel what I need to feel to be healthy and alive.

I didn't succeed at my attempts to control emotions. Emotional control has been a survival behavior for me. I can thank that behavior for helping me get through many years and situations where I didn't have any better options. But I have learned a healthier behavior — accepting my feelings.

We are meant to feel. Part of our dysfunction is trying to deny or change that. Part of our recovery means learning to go with the flow of what we're feeling and what our feelings are trying to tell us.

We are responsible for our behaviors, but we do not have to control our feelings. We can let them happen. We can learn to embrace, enjoy, and experience — feel — the emotional part of ourselves.

Today, I will stop trying to force and control my emotions. Instead, I will give power and freedom to the emotional part of myself.

*For those of us who have survived by controlling and sur-
rendering, letting go may not come easily.*
                              — Beyond Codependency

In recovery, we learn that it is important to identify what
we want and need. Where does this concept leave us? With
a large but clearly identified package of currently unmet
wants and needs. We've taken the risk to stop denying and
to start accepting what we want and need. The problem is,
the want or need hangs there, unmet.

This can be a frustrating, painful, annoying, and sometimes obsession-producing place to be.

After identifying our needs, there is a next step in getting
our wants and needs met. This step is one of the spiritual
ironies of recovery. The next step is letting go of our wants
and needs after we have taken painstaking steps to identify
them.

We let them go, we give them up — on a mental, emotional, spiritual, and physical level. Sometimes, this means
we need to *give up*. It is not always easy to get to this place,
but this is usually where we need to go.

How often I have denied a want or need, then gone
through the steps to identify my needs, only to become
annoyed, frustrated, and challenged because I don't have
what I want and don't know how to get it. If I then embark
on a plan to control or influence getting that want or need
met, I usually make things worse. Searching, trying to control the process, does not work. I must, I have learned to
my dismay, let go.

Sometimes, I even have to go to the point of saying, "I don't
want it. I realize it's important to me, but I cannot control
obtaining that in my life. Now, I don't care anymore if I have
it or not. In fact, I'm going to be absolutely happy without

it and without any hope of getting it, because hoping to get it is making me nuts — the more I hope and try to get it, the more frustrated I feel because I'm not getting it."

I don't know why the process works this way.

I know only that this is how the process works for me. I have found no way around the concept of letting go.

We often can have what we really want and need, or something better. Letting go is part of what we do to get it.

Today, I will strive to let go of those wants and needs that are causing me frustration. I will enter them on my goal list, then struggle to let go. I will trust God to bring me the desires of my heart, in God's time and in God's way.

August

We learn the magical lesson that making the most of what we have turns it into more.

                         — Codependent No More

Say thank you, until you mean it.

Thank God, life, and the universe for everyone and everything sent your way.

Gratitude unlocks the fullness of life. It turns what we have into enough, and more. It turns denial into acceptance, chaos to order, confusion to clarity. It can turn a meal into a feast, a house into a home, a stranger into a friend. It turns problems into gifts, failures into successes, the unexpected into perfect timing, and mistakes into important events. It can turn an existence into a real life, and disconnected situations into important and beneficial lessons. Gratitude makes sense of our past, brings peace for today, and creates a vision for tomorrow.

Gratitude makes things right.

Gratitude turns negative energy into positive energy. There is no situation or circumstance so small or large that it is not susceptible to gratitude's power. We can start with who we are and what we have *today,* apply gratitude, then let it work its magic.

Say thank you, until you mean it. If you say it long enough, you will believe it.

Today, I will shine the transforming light of gratitude on all the circumstances of my life.

In-Between   August 2

Sometimes, to get from where we are to where we are going, we have to be willing to be in-between.

One of the hardest parts of recovery is the concept of letting go of what is old and familiar, but what we don't want, and being willing to stand with our hands empty while we wait for God to fill them.

This may apply to feelings. We may have been full of hurt and anger. In some ways, these feelings may have become comfortably familiar. When we finally face and relinquish our grief, we may feel empty for a time. We are in between pain and the joy of serenity and acceptance.

Being in-between can apply to relationships. To prepare ourselves for the new, we need to first let go of the old. This can be frightening. We may feel empty and lost for a time. We may feel all alone, wondering what is wrong with us for letting go of the proverbial bird-in-hand, when there is nothing in the bush.

Being in-between can apply to many areas of life and recovery. We can be in between jobs, careers, homes, or goals. We can be in between behaviors as we let go of the old and are not certain what we will replace it with. This can apply to behaviors that have protected and served us well all of our life, such as caretaking and controlling.

We may have many feelings going on when we're in-between: spurts of grief about what we have let go of or lost, and feelings of anxiety, fear, and apprehension about what's ahead. These are normal feelings for the in-between place. Accept them. Feel them. Release them.

Being in-between isn't fun, but it's necessary. It will not last forever. It may feel like we're standing still, but we're not. We're standing at the in-between place. It's how we get from here to there. It is not the destination.

We are moving forward, even when we're in-between.

Today, I will accept where I am as the ideal place for me to be. If I am in-between, I will strive for the faith that this place is not without purpose, that it is moving me toward something good.

*So much of what I call my codependency is fear and panic
because I spent so much of my life feeling abused, trapped,
and not knowing how to take care of myself in relationships.*
— *Anonymous*

No matter how long we have been recovering, we may still
tend to give up our power to others, whether they be authority figures, a new love, or a child.

When we do this, we experience the set of emotions and
thoughts we call "the codependent crazies." We may feel
angry, guilty, afraid, confused, and obsessed. We may feel
dependent and needy or become overly controlling and
rigid. We may return to familiar behaviors during stress. And
for those of us who have codependency and adult children
issues, relationships can mean *stress*.

We don't have to stay stuck in our codependency. We
don't have to shame or blame ourselves, or the other person, for our condition. We simply need to remember to own
our power.

Practice. Practice. Practice using your power to take care
of yourself, no matter who you are dealing with, where you
are, or what you are doing. This is what recovery means.
This does not mean we try to control others; it does not mean
we become abrasive or abusive. It means we own our power
to take care of ourselves.

The thought of doing this may generate fears. That's normal! Take care of yourself anyway. The answers, and the
power to do that, are within you now.

Start today. Start where you are. Start by taking care of
who you are, at the present moment, to the best of your
ability.

Today, I will focus on owning my power to take care of myself. I will not let fears, or a false sense of shame and guilt, stop me from taking care of myself.

Vulnerability

> *I've learned that the more vulnerable I allow myself to be, the more in control of myself I really am.*
>
> — *Anonymous*

Many of us feel that we can only show our strong, confident side. We believe the face we have to show to the world should *always* be one of politeness, perfection, calm, strength, and control.

While it is certainly good and often appropriate to be in control, calm, and strong, there is another side to all of us — that part of us that feels needy, becomes frightened, has doubts, and gets angry. That part of us that needs care, love, and reassurance that things will be okay. Expressing these needs makes us vulnerable and less than perfect, but this side needs our acceptance too.

Allowing ourselves to be vulnerable will help us build lasting relationships. Sharing our vulnerabilities helps us feel close to people and helps others feel close to us. It helps us grow in self-love and self-acceptance. It helps us become healing agents. It allows us to become whole and accessible to others.

Today, I will allow myself to be vulnerable with others when it's safe and appropriate to do so.

Sometimes, our life and history may be so full of pain that we think it totally unfair that we have to grow up now and be financially responsible for ourselves.

The feeling is understandable; the attitude is not healthy. Many people in recovery may believe that certain people in particular, and life in general, owe them a living after what they've been through.

To feel good about ourselves, to find the emotional peace and freedom we're seeking in recovery, we need healthy boundaries about money — what we give to others, and what we allow ourselves to receive from others.

Do we feel that others owe us money because we cannot take care of ourselves? Do we believe others owe us because we do not have as much money as they do? Do we consciously or subconsciously believe that they "owe" us money because of emotional pain we suffered as a result of our relationship with them or another person?

Punitive damages are awarded in court, but not in recovery.

Unhealthy boundaries about what we allow ourselves to receive from others will not lead to healthy relationships with others or ourselves.

Test by looking within. The key is our attitude. The issue is boundaries about receiving money. Become willing to meet the challenge of taking responsibility for yourself.

Today, I will strive for clear, healthy boundaries about receiving money from others. As part of my recovery, I will take a hard look at my financial history and examine whether I have taken money that may not reflect good boundaries. If I uncover some incidents that reflect less than an attitude of healthy self-responsibility, I will become willing to make amends and develop a reasonable plan to do that.

Problems are made to be solved!

Some of us spend more time reacting to the fact that we have a problem than we do solving the problem. "Why is this happening to me?". . ."Isn't life awful?". . ."How come this had to happen?". . ."Oh, dear. This is terrible.". . ."Why is God (the Universe, an agency, a person, or life) picking on me?"

Problems are inevitable. Some problems can be anticipated. Some are surprises. But the idea that problems occur regularly need never be a surprise.

The good news is that for every problem, there's a solution. Sometimes the solution is immediate. Sometimes, it takes awhile to discover. Sometimes, the solution involves letting go. Sometimes, the problem is ours to solve; sometimes it isn't. Sometimes, there is something we can clearly do to solve the problem; other times, we need to struggle, flounder, do our part, then trust our Higher Power for help.

Sometimes, the problem is just part of life. Sometimes, the problem is important because we are learning something through the problem and its solution. Sometimes, problems end up working out for good in our life. They get us headed in a direction that is superior to one we may otherwise have taken.

Sometimes, problems just are; sometimes they are a warning sign that we are on the wrong track.

We can learn to accept problems as an inevitable part of life. We can learn to solve problems. We can learn to trust our ability to solve problems. We can learn to identify which problems are trying to lead us in a new direction, and which simply ask for solving.

We can learn to focus on the solution rather than on the problem, and maintain a positive attitude toward life and the inevitable flow of problems and solutions.

Today, I will learn to trust solutions, rather than be victimized by problems. I will not use problems to prove I am helpless, picked on, or martyred. I will not point to my problems to prove how awful life is. I will learn to trust the flow of problems and solutions. God, help me solve the problems I can solve today. Help me let go of the rest. Help me believe in my ability to tackle and solve problems. Help me trust the flow. For each problem, there is a solution.

Saying No   August 7

For many of us, the most difficult word to say is one of the shortest and easiest in the vocabulary: *No.* Go ahead, say it aloud: *No.*

No — simple to pronounce, hard to say. We're afraid people won't like us, or we feel guilty. We may believe that a "good" employee, child, parent, spouse, or Christian never says no.

The problem is, if we don't learn to say no, we stop liking ourselves and the people we always try to please. We may even punish others out of resentment.

When do we say no? When no is what we really mean.

When we learn to say no, we stop lying. People can trust us, and we can trust ourselves. All sorts of good things happen when we start saying what we mean.

If we're scared to say no, we can buy some time. We can take a break, rehearse the word, and go back and say no. We don't have to offer long explanations for our decisions.

When we can say no, we can say yes to the good. Our no's and our yes's begin to be taken seriously. We gain control of ourselves. And we learn a secret: "No" isn't really that hard to say.

Today, I will say no if that is what I mean.

Yesterday we talked about learning to say no. Today let's discuss another important word: *Yes.*

We can learn to say yes to things that feel good, to what we want — for ourselves and others.

We can learn to say yes to fun. Yes to meetings, to calling a friend, asking for help.

We can learn to say yes to healthy relationships, to people and activities that are good for us.

We can learn to say yes to ourselves, what we want and need, our instincts, and the leading of our Higher Power.

We can learn to say yes when it feels right to help someone. We can learn to say yes to our feelings. We can learn to identify when we need to take a walk, take a nap, have our back rubbed, or buy ourselves flowers.

We can learn to say yes to work that is right for us.

We can learn to say yes to all that will nurture and nourish us. We can learn to say yes to the best life and love have to offer.

Today, I will say yes to all that feels good and right.

Asking for What We Need   August 9

Decide what it is you want and need, then go to the person you need it from and ask for it.

Sometimes, it takes hard work and much energy to get what we want and need. We have to go through the pains of identifying what we want, then struggle to believe that we deserve it. Then, we may have to experience the disappointment of asking someone, having the person refuse us, and figuring out what to do next.

Sometimes in life, getting what we want and need is not so difficult. Sometimes, all we need to do is ask.

We can go to another person, or our Higher Power, and ask for what we need.

But because of how difficult it can be, at times, to get what we want and need, we may get trapped in the mind-set of believing it will always be that difficult. Sometimes, not wanting to go through the hassle, dreading the struggle, or out of fear, we may make getting what we want and need much more difficult than it needs to be.

We may get angry before we ask, deciding that we'll never get what we want, or anticipating the "fight" we'll have to endure. By the time we talk to someone about what we want, we may be so angry that we're demanding, not asking; thus our anger triggers a power play that didn't exist except in our mind.

Or we may get so worked up that we don't ask — or we waste far more energy than necessary fighting with ourselves, only to find out that the other person, or our Higher Power, is happy to give us what we want.

Sometimes, we have to fight and work and wait for what we want and need. Sometimes, we can get it just by asking or stating that this is what we want. Ask. If the answer is no, or not what we want, *then* we can decide what to do next.

Today, I will not set up a difficult situation that doesn't exist with other people, or my Higher Power, about getting what I want and need. If there is something I need from someone, I will ask first, before I struggle.

Letting Go of Perfection   August 10

As I journey through recovery, more and more I learn that accepting myself and my idiosyncrasies — laughing at myself for my ways — gets me a lot further than picking on

*myself and trying to make myself perfect. Maybe that's really
what it's all about — absolute loving, joyous, nurturing self-
acceptance.*

— *Anonymous*

Stop expecting perfection from yourself and those around you.

We do a terrible, annoying thing to ourselves and others when we expect perfection. We set up a situation where others, including ourselves, do not feel comfortable with us. Sometimes, expecting perfection makes people so uptight that they and we make more mistakes than normal because we are so nervous and focused on mistakes.

That does not mean we allow inappropriate behaviors with the excuse that "nobody's perfect." That doesn't mean we don't have boundaries and reasonable expectations of people and ourselves.

But our expectations need to be reasonable. Expecting perfection is not reasonable.

People make mistakes. The less anxious, intimidated, and repressed they are by expectations of being perfect, the better they will do.

Striving for excellence, purity in creativity, a harmonious performance, and the best we have to offer does not happen in the stymied, negative, fear-producing atmosphere of expecting perfection.

Have and set boundaries. Have reasonable expectations. Strive to do your best. Encourage others to do the same. But know that we and others will make mistakes. Know that we and others will have learning experiences, things we go through.

Sometimes, the flaws and imperfections in ourselves determine our uniqueness, the way they do in a piece of art. Relish them. Laugh at them. Embrace them, and ourselves.

Encourage others and ourselves to do the best we can. Love and nurture ourselves and others for being who we are. Then realize we are not *merely* human — we were intended and created to be human.

Today, God, help me let go of my need to be perfect and to unreasonably insist that others are perfect. I will not use this to tolerate abuse or mistreatment, but to achieve appropriate, balanced expectations. I am creating a healthy atmosphere of love, acceptance, and nurturing around and within me. I trust that this attitude will bring out the best in other people and in me.

Healing   August 11

Let healing energy flow through your body.

The healing energy of God, the Universe, life, and recovery surrounds us. It is available, waiting for us to draw on it, waiting for us to draw it in. It's waiting at our meetings or groups, on the words of a whispered prayer, in a gentle touch, a positive word, a positive thought. Healing energy is in the sun, the wind, the rain, in all that is good.

Let healing energy come. Attract it. Accept it. Let it soak in. Breathe in the golden light. Exhale. Let go of fear, anger, hurt, doubt. Let healing energy flow to you, through you.

It is yours for the asking, for the believing.

Today, I will ask for, and accept, the healing energy from God and the Universe. I will let it flow to me, through me, and back out to others. I am part of, and at one with, the continuous cycle of healing.

Directness   August 12

Direct people are a joy to be around.

We never have to guess what they're *really* thinking or

feeling, because they're honest about their thoughts and openly express their feelings.

We never have to wonder if they're with us because they want to be, or if they're there out of guilt and obligation.

When they do something for us, we don't have to worry whether they'll end up resenting us because direct people generally do things that please themselves.

We don't have to fuss about the status of our relationship because if we ask, they'll tell us.

We don't have to worry if they're angry because they deal openly with their anger and resolve it quickly.

We don't have to ponder whether they are talking about us behind our backs because if they have something to say, it will be said to us directly.

We don't have to wonder if we can rely on them because direct people are trustworthy.

Wouldn't it be nice if we were all direct?

Today, I will let go of my notions that it is somehow good or desirable to be indirect. Instead, I will strive for honesty, directness, and clarity in my communication. I will let directness in my relationships begin with me.

Friends   August 13

Don't overlook the value of friendship. Don't neglect friends.

Friends are a joy. Adult friendships can be a good place for us to learn to have fun and to appreciate how much fun we can have with a friend.

Friends can be a comfort. Who knows us better, or is more able to give us support, than a good friend? A friendship is a comfortable place to be ourselves. Often, our choice of friends will reflect the issues we're working on. Giving and receiving support will help both people grow.

Some friendships wax and wane, going through cycles throughout the years. Some trail off when one person outgrows the other. Certainly, we will have trials and tests in friendships and, at times, be called on to practice our recovery behaviors.

But some friendships will last a lifetime. There are special love relationships, and there are friendships. Sometimes, our friendships — especially recovery friendships — can be special love relationships too.

Today, I will reach out to a friend. I will let myself enjoy the comfort, joys, and enduring quality of my friendships.

Owning Our Power   August 14

Many of us have someone in our life who challenges our ability to trust and care for ourselves.

When we hear that person's voice or are in his or her presence, we may forget all we know about what is real, about how to own our power, about how to be direct, about what we know and believe to be true, about how important we are.

We give up our power to that person. The child in us gets hooked with a mixture of powerful feelings — love, fear, or anger. We may feel trapped, helpless, or so attracted that we can't think straight. There may be a powerful tug-of-war going between feelings of anger and our need to be loved and accepted, or between our head and our heart.

We may be so enamored or intimidated that we revert to our belief that we can't react or respond to this person any differently.

We get hooked.

We don't have to stay under a spell.

We start by becoming aware of the people who hook us, and then accepting that.

We can force ourselves through the motions of reacting differently to that person, even if that new reaction is awkward and uncomfortable.

Search out our motivations. Are we somehow trying to control or influence the other person? We cannot change the other person, but we can stop playing our part of the game. One good way to do this is by detaching and letting go of any need to control.

The next step is learning to own our power to take care of ourselves, to be who we are free from their influence. We can learn to own our power with difficult people. It may not happen overnight, but we can begin, today, to change our self-defeating reactions to the people who have hooked us.

God, help me identify the relationships where I have forfeited my power. Help me unhook and begin owning my power.

Leaving Room for Feelings   August 15

We need to allow enough room for others and ourselves to have and work through our feelings.

We are people, not robots. An important part of us — who we are, how we grow, how we live — is connected to our emotional center. We have feelings, sometimes difficult ones, sometimes disruptive ones, sometimes explosive ones, that need to be worked through.

By facing and working through these feelings we and others grow. In relationships, whether it be a love relationship, a friendship, a family relationship, or a close business relationship, people need room to have and work through their feelings.

Some call it "going through the process."

It is unreasonable to expect ourselves or others to not need time and room to work through feelings. We will be setting ourselves and our relationships up for failure if we do not allow this time and room in our life.

We need time to work through feelings. We need the space and permission to work through these feelings in the awkward, uncomfortable, sometimes messy way that people work through feelings.

This is life. This is growth. This is okay.

We can allow room for feelings. We can let people have time and permission to go through their feelings. We do not have to keep ourselves or others under such a tight rein. While we work through our feelings we do not have to expend unnecessary energy reacting to each feeling we or others have. We don't have to take all our feelings, and others' feelings, so seriously while we or others are in the process of working through them.

Let the feelings flow and trust where the flow is taking you.

I can set reasonable boundaries for behavior, and still leave room for a range of emotions.

Rescuing Ourselves   August 16

No one likes a martyr.

How do we feel around martyrs? Guilty, angry, trapped, negative, and anxious to get away.

Somehow, many of us have developed the belief that depriving ourselves, not taking care of ourselves, being a victim, and suffering needlessly will get us what we want.

It is our job to notice our abilities, our strengths, and take care of ourselves by developing and acting on them.

It is our job to notice our pain and weariness and appropriately take care of ourselves.

It is our job to notice our deprivation, too, and begin to take steps to give ourselves abundance. It begins inside of us, by changing what we believe we deserve, by giving up our deprivation and treating ourselves the way we deserve to be treated.

Life is hard, but we don't have to make it more difficult by neglecting ourselves. There is no glory in suffering, only suffering. Our pain will not stop when a rescuer comes, but when we take responsibility for ourselves and stop our own pain.

Today, I will be my own rescuer. I will stop waiting for someone else to work through my issues and solve my problems for me.

Healing Thoughts

Think healing thoughts.

When you feel anger or resentment, ask God to help you feel it, learn from it, and then release it. Ask Him to bless those who you feel anger toward.

Ask Him to bless you too.

When you feel fear, ask Him to take it from you. When you feel misery, force gratitude. When you feel deprived, know that there is enough.

When you feel ashamed, reassure yourself that who you are is okay. You are good enough.

When you doubt your timing or your present position in life, assure yourself that all is well; you are right where you're meant to be. Reassure yourself that others are too.

When you ponder the future, tell yourself that it will be good. When you look back at the past, relinquish regrets.

When you notice problems, affirm there will be a timely solution and a gift from the problem.

When you resist feelings or thoughts, practice acceptance. When you feel discomfort, know it will pass. When you identify a want or a need, tell yourself it will be met.

When you worry about those you love, ask God to protect and care for them. When you worry about yourself, ask Him to do the same.

When you think about others, think love. When you think about yourself, think love.

Then watch your thoughts transform reality.

Today, I will think healing thoughts.

Valuing this Moment   August 18

Detachment involves present-moment living — living in the here and now. We allow life to happen instead of forcing and trying to control it. We relinquish regrets over the past and fears about the future. We make the most of each day.
— Codependent No More

This moment, we are right where we need to be, right where we are meant to be.

How often we waste our time and energy wishing we were someone else, were doing something else, or were someplace else. We may wish our present circumstances were different.

We needlessly confuse ourselves and divert our energy by thinking that our present moment is a mistake. But we are right where we need to be for now. Our feelings, thoughts, circumstances, challenges, tasks — all of it is on schedule.

We spoil the beauty of the present moment by wishing for something else.

Come back home to yourself. Come back home to the present moment. We will not change things by escaping or leaving the moment. We will change things by surrendering to and accepting the moment.

Some moments are easier to accept than others.

To trust the process, to trust all of it, without hanging on to the past or peering too far into the future, requires a great deal of faith. Surrender to the moment. If you're feeling angry, get mad. If you're setting a boundary, dive into that. If you're grieving, grieve. Get into it. Step where instinct leads. If you're waiting, wait. If you have a task, throw yourself into the work. Get into the moment; the moment is right.

We are where we are, and it is okay. It is right where we're meant to be to get where we're going tomorrow. And that place will be good.

It has been planned in love for us.

God, help me let go of my need to be someone other than who I am today. Help me dive fully into the present moment. I will accept and surrender to my present moments — the difficult ones and the easy ones, trusting the whole process. I will stop trying to control the process; instead, I will relax and let myself experience it.

Letting Go of Shame   August 19

Shame is that dark, powerful feeling that holds us back. Yes, shame can stop us from acting inappropriately. But many of us have learned to attach shame to healthy behaviors that are in our best interest.

In dysfunctional families, shame can be tagged to healthy behaviors such as talking about feelings, making choices, taking care of ourselves, having fun, being successful, or even feeling good about ourselves.

Shame may have been attached to asking for what we want and need, to communicating directly and honestly, and to giving and receiving love.

Sometimes shame disguises itself as fear, rage, indifference, or a need to run and hide, wrote Stephanie E. But if it feels dark and makes us feel bad about being who we are, it's probably shame.

In recovery, we are learning to identify shame. When we can recognize it, we can begin to let go of it. We can love and accept ourselves — starting now.

We have a right to be, to be here, and to be who we are. And we don't ever have to let shame tell us any differently.

Today, I will attack and conquer the shame in my life.

Honesty in Relationships   August 20

We can be honest and direct about our boundaries in relationships and about the parameters of a particular relationship.

Perhaps no area of our life reflects our uniqueness and individuality in recovery more than our relationships. Some of us are in a committed relationship. Some of us are dating. Some of us are not dating. Some of us are living with someone. Some of us wish we were dating. Some of us wish we were in a committed relationship. Some of us get into new relationships after recovery. Some of us stay in the relationship we were in before we began recovering.

We have other relationships too. We have friendships. Relationships with children, with parents, with extended family. We have professional relationships — relationships with people on the job.

We need to be able to be honest and direct in our relationships. One area we can be honest and direct about is the parameters of our relationships. We can define our relationships to people, an idea written about by Charlotte Kasl and others, and we can ask them to be honest and direct about defining their vision of the relationship with us.

It is confusing to be in relationships and not know where we stand — whether this is on the job, in a friendship, with family members, or in a love relationship. We have a right to be direct about how we define the relationship — what we want it to be. But relationships equal two people who have equal rights. The other person needs to be able to define the relationship too. We have a right to know, and ask. So do they.

Honesty is the best policy.

We can set boundaries. If someone wants a more intense relationship than we do, we can be clear and honest about what we want, about our intended level of participation. We can tell the person what to reasonably expect from us, because that is what we want to give. How the person deals with that is his or her issue. Whether or not we tell the person is ours.

We can set boundaries and define friendships when those cause confusion.

We can even define relationships with children, if those relationships have gotten sticky and exceeded our parameters. We need to define love relationships and what that means to each person. We have a right to ask and receive clear answers. We have a right to make our own definitions and have our own expectations. So does the other person.

Honesty and directness is the only policy. Sometimes we don't know what we want in a relationship. Sometimes the other person doesn't know. But the sooner we can define a relationship, with the other person's help, the sooner we can decide on an appropriate course of conduct for ourselves.

The clearer we can become on defining relationships, the more we can take care of ourselves in that relationship. We have a right to our boundaries, wants, and needs. So does the other person. We can not force someone to be in a relationship or to participate at a level we desire if he or she does not want to. All of us have a right not to be forced.

Information is a powerful tool, and having the information about what a particular relationship is — the boundaries and definitions of it — will empower us to take care of ourselves in it.

Relationships take a while to form, but at some point we can reasonably expect a clear definition of what that relationship is and what the boundaries of it are. If the definitions clash, we are free to make a new decision based on appropriate information about what we need to do to take care of ourselves.

Today, I will strive for clarity and directness in my relationships. If I now have some relationships that are murky and ill-defined, and if I have given them adequate time to form, I will begin to take action to define that relationship. God, help me let go of my fears about defining and understanding the nature of my present relationships. Guide me into clarity — clear, healthy thinking. Help me know that what I want is okay. Help me know that if I can't get that from the other person, what I want is still okay, but not possible at the present time. Help me learn to not forego what I want and need, but empower me to make appropriate, healthy choices about where to get that.

Detaching in Relationships   August 21

When we first become exposed to the concept of detachment, many of us find it objectionable and questionable. We may think that detaching means we don't care. We may believe that by controlling, worrying, and trying to force things to happen, we're showing how much we care.

We may believe that controlling, worrying, and forcing will somehow affect the outcome we desire. Controlling, worrying, and forcing don't work. Even when we're right, controlling doesn't work. In some cases, controlling may prevent the outcome we want from happening.

As we practice the principle of detachment with the people in our life, we slowly begin to learn the truth. Detaching, preferably detaching with love, is a relationship behavior that works.

We learn something else too. Detachment — letting go of our need to control people — enhances all our relationships. It opens the door to the best possible outcome. It reduces our frustration level, and frees us and others to live in peace and harmony.

Detachment means we care, about ourselves and others. It frees us to make the best possible decisions. It enables us to set the boundaries we need to set with people. It allows us to have our feelings, to stop reacting and initiate a positive course of action. It encourages others to do the same.

It allows our Higher Power to step in and work.

Today, I will trust the process of detaching with love. I will understand that I am not just letting go; I am letting go and letting God. I'm loving others, but I'm loving myself too.

Responsibility for Family Members   August 22

I can still remember my mother clutching her heart, threatening to have a heart attack and die, and blaming it on me.
— Anonymous

For some of us, the idea that we were responsible for other people's feelings had its roots in childhood and was established by members of our nuclear family. We may have been told that we made our mother or father miserable, leading directly to the idea that we were also responsible for making them happy. The idea that we are responsible for our parents' happiness or misery can instill exaggerated feelings of power and guilt in us.

We do not have this kind of power over our parents — over their feelings, or over the course of their lives. We do not have to allow them to have this kind of power over us.

Our parents did the best they could. But we still do not have to accept one belief from them that is not a healthy belief. They may be our parents, but they are not always right. They may be our parents, but their beliefs and behaviors are not always healthy and in our best interest.

We are free to examine and choose our beliefs.

Let go of guilt. Let go of excessive and inappropriate feelings of responsibility toward parents and other family members. We do not have to allow their destructive beliefs to control us, our feelings, our behaviors, or our life.

Today, I will begin the process of setting myself free from any self-defeating beliefs my parents passed on to me. I will strive for appropriate ideas and boundaries concerning how much power and how much responsibility I can actually have in my relationship with my parents.

Self-Care   August 23

When will we become lovable? When will we feel safe? When will we get all the protection, nurturing, and love we so richly deserve? We will get it when we begin giving it to ourselves.
— Beyond Codependency

The idea of giving ourselves what we want and need can be confusing, especially if we have spent many years not knowing that it's okay to take care of ourselves. Taking our energy and focus off others and their responsibilities and placing that energy on to ourselves and our responsibilities is a recovery behavior that can be acquired. We learn it by daily practice.

We begin by relaxing, by breathing deeply, and letting go of our fears enough to feel as peaceful as we can. Then, we ask ourselves: What do I need to do to take care of myself today, or for this moment?

What do I need and want to do?

What would demonstrate love and self-responsibility?

Am I caught up in the belief that others are responsible for making me happy, responsible for me? Then the first thing I need to do is correct my belief system. I am responsible for myself.

Do I feel anxious and concerned about a responsibility I've been neglecting? Then perhaps I need to let go of my fears and tend to that responsibility.

Do I feel overwhelmed, out of control? Maybe I need to journey back to the first of the Twelve Steps.

Have I been working too hard? Maybe what I need to do is take some time off and do something fun.

Have I been neglecting my work or daily tasks? Then maybe what I need to do is get back to my routine.

There is no recipe, no formula, no guidebook for self-care. We each have a guide, and that guide is within us. We need to ask the question: What do I need to do to take loving, responsible care of myself? Then, we need to listen to the answer. Self-care is not that difficult. The most challenging part is trusting the answer, and having the courage to follow through once we hear it.

Today, I will focus on taking care of myself. I will trust myself and my Higher Power to guide me in this process.

Step Eight   **August 24**

Made a list of all persons we had harmed, and became willing to make amends to them all.
> — *Step Eight of Al-Anon*

The Eighth Step is not meant to punish us; it is meant to set us free from guilt, anxiety, and discord.

We begin by making a list of everyone we have harmed on our journey, as we have struggled to survive. We have probably done more damage to ourselves than to anyone else, so we put ourselves first on the list.

Often, our tendency is to feel guilty about everything we've ever done, everyone we've come in contact with. That is un-earned guilt. Writing helps us clarify whether or not we are punishing ourselves for no reason. But we need to be open to guidance as we work this Step, getting everything out of us and on to paper, so we can be healed.

Once we have made the list, we strive to become willing to make amends to everyone on it because that is how we will heal. Making amends does not mean feeling guilty and ashamed and punishing ourselves; it means swallowing our pride and defenses, and doing what we can to take care of ourselves. We become ready to improve our self-esteem by taking responsibility for our behaviors. We become willing to have our relationships with ourselves, others, and our Higher Power restored.

Today, I will open myself to an honest understanding of the people I have harmed. God, help me let go of my defenses and pride. Help me become willing to make amends to those I have harmed, so that I can improve my relationships with myself and others.

Willing to Make Amends   August 25

The Eighth Step is talking about a change of heart, a heal-ing change.

This attitude can begin a great chain of repair and healing in our relationships with others and ourselves. It means we become willing to let go of our hard-heartedness — one of the greatest blocks to our ability to give and receive love.

In the Eighth Step, we make a list of all people we have harmed, and we allow ourselves to experience a healing attitude toward them. It is an attitude of love.

We do not, in this Step, dash madly about and begin yelling, "Sorry!" We make our list, not to feel guilty, but to facilitate healing. Before we actually make amends or begin to consider appropriate amends, we allow ourselves to change our attitude. That is where healing begins — within us.

It can change the energy. It can change the dynamics. It can begin the process, before we ever open our mouths and say sorry.

It opens the door to love. It opens the door to the energy of love and healing. It enables us to release negative feelings and energy, and opens the door to positive feelings and energy.

That energy can be felt around the world, and it starts inside us.

How often have we, after we have been hurt, wished that the person would simply recognize our pain and say, "I'm sorry"? How often have we wished that the person would simply see us, hear us, and turn the energy of love our way? How often have we longed for at least a change of heart, a small dose of reconciliation, in relationships tainted by unfinished business and bad feelings? Often.

Others do too. It is no secret. The energy of healing begins with us. Our willingness to make amends may or may not benefit the other person; he or she may or may not be willing to put matters to rest.

But we become healed. We become capable of love.

Today, I will work on a change of heart if hard-heartedness, defensiveness, guilt, or bitterness are present. I will become willing to let go of those feelings and have them replaced by the healing energy of love.

Made direct amends to such people wherever possible, except when to do so would injure them or others.
                              — Step Nine of Al-Anon

When we make amends we need to be clear about what we're apologizing for and the best way to say we're sorry. What we are really doing with our amends is taking responsibility for our behavior. We need to be sure that the process itself will not be self-defeating or hurtful.

Sometimes, we need to directly apologize for a particular thing we have done or our part in a problem.

Other times, instead of saying "I'm sorry," what we need to do is work on changing our behavior with a person.

There are times when bringing up what we have done and apologizing for it will make matters worse.

We need to trust timing, intuition, and guidance in this process of making amends. Once we become willing, we can let go and tackle our amends in a peaceful, consistent, harmonious way. If nothing feels right or appropriate, if it feels as if what we are about to do will cause a crisis or havoc, we need to trust that feeling.

Attitude, honesty, openness, and willingness count here. In peace and harmony, we can strive to clear up our relationships.

We deserve to be at peace with ourselves and others.

Today, I will be open to making any amends I need to make with people. I will wait for Divine Guidance in the process of making any amends that are not clear to me. I will act, when led. God, help me let go of my fear about facing people and taking responsibility for my behaviors. Help me know I am not diminishing my self-esteem by doing this; I am improving it.

Procrastination — not acting when the time is right — is a self-defeating behavior. It produces anxiety, guilt, disharmony, and a nagging consciousness of the task that life is telling us it's time to do.

We are not always procrastinating when we put off doing something. Sometimes, doing a thing before the time is right can be as self-defeating as waiting too long.

We can learn to discern the difference. Listen to yourself. Listen to the Universe. What is past due and creating anxiety and prodding within you?

Is there something in your life you are avoiding because you don't want to face it? Is there a building anxiety from putting this off?

Sometimes anger, fear, or feeling helpless can motivate procrastination. Sometimes, procrastination has simply become habitual.

Trust and listen to yourself, your Higher Power, and the Universe. Watch for signs and signals. If it is time to do something, do it now. If it is not yet time, wait until the time is right.

God, help me learn to be on time and in harmony with my life. Help me tune in to and trust Divine Timing and Order.

Taking Care of Ourselves on the Job   **August 28**

It's okay to take care of ourselves on the job. It is not only okay, it is necessary.

Taking care of ourselves on the job means we deal with feelings appropriately; we take responsibility for ourselves. We detach, when detachment is called for. We set boundaries, when we need to do that.

We negotiate conflicts; we try to separate our issues from the other person's issues, and we don't expect perfection from ourselves or others.

We let go of our need to control that which we cannot control. Instead, we strive for peace and manageability, owning our power to be who we are and to take care of ourselves.

We do not tolerate abuse, nor do we abuse or mistreat anyone else. We work at letting go of our fear and developing appropriate confidence. We try to learn from our mistakes, but we forgive ourselves when we make them.

We try to not set ourselves up by taking jobs that couldn't possibly work out, or jobs that aren't right for us. If we find ourselves in one of those circumstances, we address the issue responsibly.

We figure out what our responsibilities are, and we generally stick to those, unless another agreement is made. We leave room for great days, and not-so-great days.

We are gentle and loving with people whenever possible, but we are assertive and firm when that is called for. We accept our strengths and build on them. We accept our weaknesses and limitations, including the limitations of our power.

We strive to stop trying to control and change what is not our business to change. We focus on what is our responsibility and what we can change.

We set reasonable goals. We take ourselves into account. We strive for balance.

Sometimes, we give ourselves a good gripe session to let it all out, but we do that appropriately, in a way meant to take care of ourselves and release our feelings, not to sabotage ourselves. We strive to avoid malicious gossip and other self-defeating behaviors.

We avoid competition, strive for cooperation and a loving spirit. We understand that we may like some people we work with and dislike others, but strive to find harmony and balance with everyone. We do not deny how we feel about a certain person, but we strive to maintain good working relationships wherever possible.

When we don't know, we say we don't know. When we need help, we ask for it directly. When panic sets in, we address the panic as a separate issue and try not to let our work and behavior be controlled by panic.

We strive to take responsible care of ourselves by appropriately asking for what we need at work, while not neglecting ourselves.

If we are part of a team, we strive for healthy teamwork as an opportunity to learn how to work in cooperation with others.

If something gets or feels crazy, if we find ourselves working with a person who is addicted or has some kind of dysfunction that is troublesome, we do not make ourselves crazier by denying the problem. We accept it and strive in peace to figure out what we need to do to take care of ourselves.

We let go of our need to be martyrs or rescuers at work. We know we do not have to stay in situations that make us miserable. Instead of sabotaging a system or ourselves, we plan a positive solution, understanding we need to take responsibility for ourselves along the way.

We remove ourselves as victims, and we work at believing we deserve the best. We practice acceptance, gratitude, and faith.

One day at a time, we strive to enjoy what is good, solve the problems that are ours to solve, and give the gift of ourselves at work.

Today, I will pay attention to what recovery behaviors I could practice that would improve my work life. I will take care of myself on the job. God, help me let go of my need to be victimized by work. Help me be open to all the good stuff that is available to me through work.

Learn to keep your energy inside.
> — Women, Sex, and Addiction
> *Charlotte Davis Kasl, Ph.D.*

For many reasons, we may have mastered the art of giving away our energy. We may have learned it when we were young because the feelings we had were too overwhelming to feel, and we did not know how to process them.

Much of our obsessing, our intense focus on others, is done to facilitate this "out-of-body" experience we call codependency.

We obsess, we babble, we become anxious. We try to control, caretake, and fuss over others. Our energy spills out of us on to whomever.

Our energy is our energy. Our feelings, thoughts, issues, love, sexuality; our mental, physical, spiritual, sexual, creative, and emotional energy is ours.

We can learn to have healthy boundaries — healthy parameters — around ourselves and our energy. We can learn to keep our energy within ourselves and deal with our issues.

If we are trying to escape from our body, if our energy is spilling out of us in unhealthy ways, we can ask ourselves what is going on, what is hurting us, what we are avoiding, what we need to face, what we need to deal with.

Then, we can do that. We can come back home to live — in ourselves.

Today, I will keep my energy in my body. I will stay focused and within my boundaries. God, help me let go of my need to escape myself. Help me face my issues so I am comfortable living in my body.

We don't have to do it any better than we can — ever.

Do our best for the moment, then let it go. If we have to redo it, we can do our best in another moment, later.

We can never do more or better than we are able to do at the moment. We punish ourselves and make ourselves feel crazy by expecting more than our reasonable best for now.

Striving for excellence is a positive quality.

Striving for perfection is self-defeating.

Did someone tell us or expect us to do or give or be *more*? Did someone always withhold approval?

There comes a time when we feel we have done our best. When that time comes, let it go.

There are days when our best is less than we hoped for. Let those times go too. Start over tomorrow. Work things through, until our best becomes better.

There is a time for constructive criticism, but if that's all we give ourselves, we'll give up.

Empowering and complimenting ourselves will not make us lazy. It will nurture us and enable us to give, do, and be our best.

Today, I will do my best, then let it go. God, help me stop criticizing myself so I can start appreciating how far I've come.

Denial   **August 31**

I've been recovering many years. I've used denial many times. It has been a defense, a survival device, a coping behavior, and, at times, almost my undoing. It has been both a friend and an enemy.

When I was a child, I used denial to protect myself and my family. I protected myself from seeing things too painful to see and feelings too overwhelming to feel. Denial got me safely through many traumatic situations, when I had no other resources for survival.

The negative aspect of using denial was that I lost touch with myself and my feelings. I became able to participate in harmful situations without even knowing I was hurting. I was able to tolerate a great deal of pain and abuse without the foggiest notion it was abnormal.

I learned to participate in my own abuse.

Denial protected me from pain, but it also rendered me blind to my feelings, my needs, and myself. It was like a thick blanket that covered and smothered me.

Eventually, I began to recover. I had a glimpse of awareness about my pain, my feelings, my behaviors. I began to see myself, and the world, as we were. There was so much denial from my past that had the blanket been entirely ripped from me, I would have died from the shock of exposure. I needed to embrace insights, remembrances, awareness, and healing gently, gradually.

Life participated in this process with me. It is a gentle teacher. As I recovered, I was brought to the incidents and people I needed in order to remind me of what I was still denying, to tell me where I required more healing from my past, as I could handle these insights.

I still use, and break through, denial — as needed. When the winds of change blow through, upsetting a familiar structure and preparing me for the new, I pick up my blanket and hide, for a while. Sometimes, when someone I love has a problem, I hide under the blanket, momentarily. Memories emerge of things denied, memories that need to be remembered, felt, and accepted so I can continue to become healed — strong and healthy.

Sometimes, I feel ashamed about how long it takes me to struggle through to acceptance of reality. I feel embarrassed when I find myself again clouded by the fog of denial.

Then something happens, and I see that I am moving forward. The experience was necessary, connected, not at all a mistake, but an important part of healing.

It's an exciting process, this journey called recovery, but I understand I may sometimes use denial to help me get through the rough spots. I'm also aware that denial is a friend, and an enemy. I'm on the alert for danger signs: those cloudy, confused feelings...sluggish energy...feeling compulsive... running too fast or hard...avoiding support mechanisms.

I've gained a healthy respect for our need to use denial as a blanket to wrap ourselves in when we become too cold. It isn't my job to run around ripping people's blankets off or shaming others for using the blanket. Shaming makes them colder, makes them wrap themselves more tightly in the blanket. Yanking their blanket away is dangerous. They could die of exposure, the same way I could have.

I've learned the best thing I can do around people who are wrapped in this blanket is to make them feel warm and safe. The warmer and safer they feel, the more able they are to drop their blanket. I don't have to support or encourage their denial. I can be direct. If others are in denial about a particular thing, and their activity is harmful to me, I don't have to be around them. I can wish them well and take care of myself. You see, if I stand too long around someone who is harming me, I will inevitably pick up my blanket again.

I tend to be attracted to warm people. When I'm around warm people, I don't need to use my blanket.

I've gained respect for creating warm environments, where blankets are not needed, or at least not needed for long. I've gained trust in the way people heal from and deal with life.

God, help me be open to and trust the process that is healing me from all I have denied from my past. Help me strive for awareness and acceptance, but also help me practice gentleness and compassion for myself — and others — for those times I have used denial.

September

Sometimes we get what we want right away. At other times, we wonder if our desires will ever be fulfilled.

We will be fulfilled in the best way possible and as quickly as possible. But some things take time. Sometimes, we have lessons to learn first, lessons that prepare us so we can accept the good we deserve. Things are being worked out in us, and in others. Blocks in us are being removed. A solid foundation is being laid.

Be patient. Relax and trust. Let go. Then, let go some more. Good things are planned for us. We will receive them at the first available moment. We will have all our heart longs for.

Relax and trust.

Today, I will identify what I want and need; then, I'll be willing to let go of it. I will devote my energy to living my life today, so I may master my lessons as quickly as possible. I will trust that what I want and need is coming to me. I will let go of my need to control the details.

Detaching with Love with Children   September 2

It's one thing to let go of my husband and let him suffer the consequences. But how do I let go of my children? Isn't it different with children? Don't we have responsibilities as parents?

                                                    — Al-Anon member

We do have different responsibilities to our children than to other adults. We are financially responsible for our children; we are responsible for providing for their material and physical needs.

Our children need to be taught how to help themselves — from tying their shoes to making social plans. They need our love and guidance. They need consistent enforcement of boundaries, once we've established limits. They need a supportive, nurturing environment in which to grow. They need help learning values.

But we are not responsible for controlling our children. Contrary to popular belief, controlling doesn't work. Discipline and nurturing do — if combined. Shame and guilt interfere with our children's learning and our parenting. We need to respond to our children in a responsible way and hold them accountable for their actions at an age-appropriate level. We need only do our best.

We can let our children have their own process of living; we can have our own process. And, we can take care of ourselves during that process. Seek balance. Seek wisdom. Seek not to have control, but to own our power as people who are parents.

Today, God, help me find an appropriate balance of responsibility to my children. Help me parent through nurturing and discipline, instead of control.

Word Power   September 3

I know I'm controlling, but so is my husband. Possibly more controlling than I am. Each time I set out to leave him, each time I started to walk away, he knew exactly what to say to pull me back in. And he knew I'd respond. He knew how to say exactly what I needed to hear to keep me where he wanted me. He knew what he was doing, and he knew what

I would do. I know, because after we began recovering, he told me so.

— Anonymous

Some of us are so vulnerable to words.

A well-timed "I love you." A chosen moment for "I'm sorry." An excuse delivered in the right tone of voice. A pat on the head. A dozen roses. A kiss. A greeting card. A few words that promise love that has yet to be delivered can spin us into denial. Sometimes, it can keep us denying that we are being lied to, mistreated, or abused.

There are those who deliberately set out to sway us, to control and manipulate us through cheap talk! They know, they fully understand our vulnerability to a few well-timed words! Break through your naivefe. They know what they're doing. They understand their impact on us!

We do not have to give such power to words, even though the words may be just what we want and need to hear, even though they *sound so good*, even though the words seem to stop the pain.

Sooner or later, we will come to realize that if behavior doesn't match a person's words, we are allowing ourselves to be controlled, manipulated, deceived. Sooner or later, we will come to realize that talk is cheap, unless the person's behavior matches it.

We can come to demand congruency in the behavior and the words of those around us. We can learn to not be manipulated, or swayed, by cheap talk.

We cannot control what others do, but we can choose our own behaviors and our own course of action. We do not have to let cheap, well-timed talk control us — even if the words we hear are exactly what we want to hear to stop our pain.

Today, I will let go of my vulnerability to words. God, help me trust myself to know the truth, even when I am being deceived. Help me cherish those relationships where there is congruity. Help me believe I deserve congruity and truth in the behavior and the words of those I care about.

Finding Direction   September 4

I used to spend so much time reacting and responding to everyone else that my life had no direction. Other people's lives, problems, and wants set the course for my life. Once I realized it was okay for me to think about and identify what I wanted, remarkable things began to take place in my life.
> — *Anonymous*

We each have a life to live, one that has purpose and meaning. We can help our Higher Power give direction and purpose to our life by setting goals.

We can set goals annually, monthly, or daily in times of crisis. Goals create direction and pace; goals help us achieve a manageable life that is directed in the course we choose for ourselves.

We can help give our lives direction by setting goals.

Today, I will pay attention to setting a course of action for my life, rather than letting others control my life and affairs.

Step Ten   September 5

Continued to take personal inventory and when we were wrong promptly admitted it.
> — *Step Ten of Al-Anon*

Once we have worked our way to this Step, we can maintain and increase our self-esteem by regularly working Step Ten.

This Step incorporates the process we have gone through in Steps Four through Nine. We do not work this Step to punish ourselves or to hold ourselves under a constantly critical and demeaning microscope. We do it to maintain self-esteem and harmony in our relationship with ourselves and others. We do it to stay on track.

When an issue or problem emerges and needs our attention, identify it and openly discuss it with at least one safe person and God. Accept it. Become willing to let go of it. Ask God to take it from us. Have a change of heart by the willingness to make whatever amend is called for — to do what is necessary to take care of ourselves. Take an appropriate action to resolve the matter. Then let go of the guilt and shame.

This is a simple formula for taking care of ourselves. This is how we change. This is how we become changed. This is the process for healing and health. This is the process for achieving self-responsibility and self-esteem.

The next time we do something that bothers us, the next time we feel off track or off course, we don't have to waste our time or energy feeling ashamed. We can take a Tenth Step. Let the process happen. And move on with our life.

God, help me make this Step and other Steps a habitual way of responding to life and my issues. Help me know that I am free to live, to allow myself to fully experiment with and experience life. If I get off course, or if an issue arises that demands my attention, help me deal with it by using the Tenth Step.

The Good in Step Ten   **September 6**

Step Ten says: "Continued to take personal inventory and when we were wrong promptly admitted it." It does not suggest that we ignore what is right in our life. It says we continue to take a personal inventory and keep a focus on ourselves.

When we take an inventory, we will want to look for many things. We can search out feelings that need our attention. We can look for low self-esteem creeping back in. We can look for old ways of thinking, feeling, and behaving. We can look for mistakes that need correcting.

But a critical part of our inventory can focus on what we're doing right and on all that is good around us.

Part of our codependency is an obsessive focus on what's wrong and what we might be doing wrong — real or imagined. In recovery we're learning to focus on what's right.

Look fearlessly, with a loving, positive eye. What did you do right today? Did you behave differently today than you would have a year ago? Did you reach out to someone and allow yourself to be vulnerable? You can compliment yourself for that.

Did you have a bad day but dealt effectively with it? Did you practice gratitude or acceptance? Did you take a risk, own your power, or set a boundary? Did you take responsibility for yourself in a way that you might not have before?

Did you take time for prayer or meditation? Did you trust God? Did you let someone do something for you?

Even on our worst days, we can find one thing we did right. We can find something to feel hopeful about. We can find something to look forward to. We can focus realistically on visions of what can be.

God, help me let go of my need to stay immersed in negativity. I can change the energy in myself and my environment from negative to positive. I will affirm the good until it sinks in and feels real. I will also strive to find one quality that I like about someone else who's important to me, and I will take the risk of telling him or her that.

Stop making excuses for other people.

Stop making excuses for ourselves.

While it is our goal to develop compassion and achieve forgiveness, acceptance, and love, it is also our goal to accept reality and hold people accountable for their behavior. We can also hold ourselves accountable for our own behavior and, at the same time, have compassion and understanding for ourselves.

When we claim powerlessness, we are not claiming irresponsibility. We have no power to control others, what they do, what they did, or what they might do. We're stating that we are willing to end an ineffective life based on willpower and control. And we're beginning a spiritual, mental, and emotional journey in which we take responsibility for ourselves.

We are not victims. We are not helpless. Accepting powerlessness when that is appropriate enables us to begin owning our true power to take care of ourselves.

Today, I will avoid making excuses for my own or someone else's behavior. I will let consequences and responsibility fall where they belong.

Some of my feelings have been stored so long they have freezer burn.

— Beyond Codependency

There are many sources of pain in our life. Those of us recovering from adult children and codependency issues frequently have a cesspool of unresolved pain from the past. We have feelings, sometimes from early childhood to the present, that either hurt too much to feel or that we had no support and permission to deal with.

There are other inevitable sources of pain in our life too. There is the sadness and grief that comes when we experience change, even good change, as we let go of one part of our life, and begin our journey into the new.

There is pain in recovery, as we begin allowing ourselves to feel while dropping our protective shield of denial.

There is the pain that leads and guides us into better choices for our future.

We have many choices about how to stop this pain. We may have experimented with different options. Compulsive and addictive behaviors stop pain — temporarily. We may have used alcohol, other drugs, relationships, or sex to stop our pain.

We may talk compulsively or compulsively focus on other people and their needs as a way to avoid or stop our pain.

We may use religion to avoid our feelings.

We may resort to denial of how we are feeling to stop our pain.

We may stay so busy that we don't have time to feel. We may use money, exercise, or food to stop our pain.

We have many choices. To survive, we may have used some of these options, only to find that these were Band-Aids — temporary pain relievers that did not solve the problem. They did not really stop our pain; they postponed it.

In recovery, there is a better choice about how we may stop pain. We can face it and feel it. When we are ready, with our Higher Power's help, we can summon the courage to feel the pain, let it go, and let the pain move us forward — into a new decision, a better life.

We can stop the behaviors we are doing that cause pain, if that's appropriate. We can make a decision to remove ourselves from situations that cause repeated, similar pain. We can learn the lesson our pain is trying to teach us.

If we are being pelleted by pain, there is a lesson. Trust that idea. Something is being worked out in us. The answer will not come from addictive or other compulsive behaviors; we will receive the answer when we feel our feelings.

It takes courage to be willing to stand still and feel what we must feel. Sometimes, we have what seems like endless layers of pain inside us. Pain hurts. Grief hurts. Sadness hurts. It does not feel good. But neither does denying what is already there; neither does living a lifetime with old and new pockets of pain packed, stored, and stacked within.

It will only hurt for a while, no longer than necessary, to heal us. We can trust that if we must feel pain, it is part of healing, and it is good. We can become willing to surrender to and accept the inevitable painful feelings that are a good part of recovery.

Go with the flow, even when the flow takes us through uncomfortable feelings. Release, freedom, healing, and good feelings are on the other side.

Today, I am open and willing to feel what I need to feel. I am willing to stop my compulsive behaviors. I am willing to let go of my denial. I am willing to feel what I need to feel to be healed, healthy, and whole.

Perspective   September 9

Too often, we try to gain a clear perspective before it is time. That will make us crazy.

We do not always know why things are happening the way they are. We do not always know how a particular relationship will work out. We do not always understand the source of our feelings, why we've been led down a particular path, what is being worked out in us, what we are learning, why we needed to recycle, why we had to wait, why we needed to go through a time of discipline, or why a door closed. How our present circumstances will work into the larger scheme of events is not always clear to us. That is how it needs to be.

Perspective will come in retrospect.

We could strain for hours today for the meaning of something that may come in an instant next year.

Let it go. We can let go of our need to figure things out, to feel in control.

Now is the time to be. To feel. To go through it. To allow things to happen. To learn. To let whatever is being worked out in us take its course.

In hindsight, we will know. It will become clear. For today, being is enough. We have been told that all things shall work out for good in our life. We can trust that to happen, even if we cannot see the place today's events will hold in the larger picture.

Today, I will let things happen without trying to figure everything out. If clarity is not available to me today, I will trust it to come later, in retrospect. I will put simple trust in the truth that all is well, events are unfolding as they should, and all will work out for good in my life — better than I can imagine.

Self-Approval   **September 10**

Most of us want to be liked. We want other people to think of us as nice, friendly, kind, and loving. Most of us want the approval of others.

Since childhood, some of us have been trying to get approval, trying to get people to like us and think highly of us. We may be afraid people will leave us if they disapprove of our actions. We may look for approval from people who have none to give. We may not know that we're lovable now and can learn to approve of ourselves.

In order to live happily, to live consistently with the way our Higher Power wants us to live, and to tap into a way of life that is in harmony with the universe, we need to let go of our extreme need for approval. These unmet needs for approval and love from our past give others control over us today. These needs can prevent us from acting in our best interest and being true to ourselves.

We can approve of ourselves. In the end, that's the only approval that counts.

Today, I will let go of my need for approval and my need to be liked. I will replace them with a need to like and approve of myself. I will enjoy the surprise I find when I do this. The people who count, including myself, will respect me when I am true to myself.

Conflict and Detachment   September 11

In a relationship, there are those wonderful times when things go smoothly for both people, and neither person needs to focus too heavily on the concept of detachment. But there are those challenging times when one person is in crisis or changing — and we need to detach.

Then there are stressful cycles when both people in a relationship are in the midst of dealing with intense issues. Both are needy and neither has anything to give.

These are times when detachment and taking care of ourselves are difficult.

It is helpful, in these moments, to identify the problem. Both people are in the midst of dealing and healing. Neither has much to give, at least at the moment. And both are feeling particularly needy.

That is the problem.

What's the solution?

There may not be a perfect solution. Detachment is still the key, but that can be difficult when we need support ourselves. In fact, the other person may be asking for support rather than offering it.

We can still work toward detachment. We can still work through our feelings. We can accept this as a temporary cycle in the relationship, and stop looking to the other person for something he or she cannot give at the moment.

We can stop expecting ourselves to give at the moment as well.

Communication helps. Identifying the problem and talking about it without blame or shame is a start. Figuring out alternative support systems, or ways to get our needs met, helps.

We are still responsible for taking care of ourselves — even when we are in the best of relationships. We can reasonably expect conflicts of need and the clashing of issues to occur in the most loving, healthy relationships.

It is one of the cycles of love, friendship, and family.

If it is a healthy relationship, the crisis will not go on endlessly. We will regain our balance. The other person will too. We can stop making ourselves so crazy by looking for the other person to be balanced when he or she isn't.

Talk things out. Work things out. Keep our expectations of ourselves, other people, and our relationships healthy and reasonable.

A good relationship will be able to sustain and survive low points. Sometimes we need them, so we can both grow and learn separately.

Sometimes, people who are usually there for us cannot be there for us. We can find another way to take care of ourselves.

Today, I will remember that my best relationships have low points. If the low point is the norm, I may want to consider the desirability of the relationship. If the low point is a temporary cycle, I will practice understanding for myself and the other person. God, help me remember that the help and support I want and need does not come in the form of only one person. Help me be open to healthy options for taking care of myself, if my normal support system is not available.

*We should learn not to grow impatient with the slow heal-
ing process of time. We should discipline ourselves to recognize that there are many steps to be taken along the highway
leading from sorrow to renewed serenity. . . . We should an-
ticipate these stages in our emotional convalescence: unbear-
able pain, poignant grief, empty days, resistance to
consolation, disinterestedness in life, gradually giving
way. . .to the new weaving of a pattern of action and the
acceptance of the irresistible challenge of life.*
                                    — *Joshua Loth Liebman*

Recovery is a process. It is a gradual process, a healing
process, and a spiritual process — a journey rather than a
destination.

Just as codependency takes on a life of its own and is
progressive, so recovery progresses. One thing leads to
another and things — as well as us — get better.

We can relax, do our part, and let the rest happen.

*Today, I will trust this process and this journey that I have
undertaken.*

Times of Reprogramming   September 13

Recovery is not all tiresome, unrewarded work. There are
times of joy and rest, times when we comfortably practice
what we have learned. There are times of change, times
when we struggle to learn something new or overcome a
particular problem.

These are the times when what we've been practicing in
recovery begins to show in our life. These times of change
are intense, but purposeful.

There are also times when, at a deep level, we are being "reprogrammed." We start letting go of beliefs and behaviors. We may feel frightened or confused during these times. Our old behaviors or patterns may not have worked for us, but they were comfortable and familiar.

During these times we may feel vulnerable, lonely, and needy — like we are on a journey without a road map or a flashlight, and we feel as if no one has traveled this ground before.

We may not understand what is being worked out in us. We may not know where or if we are being led.

We are being led. We are not alone. Our Higher Power is working His finest and best to bring true change in us. Others have traveled this road too. We will be led to someone who can help us, someone who can provide the markers we need.

We are being prepared for receiving as much joy and love as our heart can hold.

Recovery is a healing process. We can trust it, even when we don't understand it. We are right where we need to be in this process; we're going through exactly what we need to experience. And where we're going is better than any place we've been.

Today, God, help me believe that the changes I'm going through are for the good. Help me believe that the road I'm traveling will lead to a place of light, love, and joy.

What's Good for Me?   September 14

When we are soul-searching, be it for the smaller or larger decisions we face during the day, we can learn to ask, is this good for me?...Is this what I really want?...Is this what I need?...Does this direction feel right for me?...Or am I succumbing to the control and influence that I sometimes allow others to have over me?

It is not unhealthy selfishness to question if something is good for us. That is an old way of thinking. To ask if something is good for us is a healthy behavior, not to be ashamed of, and will probably work out in the other person's best interests too.

We shall not wander down a selfish path of self-indulgence by asking if a thing is good for us. We shall not stray from God's intended plan, God's highest good, by asking if a thing is good for us. By asking ourselves this simple question, we participate in directing our life toward the highest good and purpose; we own our power to hold ourselves in self-esteem.

Today, I will begin acting in my best interests. I will do this with the understanding that, on occasion, my choices will not please everyone around me. I will do this with the understanding that asking if a thing is good for me will ultimately help me take true responsibility for my life and my choices.

Getting Through Hard Times   September 15

We are sturdy beings. But in many ways, we are fragile. We can accept change and loss, but this comes at our own pace and in our own way. And only we and God can determine the timing.

— Codependent No More

Hard times, stressful times, are not all there is to life, but they are *part* of life, growth, and moving forward.

What we do with hard times, or hard energy, is our choice.

We can use the energy of hard times to work out, and work through, our issues. We can use it to fine-tune our skills and our spirituality. Or we can go through these situations suffering, storing up bitterness, and refusing to grow or change.

Hard times can motivate and mold us to bring out our best. We can use these times to move forward and upward to higher levels of living, loving, and growth.

The choice is ours. Will we let ourselves feel? Will we take a spiritual approach, including gratitude, toward the event? Will we question life and our Higher Power by asking what we're supposed to be learning and doing? Or will we use the incident to prove old, negative beliefs? Will we say, "Nothing good ever happens to me.... I'm just a victim.... People can't be trusted.... Life isn't worth living"?

We do not always require hard energy, or stress, to motivate us to grow and change. We do not have to create stress, seek it, or attract it. But if it's there, we can learn to channel it into growth and use it for achieving what's good in life.

God, let my hard times be healing times.

Revenge   September 16

No matter how long we've been recovering, no matter how solid our spiritual ground, we may still feel an overwhelming desire at times to punish, or get even, with another person.

We want revenge.

We want to see the other person hurt the way he or she has hurt us. We want to see life deal that person just rewards. In fact, we would like to help life out.

Those are normal feelings, but we do not have to act on them. These feelings are part of our anger but it's not our job to deal justice.

We can allow ourselves to feel the anger. It is helpful to go one step deeper and let ourselves feel the other feelings — the hurt, the pain, the anguish. But our goal is to release the feelings, and be finished with them.

We can hold the other person accountable. We can hold the other person responsible. But it is not our responsibility to be judge and jury. Actively seeking revenge will not help us. It will block us and hold us back.

Walk away. Stop playing the game. Unhook. Learn your lesson. Thank the other person for having taught you something valuable. And be finished with it. Put it behind, with the lesson intact.

Acceptance helps. So does forgiveness — not the kind that invites that person to use us again, but a forgiveness that releases the other person and sets him or her free to walk a separate path, while releasing our anger and resentments. That sets us free to walk our own path.

Today, I will be as angry as I need to be, with a goal of finishing my business with others. Once I have released my hurt and anger, I will strive for healthy forgiveness — forgiveness with boundaries. I understand that boundaries, coupled with forgiveness and compassion, will move me forward.

New Relationship Behaviors   September 17

We talk much about new relationship behaviors in recovery: allowing others to be themselves without over-reacting and taking it personally, and owning our power to take care of ourselves. We talk about letting go of our need to control, focusing on self-responsibility, and not setting ourselves up to be victims by focusing on the other person while neglecting ourselves. We talk about having and setting healthy boundaries, talking directly, and taking responsibility for what we want and need.

While these behaviors certainly help us deal with addicted people, these are not behaviors intended only for use in what we call "dysfunctional relationships."

These behaviors are *our new relationship behaviors.* They help us in stressful relationships. They can help us get through times of stress in healthy relationships.

The recovery behaviors we are learning are tools — healthy relationships skills — that help us improve the quality of *all* our relationships.

Recovery means self-care — learning to take care of ourselves and love ourselves — with people. The healthier we become, the healthier our relationships will become. And we'll never outgrow our need for healthy behaviors.

Today, I will remember to apply my recovery behaviors in all my relationships — with friends and co-workers, as well as in any special love relationship. I will work hard at taking care of myself in the troublesome relationships, figuring out which skill might best apply. I will also consider ways that my healthy relationships might benefit from my new relationship skills.

Letting the Good Stuff Happen   September 18

Before recovery, my relationships were lousy. I didn't do very well on my job. I was enmeshed in my dysfunctional family. But at least I knew what to expect!

— *Anonymous*

I want the second half of my life to be as good as the first half was miserable. Sometimes, I'm afraid it won't be. Sometimes, I'm frightened it *might* be.

The good stuff can scare us. Change, even good change, can be frightening. In some ways, good changes can be more frightening than the hard times.

The past, particularly before recovery, may have become comfortably familiar. We knew what to expect in our relationships. They were predictable. They were repeats of the same pattern — the same behaviors, the same pain, over and over again. They may not have been what we wanted, but we knew what was going to happen.

This is not so when we change patterns and begin recovering.

We may have been fairly good at predicting events in most areas of our life. Relationships would be painful. We'd be deprived.

Each year would be almost a repeat of the last. Sometimes it got a little worse, sometimes a little better, but the change wasn't drastic. Not until the moment when we began recovery.

Then things changed. And the further we progress in this miraculous program, the more we and our circumstances change. We begin to explore uncharted territory.

Things get good. They do get better all the time. We begin to become successful in love, in work, in life. One day at a time, the good stuff begins to happen and the misery dissipates.

We no longer want to be a victim of life. We've learned to avoid unnecessary crisis and trauma.

Life gets good.

"How do I handle the good stuff?" asked one woman. "It's harder and more foreign than the pain and tragedy."

"The same way we handled the difficult and the painful experiences," I replied. "One day at a time."

Today, God, help me let go of my need to be in pain and crisis. Help me move as swiftly as possible through sad feelings and problems. Help me find my base and balance in peace, joy, and gratitude. Help me work as hard at accepting what's good as I have worked in the past at accepting the painful and the difficult.

Sometimes, we act in a manner with which we are less than comfortable. That's human. That's why we have the words: "I'm sorry." They heal and bridge the gap. But we don't have to say "I'm sorry" if we didn't do anything wrong. A sense of shame can keep us apologizing for everything we do, every word we say, for being alive and being who we are.

We don't have to apologize for taking care of ourselves, dealing with feelings, setting boundaries, having fun, or getting healthy.

We never have to change our course, if it is in our best interest, but sometimes a general apology acknowledges other feelings and can be useful when the issues of a circumstance or relationship are not clear. We might say: "I'm sorry for the fuss we had. I'm sorry if what I needed to do to take care of myself hurt you; it was not intended that way."

Once we make an apology, we don't have to keep repeating it. If someone wants to keep on extricating an apology from us for the same incident, that is the person's issue, and we don't have to get hooked.

We can learn to take our apologies seriously and not hand them out when they're not valid. When we feel good about ourselves, we know when it's time to say we're sorry and when it's not.

Today, I will try to be clear and healthy in my apologies, taking responsibility for my actions and nobody else's. God, help me figure out what I need to apologize for and what is not my responsibility.

Spontaneity   **September 20**

In recovery, we're learning to let ourselves go! We're learning to be spontaneous.

Spontaneity may frighten some of us. We may be afraid of the loss of control involved with spontaneity. We may still be operating under the codependent rules that prohibit spontaneity: be good; be right; be perfect; be strong; don't have fun; and always *be in control.*

We may associate spontaneity with acting out in an addictive, compulsive, self-destructive, or irresponsible manner.

That's not what we're talking about in recovery. Positive spontaneity involves freely expressing who we are — in a way that is fun, healthy, doesn't hurt us, and doesn't infringe on the rights of others.

We learn to be spontaneous and free as we grow in self-awareness and self-esteem. Spontaneity emerges as our confidence and trust in ourselves increase, and we become more secure in our ability to maintain healthy boundaries.

Being spontaneous is connected to our ability to play and to achieve intimacy. For all those desirable acts, we need to be able to let go of our need to control ourselves and others, and fully and freely enter into the present moment.

Let go of your tight rein on yourself. So what if you make a mistake? So what if you're wrong? Relish your imperfections. Let yourself be a little needy, a little vulnerable. Take a risk!

We can be spontaneous without hurting ourselves, or others. In fact, everyone will benefit by our spontaneity.

Today, I will throw out the rule book and enjoy being who I am. I will have some fun with the gift of life, myself, and others.

Letting Go of Urgency   September 21

One thing at a time.

That's all we have to do. Not two things at once, but one thing done in peace.

One task at a time. One feeling at a time. One day at a time. One problem at a time. One step at a time.

One pleasure at a time.

Relax. Let go of urgency. Begin calmly now. Take one thing at a time.

See how everything works out?

Today, I will peacefully approach one thing at a time. When in doubt, I will take first things first.

Trusting Ourselves   September 22

Many of us believed that heeding the words of God or our Higher Power meant following rigid rules, an instruction booklet for life.

Many of us now believe differently. The rigid rules, the endless instructions, the exhortation to perfection, are not the words our Higher Power whispers.

The words of God are often those still, small words we call intuition or instinct, leading and guiding us forward.

We are free to be who we are, to listen to and trust ourselves. We are free to listen to the gentle, loving words of a Higher Power, words whispered to and through each of us.

Today, help me, God, to let go of shame-based rigid rules. I will choose the freedom of loving, listening, and trusting.

Tolerance   September 23

Practice tolerance.

Tolerate our quirks, our feelings, our reactions, our peculiarities, our humanness. Tolerate our ups and downs, our resistance to change, our struggling and sometimes awkward nature.

Tolerate our fears, our mistakes, our natural tendency to duck from problems and pain. Tolerate our hesitancy to get close, expose ourselves, be vulnerable.

Tolerate our need to occasionally feel superior, to sometimes feel ashamed, and to occasionally share love as an equal. Tolerate the way we progress — a few steps forward, and a couple back.

Tolerate our instinctive desire to control and how we reluctantly learn to practice detachment. Tolerate the way we say we want love, and then sometimes push others away. Tolerate our tendency to get obsessive, forget to trust God, and occasionally get stuck.

Some things we do not tolerate. Do not tolerate abusive or destructive behaviors toward others or ourselves.

Practice healthy, loving tolerance of ourselves, said one man. When we do, we'll learn tolerance for others. Then, take it one step further. Learn that all the humanness we're tolerating is what makes ourselves and others beautiful.

Today, I will be tolerant of myself. From that, I will learn appropriate tolerance of others.

Allowing Ourselves to be Needy   September 24

We can accept ourselves as people who have needs — the need for comfort, love, understanding, friendship, healthy touch. We need positive reinforcement, someone to listen to us, someone to give to us. We are not weak for needing these things. These needs make us human and healthy. Getting our needs met — believing we deserve to have them met — makes us happy.

There are times, too, when in addition to our regular needs, we become particularly needy. At these times, we need more than we have to give out. That is okay too.

We can accept and incorporate our needs, and our needy side, into the whole of us. We can take responsibility for our needs. That doesn't make us weak or deficient. It doesn't mean we are not properly recovering, nor does it mean we're being dependent in an unhealthy way. It makes our needs, and our needy side, manageable. Our needs stop controlling us, and we gain control.

And, our needs begin to get met.

Today, I will accept my needs and my needy side. I believe I deserve to get my needs met, and I will allow that to happen.

Peace with the Past   September 25

Even God cannot change the past.

— *Agathon*

Holding on to the past, either through guilt, longing, denial, or resentment, is a waste of valuable energy — energy that can be used to transform today and tomorrow.

"I used to live in my past," said one recovering woman. "I was either trying to change it, or I was letting it control me. Usually both.

"I constantly felt guilty about things that had happened. Things I had done; things others had done to me — even though I had made amends for most everything, the guilt ran deep. Everything was somehow my fault. I could never just let it go.

"I held on to anger for years, telling myself it was justified. I was in denial about a lot of things. Sometimes, I'd try to absolutely forget about my past, but I never really stopped and sorted through it; my past was like a dark cloud that followed me around, and I couldn't shake clear of it. I guess I was scared to let it go, afraid of today, afraid of tomorrow.

"I've been recovering now for years, and it has taken me almost as many years to gain the proper perspective on my past. I'm learning I can't forget it; I need to heal from it. I need to feel and let go of any feelings I still have, especially anger.

"I need to stop blaming myself for painful events that took place, and trust that everything has happened on schedule, and truly all is okay. I've learned to stop regretting, and to start being grateful.

"When I think about the past, I thank God for the healing and the memory. If something occurs that needs an amend, I make it and am done with it. I've learned to look at my past with compassion for myself, trusting that my Higher Power was in control, even then.

"I've healed from some of the worst things that happened to me. I've made peace with myself about these issues, and I've learned that healing from some of these issues has enabled me to help others to heal too. I'm able to see how the worst things helped form my character and developed some of my finer points.

"I've even developed gratitude for my failed relationships because they have brought me to who and where I am today.

"What I've learned has been acceptance — without guilt, anger, blame, or shame. I've even had to learn to accept the years I spent feeling guilty, angry, shameful, and blaming."

We cannot control the past. But we can transform it by allowing ourselves to heal from it and by accepting it with love for ourselves and others. I know, because that woman is me.

Today, I will begin being grateful for my past. I cannot change what happened, but I can transform the past by owning my power, now, to accept, heal, and learn from it.

Our task is not a naive one of feeling safe, of living and loving in a utopian world. One woman commented that our task is making ourselves feel safe while learning to live and love in a world that is unsafe.

We do not want to dwell on the dangers, for that gives power to the negative. Neither do we want to ignore them or pretend they don't exist.

If we were going to sunbathe, we would not be naive about the dangers from the sun. We know that harmful rays can burn. We would take steps to protect ourselves, so that we could enjoy the benefits of the sun.

That is our task in recovery.

This is what a woman, a helping professional, told me:

Picture a sunscreen surrounding you. Place it around yourself — not too heavy and thick so no light can penetrate, and not so thin that you are exposed to danger.

See yourself protected by a sunscreen that is effective. Make certain that the screen is open to the good. For a while, your screen was too heavy. It held back what you wanted. Now change it to let the good come through.

This is your screen for life and the world. See it. Imagine it surrounding you always. It wraps you in love, in comfort, in protection. No harm can enter. No negative energy can penetrate the screen.

Go in peace; go in safety; go, now, knowing you are protected. Go anywhere you need to go. The evil has been blocked; the goodwill comes pouring forth. You do not have to work so hard at protecting yourself. You can relax and enjoy life, trusting that you are safe. Go without fear, for you are wrapped in love and protection. And you shall always be.

Today, I will envision myself wrapped in a shield that blocks the negative and harmful rays of the world, but it is constructed so that the good can enter.

Temporary Setbacks   September 27

Sometimes, after we begin recovery, things in our life seem to get worse for a time. Our finances, our relationships, or our health may seem to deteriorate.

This is temporary; this is a normal part of recovery and healing. It may be the way things will be for a time, but not for long.

Keep working at recovery, and the trend will reverse. Before too long, things, and us, will be better than they were before. This time, the foundation will be solid.

God, help me trust You and recovery, even when I have setbacks. Help me remember that the problems are temporary, and when they are solved, I will be on more solid ground.

Prayer   September 28

Here are some of my favorite prayers:
Help. Please. Don't.
Show me. Guide me. Change me.
Are you there?
Why'd you do that?
Oh.
Thank you.

Today, I will tell God what I want to tell God, and listen for God's answer. I will remember that I can trust God.

We cannot afford to allow our focus in life to be money. That will not lead us into the abundance we're seeking. Usually, it will not even lead to financial stability.

Money is important. We deserve to be paid what we're worth. We will be paid what we're worth when we believe we deserve to be. But often our plans fail when our primary consideration is money.

What do we really want to do? What do we feel led to do? What are our instincts telling us? What do we feel guided to do? What are we *excited* about doing? Seek to find a way to do that, without worrying about the money.

Consider the financial aspects. Set boundaries about what you need to be paid. Be reasonable. Expect to start at the bottom, and work up. But if you feel led toward a job, go for it.

Is there something we truly don't want to do, something that goes against our grain, but we are trying to force ourselves into it "for the money"? Usually, that's a behavior that backfires. It doesn't work. We make ourselves miserable, and the money usually goes wrong too.

I have learned that when I am true to myself about work and what I need to be doing, the money will follow. Sometimes it's not as much as I want; sometimes I'm pleasantly surprised, and it's more. But I'm content, and I have *enough*.

Money is a consideration, but it cannot be our primary consideration if we are seeking spiritual security and peace of mind.

Today, I will make money a consideration, but I will not allow it to become my primary consideration. God, help me be true to myself and trust that the money will follow.

You are not a victim.

How deeply ingrained our self-image as a victim can be! How habitual our feelings of misery and helplessness! Victimization can be like a gray cloak that surrounds us, both attracting that which will victimize us and causing us to generate the feelings of victimization.

Victimization can be so habitual that we may feel victimized even by the good things that happen to us!

Got a new car? Yes, we sigh, but it doesn't run as well as I expected, and after all, it cost so much....

You've got such a nice family! Yes, we sigh, but there are problems. And we've had such hard times....

Well, your career certainly is going well! Ah, we sigh, but there is such a price to pay for success. All that extra paperwork....

I have learned that, if we set our mind to it, we have an incredible, almost awesome ability to find misery in any situation, even the most wonderful of circumstances.

Shoulders bent, head down, we shuffle through life taking our blows.

Be done with it. Take off the gray cloak of despair, negativity, and victimization. Hurl it; let it blow away in the wind.

We are not victims. We may have been victimized. We may have allowed ourselves to be victimized. We may have sought out, created, or re-created situations that victimized us. But we are not victims.

We can stand in our power. We do not have to allow ourselves to be victimized. We do not have to let others victimize us. We do not have to seek out misery in either the most miserable or the best situations.

We are free to stand in the glow of self-responsibility.

Set a boundary! Deal with the anger! Tell someone no, or stop that! Walk away from a relationship! Ask for what you need! Make choices and take responsibility for them. Explore options. Give yourself what you need! Stand up straight, head up, and claim your power. Claim responsibility for yourself!

And learn to enjoy what's good.

Today, I will refuse to think, talk, speak, or act like a victim. Instead, I will joyfully claim responsibility for myself and focus on what's good and right in my life.

October

In recovery, we're learning a new behavior. It's called Be Who You Are.

For some of us, this can be frightening. What would happen if we felt what we felt, said what we wanted, became firm about our beliefs, and valued what we needed? What would happen if we let go of our camouflage of adaptation? What would happen if we owned our power to be ourselves?

Would people still like us? Would they go away? Would they become angry?

There comes a time when we become willing and ready to take that risk. To continue growing, and living with ourselves, we realize we must liberate ourselves. It becomes time to stop allowing ourselves to be so controlled by others and their expectations and be true to ourselves — regardless of the reaction of others.

Before long, we begin to understand. Some people may go away, but the relationship would have ended anyway. Some people stay and love and respect us more for taking the risk of being who we are. We begin to achieve intimacy, and relationships that *work*.

We discover that who we are has always been good enough. It is who we were intended to be.

Today, I will own my power to be myself.

Coping with Families   October 2

There are many paths to self-care with families. Some people choose to sever connections with family members for a period of time. Some people choose to stay connected with family members and learn different behaviors. Some disconnect for a time, then return slowly on a different basis.

There is no one or perfect way to deal with members of our family in recovery. It is up to each of us to choose a path that suits us and our needs at each point in time.

The idea that is new to us in recovery is that we *can choose*. We can set the boundaries we need to set with family members. We can choose a path that works for us, without guilt and obligation or undue influence from any source, including recovery professionals.

Our goal is to detach in love with family members. Our goal is to be able to take care of ourselves, love ourselves, and live healthy lives despite what family members do or don't do. We decide what boundaries or decisions are necessary to do this.

It's okay to say no to our families when that is what we want. It's okay to say yes to our families if that feels right. It's okay to call time-out and it's okay to go back as a different person.

God, help me choose the path that is right for me with family. Help me understand there is no right or wrong in this process. Help me strive for forgiveness and learn to detach with love, whenever possible. I understand that this never implies that I have to forfeit self-care and health for the good of the system.

Getting Through the Discomfort   October 3

Surrender to the pain. Then learn to surrender to the good. It's there and more is on the way.
— Beyond Codependency

Our goal in recovery is to make ourselves feel comfortable, peaceful, content. Happy. We want to be at peace with ourselves and our environment. Sometimes, to do that, we need to be willing to face, feel, and get through discomfort.

I am not talking here about being addicted to misery and pain. I am not talking about creating unnecessary pain. I'm talking about the legitimate discomfort we sometimes need to feel as we heal.

When we have surgery, the pain hurts most the day after the operation. When we do the kind of work we are facing in recovery, we are doing an emotional, mental, and spiritual surgery on ourselves. We're removing parts of us that are infected and inflamed.

Sometimes the process hurts.

We are strong enough to survive discomfort and temporary feelings of emotional pain. Once we are willing to face and feel our discomfort and pain, we are almost to the point of release.

Today, I am willing to face my discomfort, trusting that healing and release are on the other side. Help me, God, be open to feeling whatever I need to feel to be healed and healthy. While I am doing this, I will trust I am cared for and protected by myself, my friends, my Higher Power, and the Universe.

Faith and Money   October 4

Sometimes, there is not enough money to make ends meet, much less afford any luxuries.

People may tell us to do a budget, and we chuckle. The expenses we need to pay for survival surpass the income.

We look at the situation, shake our heads, and say, "No way."

Many of us have had to live through these situations. This is not the time to panic; this is not the time to despair.

Panic and desperation will lead to bad judgment and desperate moves. This is the time to substitute faith for fear. This is the time to trust God to meet our needs.

Take life one day and one need at a time. Use your survival skills positively. Know your possibilities are not limited by the past or by your present circumstances.

Examine any blocks that might be stopping the flow of money in your life. Do you have an attitude, an issue, a lesson that might be yours to change or learn?

Maybe the lesson is a simple one of faith. In Biblical times, it is said that Jesus walked on the water. It is said His followers could, too, but the moment they let fear take over, they sank.

During financial hard times, *we* can learn to "walk on water" with money issues. If we make out a budget, and there's not enough money to survive and pay legitimate expenses, do your best, then let go. Trust your Source to supply your needs. If an emergency arises, and there is no cash to meet the need, look beyond your wallet. Look to your source. Claim a Divine supply, an unlimited supply, for all that you need.

Do your part. Strive for an attitude of financial responsibility in thought and action. Ask for Divine Wisdom. Listen to God's leadings. Then let go of your fears and your need to control.

We know that money is a necessary part of being alive and living; so does our Higher Power.

God, bring any blocks and barriers within me concerning money to the surface. Help me take care of myself financially. If money is tight, I will dispel fear and learn to "walk on water" concerning finance issues. I will not use this attitude to justify irresponsibility. I will do my part, including letting go of fear and trusting you to do the rest.

Learn to let yourself be guided into truth.

We will know what we need to know, when we need to know that. We don't have to feel badly about taking our own time to reach our insights. We don't have to force insight or awareness before it's time.

Yes! Maybe the whole world saw a particular truth in our life, and we denied it — until we were ready to deal with it. That is our business, and our right! Our process is our own, and we will discover our truths at the right time, when we are ready, when the learning experience is complete.

The most growth-producing concept we can develop for ourselves and others is to allow ourselves to have our own process. We can give and receive support and encouragement while we go through this process. We can listen to others and say what we think. We can set boundaries and take care of ourselves, when needed. But we still give ourselves and others the right to grow at our own pace, without judgment, and with much trust that all is well and is on schedule.

When we are ready, when the time is right, and when our Higher Power is ready — we will know what we need to know.

Today, I will let myself and others have our own pace and time schedule for growth and change. I will trust that I will be empowered with insights and the tools for dealing with these insights, at the right time.

It's healthy, wise, and loving to be considerate and responsive to the feelings and needs of others. That's different from caretaking. Caretaking is a self-defeating and, certainly, a relationship-defeating behavior — a behavior that backfires and can cause us to feel resentful and victimized — because ultimately, what we feel, want, and need will come to the surface.

Some people seem to invite emotional caretaking. We can learn to refuse the invitation. We can be concerned; we can be loving, when possible; but we can place value on our own needs and feelings too. Part of recovery means learning to pay attention to, and place importance on, what we feel, want, and need, because we begin to see that there are clear, predictable, and usually undesirable consequences when we don't.

Be patient and gentle with yourself as you learn to do this. Be understanding with yourself when you slip back into the old behavior of emotional caretaking and self-neglect.

But stop the cycle today. We do not have to feel responsible for others. We do not have to feel guilty about not feeling responsible for others. We can even learn to let ourselves feel good about taking responsibility for our needs and feelings.

Today, I will evaluate whether I've slipped into my old behavior of taking responsibility for another's feelings and needs, while neglecting my own. I will own my power, right, and responsibility to place value on myself.

Letting Go of Naiveté   October 7

We can be loving, trusting people and still not allow ourselves to be used or abused. We don't have to let people do whatever they want to us. Not all requests are legitimate! Not all requests require a yes!

Life may test us. People may seek out our weak spots. We may see a common denominator to the limits that are being tested in our life. If we have a weak spot in one area, we may find ourselves tested repeatedly in that area by family, friends, co-workers, and neighbors. Life, people, our Higher Power, and the Universe may be trying to teach us something specific.

When we learn that lesson, we will find that problems with that area dwindle. The boundary has been set, the power has been owned. For now, the lesson has been learned. We may need to be angry with certain people for a while, people who have pushed our tolerance over the edge. That's okay. Soon, we can let go of the anger and exchange it for gratitude. These people have been here to help us learn about what we don't want, what we won't tolerate, and how to own our power.

We can thank them for what we have learned.

How much are we willing to tolerate? How far shall we let others go with us? How much of our anger and intuition shall we discount? Where are our limits? Do we have any? If we don't, we're in trouble.

There are times to not trust others, but instead trust ourselves and set boundaries with those around us.

Today, I will be open to new awareness about the areas where I need healthier boundaries. I will forego my naive assumption that the other person is always right. I will exchange that view for trusting myself, listening to myself, and having and setting healthy boundaries.

*I've started to realize that waiting is an art, that waiting
achieves things. Waiting can be very, very powerful. Time
is a valuable thing. If you can wait two years, you can sometimes achieve something that you could not achieve today,
however hard you worked, however much money you threw
up in the air, however many times you banged your head
against the wall. . . .*
    — The Courage to Change *by Dennis Wholey*

The people who are most successful at living and loving
are those who can learn to wait successfully. Not many
people enjoy waiting or learning patience. Yet, waiting can
be a powerful tool that will help us accomplish much good.

We cannot always have what we want when we want it.
For different reasons, what we want to do, have, be, or accomplish is not available to us now. But there are things we
could not do or have today, no matter what, that we *can* have
in the future. Today, we would make ourselves crazy trying
to accomplish what will come naturally and with ease later.

We can trust that all is on schedule. Waiting time is not
wasted time. Something is being worked out — in us, in
someone else, in the Universe.

We don't have to put our life on hold while we wait. We
can direct our attention elsewhere; we can practice acceptance and gratitude in the interim; we can trust that we do
have a life to live while we are waiting — then we go about
living it.

Deal with your frustration and impatience, but learn how
to wait. The old saying, "You can't always get what you
want" isn't entirely true. Often, in life, we can get what we

want — especially the desires of our heart — if we can
learn to wait.

*Today, I am willing to learn the art of patience. If I am feeling power-
less because I am waiting for something to happen and I am not
in control of timing, I will focus on the power available to me by
learning to wait.*

Self-Disclosure   October 9

Learning to gently reveal who we are is how we open ourselves up to love and intimacy in our relationships.

Many of us have hidden under a protective shell, a casing
that prevents others from seeing or hurting us. We do not
want to be *that* vulnerable. We do not want to expose our
thoughts, feelings, fears, weaknesses, and sometimes our
strengths, to others.

We do not want others to see who we really are.

We may be afraid they might judge us, go away, or not like
us. We may be uncertain that who we are is okay or exactly
how we should reveal ourselves to others.

Being vulnerable can be frightening, especially if we have
lived with people who abused, mistreated, manipulated, or
did not appreciate us.

Little by little, we learn to take the risk of revealing ourselves. We disclose the real person within to others. We pick
safe people, and we begin to disclose bits and pieces about
ourselves.

Sometimes, out of fear, we may withhold, thinking that
will help the relationship or will help others like us more.
That is an illusion. Withholding who we are does not help
us, the other person, or the relationship. Withholding is a
behavior that backfires. For true intimacy and closeness to
exist, for us to love ourselves and be content in a relationship, we need to disclose who we are.

That does not mean we tell all to everyone at once. That can be a self-defeating behavior too. We can learn to trust ourselves, about who to tell, when to tell, where to tell, and how much to tell.

To trust that people will love and like us if we are exactly who we are is frightening. But it is the only way we can achieve what we want in relationships. To let go of our need to control others — their opinions, their feelings about us, or the course of the relationship — is the key.

Gently, like a flower, we can learn to open up. Like a flower, we will do that when the sun shines and there is warmth.

Today, I will begin to take the risk of disclosing who I am to someone with whom I feel safe. I will let go of some of my protective devices and risk being vulnerable — even though I may have been taught differently, even though I may have taught myself differently. I will disclose who I am in a way that reflects self-responsibility, self-love, directness, and honesty. God, help me let go of my fears about disclosing who I am to people. Help me accept who I am, and help me let go of my need to be who people want me to be.

Payoffs from Destructive Relationships   October 10

Sometimes it helps to understand that we may be receiving a payoff from relationships that cause us distress.

The relationship may be feeding into our helplessness or our martyr role.

Maybe the relationship feeds our need to be needed, enhancing our self-esteem by allowing us to feel in control or morally superior to the other person.

Some of us feel alleviated from financial or other kinds of responsibility by staying in a particular relationship.

"My father sexually abused me when I was a child," said one woman. "I went on to spend the next twenty years blackmailing him emotionally and financially on this. I could get money from him whenever I wanted, and I never had to take financial responsibility for myself."

Realizing that we may have gotten a codependent payoff from a relationship is not a cause for shame. It means we are searching out the blocks in ourselves that may be stopping our growth.

We can take responsibility for the part we may have played in keeping ourselves victimized. When we are willing to look honestly and fearlessly at the payoff and let it go, we will find the healing we've been seeking. We'll also be ready to receive the positive, healthy payoffs available in relationships, the payoffs we really want and need.

Today, I will be open to looking at the payoffs I may have received from staying in unhealthy relationships, or from keeping destructive systems operating. I will become ready to let go of my need to stay in unhealthy systems; I am ready to face myself.

Recovery   October 11

How easy it is to blame our problems on others. "Look at what he's doing.". . . "Look how long I've waited.". . . "Why doesn't she call?". . . "If only he'd change then I'd be happy.". . .

Often, our accusations are justified. We probably are feeling hurt and frustrated. In those moments, we may begin to believe that the solution to our pain and frustration is getting the other person to do what we want, or having the outcome we desire. But these self-defeating illusions put the power and control of our life in other people's hands. We call this *codependency*.

The solution to our pain and frustration, however valid, is to acknowledge our own feelings. We feel the anger, the grief; then we let go of the feelings and find peace — within ourselves. We know our happiness isn't controlled by another person, even though we may have convinced ourselves it is. We call this *acceptance*.

Then we decide that although we'd like our situation to be different, maybe our life is happening this way for a reason. Maybe there is a higher purpose and plan in play, one that's better than we could have orchestrated. We call this *faith*.

Then we decide what we need to do, what is within our power to do to take care of ourselves. That's called *recovery*.

It's easy to point our finger at another, but it's more rewarding to gently point it at ourselves.

Today, I will live with my pain and frustration by dealing with my own feelings.

Being Gentle with Ourselves During Times of Grief

October 12

The process of adapting to change and loss takes energy. Grief is draining, sometimes exhausting. Some people need to "cocoon for transformation," in Pat Carnes's words, while going through grief.

We may feel more tired than usual. Our ability to function well in other areas of our life may be reduced, temporarily. We may want to hide out in the safety of our bedroom.

Grief is heavy. It can wear us down.

It's okay to be gentle with ourselves when we're going through change and grief. Yes, we want to maintain the disciplines of recovery. But we can be compassionate with ourselves. We do not have to expect more from ourselves than we can deliver during this time. We do not even have to expect as much from ourselves as we would normally and reasonably expect.

We may need more rest, more sleep, more comfort. We may be more needy and have less to give. It is okay to accept ourselves, and our changed needs, during times of grief, stress, and change.

It is okay to allow ourselves to cocoon during times of transformation. We can surrender to the process, and trust that a new, exciting energy is being created within us.

Before long, we will take wings and fly.

God, help me accept my changed needs during times of grief, change, and loss.

Substance over Form   October 13

I'm learning that for a variety of reasons, I've spent much of my life focusing on form rather than substance. My focus has been on having my hair done perfectly, wearing the right clothes, having my makeup applied perfectly, living in the right place, furnishing it with the right furniture, working at the right job, and having the right man. Form, rather than substance, has controlled my behavior in many areas of my life. Now, I'm finally getting to the truth. It's substance that counts.

— Anonymous

There is nothing wrong in wanting to look our best. Whether we are striving to create a self, a relationship, or a life, we need to have some solid ideas about what we want that to look like.

Form gives us a place to begin. But for many of us, form has been a substitute for substance. We may have focused on form to compensate for feeling afraid or feeling inferior. We may have focused on form because we didn't know how to focus on substance.

Form is the outline; substance is what fills it in. We fill in the outline of ourselves by being authentic; we fill in the outline of our life by showing up for life and participating to the best of our ability.

Now, in recovery, we're learning to pay attention to how things work and feel, not just to what they look like.

Today, I will focus on substance in my life. I will fill in the lines of myself with a real person — me. I will concentrate on the substance of my relationships, rather than what they look like. I will focus on the real workings of my life, instead of the trappings.

Controlling Versus Trust   October 14

There was a time in my life when I felt so afraid of and overwhelmed by the very act of living that I actually wanted to make out a schedule for each day of my life for the next five years. I wanted to include all the chores I had to do, when I would do them, even when I would schedule relaxation. I wanted to get some order into what felt overwhelming. I wanted to feel like I was in control.

— Anonymous

Controlling is a direct response to our fear, panic, and sense of helplessness. It is a direct response to feeling overwhelmed, and to distrust.

We may not trust ourselves, our Higher Power, the Plan, the Universe, or the process of life. Instead of trusting, we revert to control.

We can approach this need to control by dealing with our fear. We deal with fear by trusting — ourselves, our Higher Power, the love and support of the Universe, the Plan, and this process we call life and recovery.

We can trust that when things don't work out the way we want, God has something better planned.

We can trust ourselves to get where we need to go, say what we need to say, do what we need to do, know what we need to know, be who we need to be, and become all we can become, when we are intended to do that, when we are ready, and when the time is right.

We can trust our Higher Power and the Universe to give us all the direciton we need.

We can trust ourselves to listen, and respond, accordingly.

We can trust that all we need on this journey shall come to us. We will not get all we need for the entire journey today. We shall receive today's supplies today, and tomorrow's supplies tomorrow. We were never intended to carry supplies for the entire journey. The burden would be too heavy, and the way was intended to be light.

Trust in yourself. We do not have to plan, control, and schedule all things. The schedule and plan have been written. All we need to do is show up.

The way will become clear and the supplies will be amply and clearly provided, one day at a time.

Trust, my friend, in today.

Today, I will trust that I will receive all I need to to get me through today. I will trust that the same shall happen tomorrow.

Letting Go of Chaos   October 15

No good work comes from unrest.

Unrest, fear, anger, or sadness may motivate us. These feelings are sometimes intended to compel action. But our best work emerges after these feelings have been replaced by peace.

We will not accomplish our task any sooner, or any better, by performing it out of a sense of urgency, fear, anger, or sadness.

Let go of unrest. Let peace fill the void. We do not have to forfeit our power, our God-given personal power — or our peace — to do the work as we are called upon to do today. We will be given all the power we need to do what we are meant to do, when it is time.

Let peace come first. Then proceed. The task will get done, naturally and on time.

Today, I will get peaceful first, and let my work and life emerge from that base.

Being Honest with Ourselves   October 16

Our relationship with ourselves is the most important relationship we need to maintain. The quality of that relationship will determine the quality of our other relationships.

When we can tell ourselves how we feel, and accept our feelings, we can tell others.

When we can accept what we want and need, we will be ready to have our wants and needs met.

When we can accept what we think and believe, and accept what's important to us, we can relay this to others.

When we learn to take ourselves seriously, others will too.

When we learn to chuckle at ourselves, we will be ready to laugh with others.

When we have learned to trust ourselves, we will be trustworthy and ready to trust.

When we can be grateful for who we are, we will have achieved self-love.

When we have achieved self-love and accepting our wants and needs, we will be ready to give and receive love.

When we've learned to stand on our own two feet, we're ready to stand next to someone.

Today, I will focus on having a good relationship with myself.

Surrendering is a highly personal *and* spiritual experience.

Surrender is not something we can do in our heads. It is not something we can force or control by willpower. It is something we experience.

Acceptance, or surrender, is not a tidy package. Often, it is a package full of hard feelings — anger, rage, and sadness, followed by release and relief. As we surrender, we experience our frustration and anger at God, at other people, at ourselves, and at life. Then we come to the core of the pain and sadness, the heavy emotional burden inside that must come out before we can feel good. Often, these emotions are connected to healing and release at a deep level

Surrender sets the wheels in motion. Our fear and anxiety about the future are released when we surrender.

We are protected. We are guided. Good things have been planned. The next step is now being taken. Surrender is the process that allows us to move forward. It is how our Higher Power moves us forward.

Trust in the rightness of timing, and the freedom at the other end, as you struggle humanly through this spiritual experience.

I will be open to the process of surrender in my life. I will allow myself all the awkward and potent emotions that must be released.

Throwing Out the Rule Book   October 18

Many of us feel like we need a rule book, a microscope, and a warranty to get through life. We feel uncertain, frightened. We want the security of knowing what's going to happen, and how we shall act.

We don't trust ourselves or life.
We don't trust the Plan.
We want to be in control.

"I've made terrible mistakes about my choices, mistakes that nearly destroyed me. Life has really shocked me. How can I trust myself? How can I trust life, and my instincts, after where I've been?" asked one woman.

It is understandable that we fear being crushed again, considering the way many of us were when we bottomed out on our codependency. We don't have to be fearful. We can trust our self, our path, and our instincts.

Yes, we want to avoid making the same mistakes again. We are not the same people we were yesterday or last year. We've learned, grown, changed. We did what we needed to do then. If we made a mistake, we cannot let that stop us from living and fully experiencing today.

We have arrived at the understanding that we needed our experiences — even our mistakes — to get to where we are today. Do we know that we needed our life to unfold exactly as it did to find ourselves, our Higher Power, and this new way of life? Or is part of us still calling our past a mistake?

We can let go of our past and trust ourselves now. We do not have to punish ourselves with our past. We don't need a rule book, a microscope, a warranty. All we really need is a mirror. We can look into the mirror and say, "I trust you. No matter what happens, you can take care of yourself. And what happens will continue to be good, better than you think."

Today, I will stop clinging to the painful lessons of the past. I will open myself to the positive lessons today and tomorrow hold for me. I trust that I can and will take care of myself now. I trust that the Plan is good, even when I don't know what it is.

What's a codependent? The answer's easy. They're some of the most loving, caring people I know.
— Beyond Codependency

We don't need to limit an inventory of ourselves to the negatives. Focusing only on what's wrong is a core issue in our codependency.

Honestly, fearlessly, ask: "What's *right* with me? What are my good points?"

"Am I a loving, caring, nurturing person?" We may have neglected to love ourselves in the process of caring for others, but nurturing is an asset.

"Is there something I do particularly well?" "Do I have a strong faith?" "Am I good at being there for others?" "Am I good as part of a team, or as a leader?" "Do I have a way with words or with emotions?"

"Do I have a sense of humor?" "Do I brighten people up?" "Am I good at comforting others?" "Do I have an ability to make something good out of barely nothing at all?" "Do I see the best in people?"

These are character assets. We may have gone to an extreme with these, but that's okay. We are now on our way to finding balance.

Recovery is not about eliminating our personality. Recovery aims at changing, accepting, working around, or transforming our negatives, and building on our positives. We all have assets; we only need to focus on them, empower them, and draw them out in ourselves.

Codependents are some of the most loving, caring people around. Now, we're learning to give some of that concern and nurturing to ourselves.

Today, I will focus on what's right about me. I will give myself some of the caring I've extended to the world.

Detaching with Love   October 20

Sometimes people we love do things we don't like or approve of. We react. They react. Before long, we're all reacting to each other, and the problem escalates.

When do we detach? When we're hooked into a reaction of anger, fear, guilt, or shame. When we get hooked into a power play -- an attempt to control or force others to do something they don't want to do. When the way we're reacting isn't helping the other person or solving the problem. When the way we're reacting is hurting us.

Often, it's time to detach when detachment appears to be the least likely, or possible, thing to do.

The first step toward detachment is understanding that reacting and controlling don't help. The next step is getting peaceful — getting centered and restoring our balance.

Take a walk. Leave the room. Go to a meeting. Take a long, hot bath. Call a friend. Call on God. Breathe deeply. Find peace. From that place of peace and centering will emerge an answer, a solution.

Today, I will surrender and trust that the answer is near.

Financial Responsibility   October 21

"When I began recovery from chemical dependency, I had to face my money mess stone cold sober, and I really had a mess," said one woman.

"I wasn't able to earn much at first, and it was important to me to make amends. I had past due bills from years before. I needed to try to stay current with my new bills. I had a lot more money before I sobered up. But in time, slowly, gradually, my financial situation cleared up. I restored my credit. I had a checking account. I had a little money in the bank.

"Then I married an alcoholic and began to learn about my codependency — the hard way. I lost myself, my feelings, my sanity, and all the progress I had made with my financial affairs. My husband and I opened a checking account together, and he overdrafted checks until I lost the right to have a checking account. I let him charge and charge on my credit card, and he drove that into the ground.

"We borrowed and borrowed to keep our sinking ship afloat — and we borrowed a lot from my parents," she said. "By the time I began my recovery from codependency, I was again facing a real financial mess. I was furious, but it didn't matter who did what. I had some serious financial matters to face if that part of my life was ever going to become manageable again.

"Slowly — very slowly — I began to work out of my mess. It seemed impossible! I didn't even want to face it, it felt so overwhelming and hopeless. But I did. And each day I did the best I could to be responsible for myself.

"One decision I made was to separate and protect myself financially from my husband, the best I could, before and after we divorced. The other decision I made was to face and begin reconstructing the financial affairs in my life.

"It was difficult. We owed over fifty thousand dollars, and my ability to produce income had dramatically decreased. I was grieving; my self-esteem was at an all-time low; my energy was low. I did not know how I would ever untangle this nightmare. But it did happen. Slowly, gradually, with the help of a Higher Power, manageability crept in and replaced chaos.

"I began by not spending more than I earned. I paid back some creditors, a little at a time. I let go of what I couldn't do, and focused on what I could do.

306

"Now, eight years have passed. I am debt free, which I never imagined possible. I am living comfortably, with money in the bank. My credit has been restored, again. And I intend to keep it that way.

"I am not willing to lose my financial sanity and security again, ever, for love or for alcoholism. With the help of God and the Twelve Steps, I won't have to."

One day at a time, we can be restored in recovery — mentally, emotionally, spiritually, physically, *and financially*. It may get worse before it gets better — because we are finally facing reality instead of dodging it. But once we make the decision to take financial responsibility for ourselves, we are on our way.

God, help me remember that what seems hopeless today can often be solved tomorrow, even if I can't see the solution. If I have allowed the problems of others to hurt me financially, help me repair and restore my boundaries around money — and what I am willing to lose. Help me understand that I do not have to allow anyone else's financial irresponsibility, addiction, disease, or problem to hurt me financially. Help me go on with my life in spite of my present financial circumstances, trusting that if I am willing to make amends and be responsible, things will work out.

Holding Your Own   October 22

Trust yourself. Trust what you know.

Sometimes, it is hard to stand in our own truth and trust what we know, especially when others would try to convince us otherwise.

In these cases, others may be dealing with issues of guilt and shame. They may have their own agenda. They may be immersed in denial. They would like us to believe that we do not know what we know; they would like us not to trust ourselves; they would prefer to engage us in their nonsense.

We don't have to forfeit our truth or our power to others. That is codependency.

Believing lies is dangerous. When we stop trusting our truth, when we repress our instincts, when we tell ourselves there must be something wrong with us for feeling what we feel or believing what we believe, we deal a deadly blow to our self and our health.

When we discount that important part of ourselves that knows what is the truth, we cut ourselves off from our center. We feel crazy. We get into shame, fear, and confusion. We can't get our bearings when we allow someone to pull the rug from under us.

This does not mean that we are never wrong. But we are not *always* wrong.

Be open. Stand in our truth. Trust what you know. And refuse to buy into denial, nonsense, bullying, or coercion that would like to take you off course.

Ask to be shown the truth, clearly — not by the person trying to manipulate or convince you, but by yourself, your Higher Power, and the Universe.

Today, I will trust my truth, my instincts, and my ability to ground myself in reality. I will not allow myself to be swayed by bullying, manipulating, games, dishonesty, or people with peculiar agendas.

Morning Cues   October 23

There is an important message for us first thing every day.

Often, once we get started with the day, we may not listen as closely to ourselves and life as we do in those still moments when we first awaken.

An ideal time to listen to ourselves is when we are laying quietly, our defenses are down, and we're open and most vulnerable.

What is the first feeling that floods through us, the feeling that perhaps we are trying to avoid during the business of the day? Are we angry, frustrated, hurt, or confused? That is what we need to focus on and work through. That's the issue we need to address.

When you awaken, what is the first idea or thought that enters your mind? Do you need to finish a timely project? Are you in need of a fun day? A restful day?

Do you feel sick and need to nurture yourself? Are you in a negative frame of mind? Do you have an issue to resolve with someone?

Do you need to tell someone something? Is something bothering you? Is something feeling particularly good?

Does an idea occur to you, something you could get or do that would feel good?

When you awaken, what is the first issue that presents itself? You don't have to be fearful. You don't have to rush. You can lay still and listen and then accept the message.

We can define some of our recovery goals for the day by listening to the morning message.

God, help me let go of my need to be in resistance to the harmonic flow of life. Help me learn to go with the flow and accept the help and support that You have to offer me.

Opening Ourselves to Love   October 24

Open ourselves to the love that is available to us.

We do not have to limit our sources of love. God and the Universe have an unlimited supply of what we need, including love.

When we are open to receiving love, we will begin to receive it. It may come from the most surprising places, including from within ourselves.

We will be open to and aware of the love that is and has been there for us all along. We will feel and appreciate the love from friends. We will notice and enjoy the love that comes to us from family.

We will be ready to receive love in our special love relationships too. We do not have to accept love from unsafe people — people who will exploit us or with whom we don't want to have relationships.

But there is plenty of good love available — love that heals our heart, meets our needs, and makes our spirit sing.

We have denied ourselves too long. We have been martyrs too long. We have given so much and allowed ourselves to receive too little. We have paid our dues. It is time to continue the chain of giving and receiving by allowing ourselves to receive.

Today, I will open myself to the love that is coming to me from the Universe. I will accept it and enjoy it when it comes.

Letting Go of the Past   October 25

. . . in thy book were written, every one of them, the days that were formed for me, when as yet there was none of them.
— *Ps. 139:16*

Some people believe that each of our days were planned, Divinely Ordered, before we were born. God knew, they say, and planned exactly what was to transpire.

Others suggest we *chose*, we participated in planning our life — the events, the people, the circumstances that were to take place, in order to work through our issues and learn the lessons we needed to master.

Whatever our philosophy, our interpretation can be similar: Our past is neither an accident nor a mistake. We have been where we needed to be, with the necessary people. We can embrace our history, with its pain, its imperfections, its mistakes, even its tragedies. It is uniquely ours; it was intended just for us.

Today, we are right where we need to be. Our present circumstances are exactly as they need to be — for now.

Today, I will let go of my guilt and fear about my past and present circumstances. I will trust that where I have been and where I am now are right for me.

Clarity October 26

I know better than to not trust God. But sometimes, I forget that.

When we are in the midst of an experience, it is easy to forget that there is a Plan. Sometimes, all we can see is today.

If we were to watch only two minutes of the middle of a television program, it would make little sense. It would be a disconnected event.

If we were to watch a weaver sewing a tapestry for only a few moments, and focused on only a small piece of the work, it would not look beautiful. It would look like a few peculiar threads randomly placed.

How often we use that same, limited perspective to look at our life — especially when we are going through a difficult time.

We can learn to have perspective when we are going through those confusing, difficult *learning* times. When we are being pelleted by events that make us feel, think, and question, we are in the midst of learning something important.

We can trust that something valuable is being worked out in us — even when things are difficult, even when we cannot get our bearings. Insight and clarity do not come until we have mastered our lesson.

311

Faith is like a muscle. It must be exercised to grow strong. Repeated experiences of having to trust what we can't see and repeated experiences of learning to trust that things will work out, are what makes our faith muscles grow strong.

Today, I will trust that the events in my life are not random. My experiences are not a mistake. The Universe, my Higher Power, and life are not picking on me. I am going through what I need to go through to learn something valuable, something that will prepare me for the joy and love I am seeking.

Step Eleven   October 27

Sought through prayer and meditation to improve our conscious contact with God as we understood Him, praying only for knowledge of His will for us and the power to carry that out.
— *Step Eleven of Al-Anon*

". . . praying only for knowledge of His will for us and the power to carry that out" means that we ask on a daily basis to be shown the plan for that day. We also ask our Source for the power we need to carry that through. We will get a yes to both requests.

We do not ask other people to show their will for us. We ask God. Then we trust that we'll be empowered to carry God's will through.

God never, never asks us to do anything that He would not equip us to do. He never asks us to do anything we can't do. If we are to do it, we will be empowered. That's the easy part of this program. We never have to do more than we can, or anything we can't. If we want to worry and fuss we can, but we don't need to. That is our choice.

I have learned, through difficult and good times, that this Step will carry me through. When I don't know what to do next, God does. Working this Step, one day at a time, will take us to places we could never have traveled on our own. Simple acts, done daily in accordance to God's will for us, lead to a Grand Plan for our life.

Today, I will focus on asking God to show me what He wants me to do. I will ask God for the power to do that; then I will go ahead and get the job done. God, help me let go of my fears about living life one day at a time. Help me trust that when life is lived simply and in trust, a beautiful mosaic called "my life" will be woven. I am being divinely led, guided, and cared for.

Meditation and Prayer   **October 28**

The Eleventh Step asks us to meditate as a route to improving our conscious contact with God.

Meditation is different than obsessing or worrying. Obsession and worrying are fear connections. Meditation means opening our mind and our spiritual energy to the God connection.

To connect with God, we need to relax as best we can and open our conscious and subconscious mind to a Higher Consciousness — one that is available to each of us.

In the busyness of our day and life, it may seem like a waste of time to slow down, to stop what we're doing, and take this kind of break. It is no more a waste of time than stopping to put gas in our car when the tank is almost empty. It is necessary, it is beneficial, and it saves time. In fact, meditation can create more time and energy than the moments we take to do it.

Meditation and prayer are powerful recovery behaviors that work. We need to be patient. It is not reasonable to expect immediate answers, insight, or inspiration.

But solutions are coming. They are already on the way, if we have done our part — meditate and pray — and then let the rest go.

Whether we pray and meditate first thing in the morning, during a coffee break, or in the evening is our choice.

When our conscious contact with God improves, our subconscious contact will too. We will find ourselves increasingly tuned in to God's harmony and will for us. We will find and maintain that soul connection, the God connection.

Today, I will take a moment for meditation and prayer. I will decide when and how long to do it. I am a child and creation of God—a Higher Power who loves to listen and talk to me. God, help me let go of my fears about whether or not You hear and care. Help me know that You are there and that I am able to tap into the spiritual consciousness.

Acceptance   October 29

A magical potion is available to us today. That potion is called *acceptance.*

We are asked to accept many things: ourselves, as we are; our feelings, needs, desires, choices, and current status of being. Other people, as they are. The status of our relationships with them. Problems. Blessings. Financial status. Where we live. Our work, our tasks, our level of performance at these tasks.

Resistance will not move us forward, nor will it eliminate the undesirable. But even our resistance may need to be accepted. Even resistance yields to and is changed by acceptance.

Acceptance is the magic that makes change possible. It is not forever; it is for the present moment.

Acceptance is the magic that makes our present circumstances good. It brings peace and contentment and opens the door to growth, change, and moving forward.

It shines the light of positive energy on all that we have and are. Within the framework of acceptance, we figure out what we need to do to take care of ourselves.

Acceptance empowers the positive and tells God we have surrendered to the Plan. We have mastered today's lesson, and are ready to move on.

Today, I will accept. I will relinquish my need to be in resistance to myself and my environment. I will surrender. I will cultivate contentment and gratitude. I will move forward in joy by accepting where I am today.

Self-Value   October 30

We have a real life of our own. Yes, we do.

That empty feeling, that sense that everyone except us has a life — an important life, a valuable life, a better life — is a remnant from the past. It is also a self-defeating belief that is inaccurate.

We are real. So is our life. Jump into it, and we'll see.

Today, I will live my life and treasure it as mine.

All Our Needs   October 31

And my God shall supply every need of yours according to His riches in glory. . . .

— Phil. 4:19

This verse has helped me many times. It has helped me when I have wondered where my next friend, bit of wisdom, insight, or meal was coming from.

Everything I need today shall be supplied to me.

People, jobs, what we have at our immediate disposal, are not our source.

We have tapped into a Greater Source, a source of infinite and immediate supply: God and His Universe.

Our task is to allow ourselves to come into harmony with our Source. Our task is to believe in, and look to, our true Source. Our task is to release fear, negative thinking, limitations, and short-supply thinking.

Everything we need shall be provided to us. Let it become a natural response to all situations, and all situations of need.

Reject fear. Reject short-supply and limited thinking notions. Be open to abundance.

Cherish need because it is part of our relationship to God and His Universe. God has planned to meet our every need, has created the need within us, so God can supply.

No need is too small or too great. If we care and value our need, God will too.

Our part is taking responsibility for owning the need. Our part is giving the need to the Universe. Our part is letting go, in faith. Our part is giving God permission to meet our needs by believing we deserve to have our needs — and wants — met.

Our part is healthy giving, not out of caretaking, guilt, obligation, and codependency, but out of a healthy relationship with ourselves, God, and all of God's creations.

Our part is simply to be who we are, and love being that.

Today, I will practice the belief that all my needs today shall be met. I will step into harmony with God and His Universe, knowing that I count.

November

We're striving for acceptance in recovery — acceptance of ourselves, our past, other people, and our present circumstances. Acceptance brings peace, healing, and freedom — the freedom to take care of ourselves.

Acceptance is not a one-step process. Before we achieve acceptance, we go toward it in stages of denial, anger, negotiating, and sadness. We call these stages the *grief process*. Grief can be frustrating. It can be confusing. We may vacillate between sadness and denial. Our behaviors may vacillate. Others may not understand us. We may neither understand ourselves nor our own behavior while we're grieving our losses. Then one day, things become clear. The fog lifts, and we see that we have been struggling to face and accept a particular reality.

Don't worry. If we are taking steps to take care of ourselves, we will move through this process at exactly the right pace. Be understanding with yourself and others for the very human way we go through transition.

Today, I will accept the way I go through change. I will accept the grief process, and its stages, as the way people accept loss and change.

The Grief Process   **November 2**

To let ourselves wholly grieve our losses is how we surrender to the process of life and recovery. Some experts, like Patrick Carnes, call the Twelve Steps "a program for dealing with our losses, a program for dealing with our grief."

How do we grieve?

Awkwardly. Imperfectly. Usually with a great deal of resistance. Often with anger and attempts to negotiate. Ultimately, by surrendering to the pain.

The grief process, says Elisabeth Kubler-Ross, is a five-stage process: denial, anger, bargaining, sadness, and, finally, acceptance. That's how we grieve; that's how we accept; that's how we forgive; that's how we respond to the many changes life throws our way.

Although this five-step process looks tidy on paper, it is not tidy in life. We do not move through it in a compartmentalized manner. We usually flounder through, kicking and screaming, with much back-and-forth movement — until we reach that peaceful state called *acceptance*.

When we talk about "unfinished business" from our past, we are usually referring to losses about which we have not completed grieving. We're talking about being stuck somewhere in the grief process. Usually, for adult children and codependents, the place where we become stuck is denial. Passing through denial is the first and most dangerous stage of grieving, but it is also the first step toward acceptance.

We can learn to understand the grief process and how it applies to recovery. Even good changes in recovery can bring loss and, consequently, grief. We can learn to help ourselves and others by understanding and becoming familiar with this process. We can learn to fully grieve our losses, feel our pain, accept, and forgive, so we can feel joy and love.

Today, God, help me open myself to the process of grieving my losses. Help me allow myself to flow through the grief process, accepting all the stages so I might achieve peace and acceptance in my life. Help me learn to be gentle with myself and others while we go through this very human process of healing.

Denial   November 3

Denial is fertile breeding ground for the behaviors we call codependent: controlling, focusing on others, and neglecting ourselves. Illness and compulsive or addictive behaviors can also emerge during denial.

Denial can be confusing because it resembles sleeping. We're not really aware we're doing it until we're done doing it. *Forcing* ourselves — or anyone else — to *face the truth* usually doesn't help. We won't face the facts until *we are ready.* Neither, it seems, will anyone else. We may admit to the truth for a moment, but we won't let ourselves know what we know until we feel safe, secure, and prepared enough to deal and cope with it.

Talking to friends who know, love, support, encourage, and affirm us helps.

Being gentle, loving, and affirming with ourselves helps. Asking ourselves, and our Higher Power, to guide us into and through change helps.

The first step toward acceptance is denial. The first step toward moving through denial is accepting that we may be in denial, and then gently allowing ourselves to move through.

God, help me feel safe and secure enough today to accept what I need to accept.

Anger   November 4

Feeling angry — and, sometimes, the act of blaming — is a natural and necessary part of accepting loss and change — of grieving. We can allow ourselves and others to become angry as we move from denial toward acceptance.

As we come to terms with loss and change, we may blame ourselves, our Higher Power, or others. The person may be connected to the loss, or he or she may be an innocent bystander. We may hear ourselves say: "If only he would have done that. . . . If I wouldn't have done that. . . . Why didn't God do it differently?. . ." We know that blame doesn't help. In recovery, the watchwords are *self-responsibility* and *personal accountability,* not blame. Ultimately, surrender and self-responsibility are the only concepts that can move us forward, but to get there we may need to allow ourselves to feel angry and to occasionally indulge in some blaming.

It is helpful, in dealing with others, to remember that they, too, may need to go through their angry stage to achieve acceptance. To not allow others, or ourselves, to go through anger and blame may slow down the grief process.

Trust ourselves and the grief process. We won't stay angry forever. But we may need to get mad for a while as we search over what could have been, to finally accept what is.

God, help me learn to accept my own and others' anger as a normal part of achieving acceptance and peace. Within that framework, help me strive for personal accountability.

Let's Make a Deal   November 5

> *The relationship just wasn't working out, and I wanted it to so badly. I kept thinking if I just made myself look prettier, if I just tried to be a more loving, kind person, then he would love me. I turned myself inside out to be something better, when all along, who I was was okay. I just couldn't see what I was doing, though, until I moved forward and accepted reality.*
>
> — *Anonymous*

One of the most frustrating stages of acceptance is the bargaining stage. In denial, there is bliss. In anger, there is some sense of power. In bargaining, we vacillate between believing there is something we can do to change things and realizing there isn't.

We may get our hopes up again and again, only to have them dashed.

Many of us have turned ourselves inside out to try to negotiate with reality. Some of us have done things that appear absurd, in retrospect, once we've achieved acceptance.

"If I try to be a better person, then this won't happen.... If I look prettier, keep a cleaner house, lose weight, smile more, let go, hang on more tightly, close my eyes and count to ten, holler, then I won't have to face this loss, this change."

There are stories from members of Al-Anon about attempts to bargain with the alcoholic's drinking: "If I keep the house cleaner, he won't drink.... If I make her happy by buying her a new dress, she won't drink.... If I buy my son a new car, he'll stop using drugs."

Adult children have bargained with their losses too: "Maybe if I'm the perfect child, then Mom or Dad will love and approve of me, stop drinking, and be there for me the way I want them to be." We do big, small, and in-between things, sometimes crazy things, to ward off, stop, or stall the pain involved with accepting reality.

There is no substitute for accepting reality. That's our goal. But along the way, we may try to strike a deal. Recognizing our attempts at bargaining for what they are — part of the grief process — helps our lives become manageable.

Today, I will give myself and others the freedom to fully grieve losses. I will hold myself accountable, but I will give myself permission to be human.

Enjoying Life   November 6

Do something fun today.

If you're relaxing, let yourself relax, without guilt, without worrying about the work that is undone.

If you're with loved ones, let yourself love them, and let them love you. Let yourself feel close.

Let yourself enjoy your work, for that can be pleasurable too.

If you're doing something fun, let yourself enjoy it.

What would feel good? What would you enjoy? Is there a positive pleasure available? Indulge.

Recovery is not solely about stopping the pain. Recovery is about learning to make ourselves feel better; then it's about making ourselves feel good.

Enjoy your day.

Today, I will do something fun, something I enjoy, something just for me. I will take responsibility for making myself feel good.

Relationships   November 7

There is a gift for us in each relationship that comes our way.

Sometimes the gift is a behavior we're learning to acquire: detachment, self-esteem, becoming confident enough to set a boundary, or owning our power in another way.

Some relationships trigger healing in us — healing from issues of the past or an issue we're facing today.

Sometimes we find ourselves learning the most important lessons from the people we least expect to help us. Relationships may teach us about loving ourselves or someone else. Or maybe we'll learn to let others love us.

Sometimes, we aren't certain what lesson we're learning, especially while we're in the midst of the process. But we can trust that the lesson and the gift are there. We don't have to control this process. We'll understand, when it's time. We can also trust that the gift is precisely what we need.

Today, I'll be grateful for all my relationships. I will open myself to the lesson and the gift from each person in my life. I will trust that I, too, am a gift in other people's lives.

*This above all: to thine own self be true, and it must follow,
as the night the day, thou 'canst not then be false to any man.*
— *William Shakespeare*

To thine own self be true. A grounding statement for those
of us who get caught up in the storm of needs and feelings
of others.

Listen to the self. What do we need? Are those needs getting met? What do we feel? What do we need to do to take
care of our feelings? What are our feelings telling us about
ourselves and the direction we need to go?

What do we want to do or say? What are our instincts telling us? Trust them — even if they don't make sense or meet
other people's rules and expectations.

Sometimes, the demands of other people and our confused expectations of ourselves — the messages about our
responsibilities toward others — can create a tremendous,
complicated mess.

We can even convince ourselves that people-pleasing,
going against our nature and not being honest, is the kind,
honest thing to do!

Not true. Simplify. Back to basics. Let go of the confusion.
By honoring and respecting ourselves, we will be true to
those around us, even if we displease them momentarily.

To thine own self be true. Simple words describing a
powerful task that can put us back on track.

*Today, I will honor, cherish, and love myself. When confused about
what to do, I will be true to myself. I will break free of the hold
others, and their expectations, have on me.*

Many of us have worked too hard to make relationships work; sometimes those relationships didn't have a chance because the other person was unavailable or refused to participate.

To compensate for the other person's unavailability, we worked too hard. We may have done all or most of the work. This may mask the situation for a while, but we usually get tired. Then, when we stop doing all the work, we notice there is no relationship, or we're so tired we don't care.

Doing all the work in a relationship is not loving, giving, or caring. It is self-defeating and relationship-defeating. It creates the illusion of a relationship when in fact there may be no relationship. It enables the other person to be irresponsible for his or her share. Because that does not meet our needs, we ultimately feel victimized.

In our best relationships, we all have temporary periods where one person participates more than the other. This is normal. But as a permanent way of participating in relationships, it leaves us feeling tired, worn out, needy, and angry.

We can learn to participate a reasonable amount, then let the relationship find it's own life. Are we doing all the calling? Are we doing all the initiating? Are we doing all the giving? Are we the one talking about feelings and striving for intimacy?

Are we doing all the waiting, the hoping, the work?

We can let go. If the relationship is meant to be, it will be, and it will become what it is meant to be. We do not help that process by trying to control it. We do not help ourselves, the other person, or the relationship by trying to force it or by doing all the work.

Let it be. Wait and see. Stop worrying about making it happen. See what happens and strive to understand if that is what you want.

Today, I will stop doing all the work in my relationships. I will give myself and the other person the gift of requiring both people to participate. I will accept the natural level my relationships reach when I do my share and allow the other person to choose what his or her share will be. I can trust my relationships to reach their own level. I do not have to do all the work; I need only do my share.

Beliefs About Money   November 10

I was starting a new job for a corporation. I was good at what I did for a living. The personnel manager and I were down to the details of employment, and he asked me how much money I believed I deserved. I thought about it and came up with a figure of $400 a month. This was back in the sixties. I didn't want to ask for too much, so I decided to ask for the smallest amount I could live with. He hired me and gave me what I asked for. Later on, when I left that job, the personnel manager told me he had been willing to pay me whatever I wanted. Had I asked for $600 or even $700 a month, which was a tremendous salary at that time, I would have gotten it. I had limited myself by what I believed I deserved.

— *Anonymous*

What are our beliefs about money?

Do we believe that money is evil and wrong? Money is neither. It is a commodity on earth, a necessity. It is what people need to purchase many of their basic needs, as well as luxuries and treats; it is one way they are rewarded for their work. Loving money, however, can be as self-defeating as loving any other commodity. We can become obsessed with money; we can use it as an escape from relationships and feelings; we can use it compulsively to gain a temporary sense of power. Money is simply money.

Do we believe there's a scarcity of money? Many of us grew up with deprived thinking concerning money: There's not

326

enough. There will never be enough. If we get a little, we may guard it and hoard it because there's no more.

Money is not in short supply. We do not have to waste our energy resenting those who have enough. There is plenty of money here on earth.

How much do we believe we deserve? Many of us are limiting ourselves by what we believe we deserve.

Money is not evil. There is no scarcity, except in our mind and attitudes. And what we believe we deserve will be about what we shall receive.

We can change our beliefs through affirmations, by setting goals, by starting where we are, and working slowly forward to where we want to be.

Today, I will examine my beliefs about money. I will begin the process of letting go of any self-defeating beliefs that may be limiting or blocking the financial part of my life.

Discipline   November 11

Children need discipline to feel secure; so do adults.

Discipline means understanding there are logical consequences to our behavior. Discipline means taking responsibility for our behavior and the consequences.

Discipline means learning to wait for what we want.

Discipline means being willing to work for and toward what we want.

Discipline means learning and practicing new behaviors.

Discipline means being where we need to be, when we need to be there, despite our feelings.

Discipline is the day-to-day performing of tasks, whether these be recovery behaviors or washing the dishes.

Discipline involves trusting that our goals will be reached though we cannot see them.

Discipline can be grueling. We may feel afraid, confused, uncertain. Later, we will see the purpose. But this clarity of sight usually does not come during the time of discipline. We may not even believe we're moving forward.

But we are.

The task at hand during times of discipline is simple: listen, trust, and obey.

Higher Power, help me learn to surrender to discipline. Help me be grateful that You care enough about me to allow these times of discipline and learning in my life. Help me know that as a result of discipline and learning, something important will have been worked out in me.

Timing   November 12

Wait until the time is right. It is self-defeating to postpone or procrastinate; it is also self-defeating to act too soon, before the time is right.

Sometimes, we panic and take action out of fear. Sometimes, we take untimely action for revenge or because we want to punish someone. We act or speak too soon as a way to control or force someone to action. Sometimes, we take action too soon to relieve feelings of discomfort or anxiety about how a situation will turn out.

An action taken too soon can be as ineffective as one taken too late. It can backfire and cause more problems than it solves. Usually, when we wait until the time is right — sometimes only a matter of minutes or hours — the discomfort dissolves, and we're empowered to accomplish what we need to do.

In recovery, we are learning to be effective.

Our answers will come. Our guidance will come. Pray. Trust. Wait. Let go. We are being led. We are being guided.

Today, I will let go of my need to control by waiting until the time is right. When the time is right, I will take action.

Taking Care of Ourselves   November 13

We do not have to wait for others to come to our aid. We are not victims. We are not helpless.

Letting go of faulty thinking means we realize there are no knights on white horses, no magical grandmothers in the sky watching, waiting to rescue us.

Teachers may come our way, but they will not rescue. They will teach. People who care will come, but they will not rescue. They will care. Help will come, but help is not rescuing.

We are our own rescuers.

Our relationships will improve dramatically when we stop rescuing others and stop expecting them to rescue us.

Today, I will let go of the fears and self-doubt that block me from taking assertive action in my best interest. I can take care of myself and let others do the same for themselves.

Letting Our Anger Out   November 14

It's okay to be angry, but it isn't healthy to be resentful. Regardless of what we learned as children, no matter what we saw role-modeled, we can learn to deal with our anger in ways that are healthy for us and for those around us. We can have our angry feelings. We can connect with them, own them, feel them, express them, release them, and be done with them.

We can learn to listen to what anger is telling us about what we want and need in order to take care of ourselves.

Sometimes we can even indulge in angry feelings that aren't justified. Feelings are just feelings; there is no morality in the feeling, only in our behavior. We can feel angry without hurting or abusing others or ourselves. We can learn to deal with anger in ways that benefit our relationships instead of ways that harm them.

If we don't feel our angry feelings today, we will need to face them tomorrow.

Today, I will let myself feel my anger. I will express my anger appropriately, without guilt. Then I will be done with it.

Benefits of Recovery   November 15

There are two benefits from recovery: we have short-term gains and long-term gains.

The short-term gains are the things we can do today that help us feel better immediately.

We can wake up in the morning, read for a few minutes in our meditation book, and feel lifted. We can work a Step and often notice an immediate difference in the way we feel and function. We can go to a meeting and feel refreshed, talk to a friend and feel comforted, or practice a new recovery behavior, such as dealing with *our* feelings or doing something good for ourselves, and feel relieved.

There are other benefits from recovery, though, that we don't see immediately on a daily or even a monthly basis. These are the long-term gains, the larger progress we make in our life.

Over the years, we can see tremendous rewards. We can watch ourselves grow strong in faith, until we have a daily personal relationship with a Higher Power that is as real to us as a relationship with a best friend.

We can watch ourselves grow beautiful as we shed shame, guilt, resentments, self-hatred, and other negative buildups from our past.

We can watch the quality of our relationships improve with family, friends, and spouses. We find ourselves growing steadily and gradually in our capacity to be intimate and close, to give and receive.

We can watch ourselves grow in our careers, in our ability to be creative, powerful, productive people, using our gifts and talents in a way that feels good and benefits others.

We discover the joy and beauty in ourselves, others, and life.

The long-term progress is steady, but sometimes slow, happening in increments and often with much forward and backward movement. Enough days at a time of practicing recovery behaviors and piling up short-term gains leads to long-term rewards.

Today, I will be grateful for the immediate and long-term rewards of recovery. If I am new to recovery, I will have faith that I can achieve the long-term benefits. If I've been recovering for a while, I will pause to reflect, and be grateful for my overall progress.

The Victim Trap   November 16

The belief that life has to be hard and difficult is the belief that makes a martyr.

We can change our negative beliefs about life, and whether we have the power to stop our pain and take care of ourselves.

We aren't helpless. We can solve our problems. We do have power — not to change or control others, but to solve the problems that are ours to solve.

Using each problem that comes our way to "prove" that life is hard and we are helpless — this is codependency. It's the victim trap.

Life does not have to be difficult. In fact, it can be smooth. Life is good. We don't have to "awfulize" it, or ourselves. We don't have to live on the underside.

We do have power, more power than we know, even in the difficult times. And the difficult times don't prove life is bad; they are part of the ups and downs of life; often, they work out for the best.

We can change our attitude; we can change ourselves; sometimes, we can change our circumstances.

Life is challenging. Sometimes, there's more pain than we asked for; sometimes, there's more joy than we imagined.

It's all part of the package, and the package is good.

We are not victims of life. We can learn to remove ourselves as victims of life. By letting go of our belief that life has to be hard and difficult, we make our life much easier.

Today, God, help me let go of my belief that life is so hard, so awful, or so difficult. Help me replace that belief with a healthier, more realistic view.

Grief and Action   November 17

Trust in God and do something.

— *Mary Lyon*

It's important to let ourselves grieve as a passage between yesterday and tomorrow. But we do not have to be controlled unduly by our grief, or our pain.

There are times when we have grieved, surrendered to the heaviness, tiredness, and weariness of a circumstance long enough. It becomes time to break out. It comes time to take action.

We will know when it's time to break the routine of grieving. There will be signs within and around us. We will become tired of the heaviness. An idea will occur; an opportunity will present itself. We may think: No. Too much effort.... Do it anyway. Try something. Reach out. Stretch. Do something unusual, something different, something special.

A new activity may help trigger the transformation process. Stay up two hours later than usual! Make an appointment to do something for yourself that is different from what you usually do. Visit someone you haven't seen in years. Do something to encourage and help the new energy coming your way.

We may not feel like breaking out of grief. It may feel safer, easier, to remain in our cocoon. Begin pushing out anyway.

Test the walls of your cocoon. Push. Push a little harder. It may be time to emerge.

Today, I will trust God and the process, but I will also take action to help myself feel better.

Allowing Ourselves to be Nurtured   November 18

Let yourself be nurtured and loved. Let people be there for you. Allow yourself to be held when it would feel good. Let someone listen to you, support and encourage you when you need that. Receive comfort from someone's physical presence when you need that. Allow yourself to be supported emotionally and cared about.

For too long, we've stood in the background, attending to the needs of others and claiming we have no needs of our own. We've shut off, for too long, the part of us that longs to be nurtured.

It is time, now, to claim those needs, to identify them, and to understand that we deserve to have them met.

What are our needs? What would feel good? What kinds of ways would we like others to nurture and support us? The more clear we can be about our needs, the greater the possibility they will be met.

Hugs. A listening ear. Support. Encouragement. The physical and emotional presence of people who care about us. Doesn't that sound good? Tempting?

Someone once said to me, "The eighties have been a 'me' decade. Now, maybe the nineties can be a 'you' decade."

My reply was immediate. "Let's make the nineties a 'me' and 'you' decade."

No matter how long we've been recovering, we never outgrow our need for nurturing and love.

Today, I will be open to recognizing my needs for nurturing. I will be open to the needs of those around me too. I can begin taking a nurturing, loving attitude toward myself and by taking responsibility for my needs in relationships.

Accepting Our Feelings   November 19

Why do we struggle so with our feelings? Why do we work so hard to deny our emotions, especially concerning other people? They are *only* feelings!

In the course of a day, we may deny we feel frustrated in reaction to someone who is selling us a service.

We may deny that we feel frustrated, angry, or hurt in reaction to a friend.

We may deny feelings of fear, or anger, toward our children.

We may deny a whole range of feelings toward our spouse or the person with whom we're in a love relationship.

We may deny feelings provoked by people we work for, or by people who work for us.

Sometimes the feelings are a direct reaction to others. Sometimes people trigger something deeper — an old sadness or frustration.

Regardless of the source of our feelings, they are still our feelings. We own them. And acceptance is often all that is necessary to make them go away.

We don't have to let our feelings control our behavior. We don't have to act on each feeling that passes through us. We do not need to indulge in inappropriate behavior.

It does help to talk about our feelings with someone we trust. Sometimes we need to bring our feelings to the person who is triggering them. That can breed intimacy and closeness. But the most important person we need to tell is ourselves. If we allow our feelings to pass through us, accept them, and release them, we shall know what to do next.

Today, I will remember that feelings are an important part of my life. I will be open to my feelings in family life, in friendships, in love, and at work. I will feel my feelings without judging myself.

Wants and Needs   November 20

So many of us have been brainwashed to think that we can't have what we want in life. That is the belief of the martyr. It is born of deprivation and fear.

Identifying what we want and need, then writing it down, sets in motion a powerful chain of events. It indicates that we are taking responsibility for ourselves, giving God and the Universe permission to supply our wants and needs.

The belief that we deserve to have a change in character, a relationship, a new dimension to an existing relationship, a possession, a certain level of health, living, loving, or success, is a powerful force in bringing that desire to pass.

Often, when we realize that we want something, that feeling is God preparing us to receive it!

Listen. Trust. Empower the good in your life by paying attention to what you want and need. Write it down. Affirm it mentally. Pray about it. Then, let it go. Give it to God, and see what happens.

The results may be better than you think.

Today, I will pay attention to what I want and need. I will take time to write it down, then I will let it go. I will begin to believe I deserve the best.

I sat in the car, looking at the sign on the door of the food shelf office: "Closed until Friday." It was Wednesday. I had two hungry children and myself; I had no money.

I laid my head on the steering wheel. I couldn't take it anymore.

I had been so strong, so brave, so trusting for so long. I was a single parent with two children, recently divorced. I had worked so courageously at being grateful for what I had, while setting financial goals and working at believing I deserved the best.

I had put up with so much poverty, so much deprivation. Daily, I worked the Eleventh Step. I worked so hard at praying for knowledge of God's will for me only, and the power to carry it through. I believed I was doing what I needed to do in my life. I wasn't lollygagging. I was doing my best, working my hardest.

And there just wasn't enough money. Life had been a struggle in many ways, but the financial struggle seemed endless.

Money isn't everything, but it takes money to solve certain problems. I was sick of "letting go" and "letting go" and "letting go." I was sick of "acting as if" I had enough money. I was tired of having to work so hard daily at letting go of the pain and fear about not having enough. I was tired of working so hard at being happy without having enough. Actually, most of the time I was happy. I had found my soul in poverty. But now that I had my soul and my self, I wanted some money too.

While I sat in the car trying to compose myself, I heard God speak to me in that silent, still voice that whispers gently to our souls.

"You don't ever have to worry about money again, child. Not unless you want to. I told you that I would take care of you. And I will."

Great, I thought. Thanks a lot. I believe you. I trust you. But look around. I have no money. I have no food. And the food shelf is closed. You've let me down.

Again I heard His voice in my soul: "You don't have to worry about money again. You don't have to be afraid. I promised to meet all your needs."

I went home, called a friend, and asked to borrow some money. I hated borrowing, but I had no choice. My breakdown in the car was a release, but it didn't solve a thing — that day. There was no check in the mailbox.

But I got food for the day. And the next day. And the next. Within six months, my income doubled. Within nine months, it tripled. Since that day, I have had hard times, but I have never had to go without — not for more than a moment in time.

Now, I have enough. Sometimes I still worry about money because that seems to be habitual. But now I know I don't have to, and I know I never did.

God, help me work hard at what I believe is right for me in my life today, and I'll trust You for the rest. Help me let go of my fears about money. Help me turn that area over to You, God. Take away the blocks and barriers in my life to financial success.

The Magic of Gratitude and Acceptance November 22

Gratitude and acceptance are two magic tricks available to us in recovery. No matter who we are, where we are, or what we have, gratitude and acceptance work.

We may eventually become so happy that we realize our present circumstances are good. Or we master our present circumstances and then move forward into the next set of circumstances.

If we become stuck, miserable, feeling trapped and hopeless, try gratitude and acceptance. If we have tried unsuccessfully to alter our present circumstances and have begun to feel like we're beating our head against a brick wall, try gratitude and acceptance.

If we feel like all is dark and the night will never end, try gratitude and acceptance.

If we feel scared and uncertain, try gratitude and acceptance.

If we've tried everything else and nothing seems to work, try gratitude and acceptance.

If we've been fighting something, try gratitude and acceptance.

When all else fails, go back to the basics.

Gratitude and acceptance work.

Today, God, help me let go of my resistance. Help me know the pain of a circumstance will stop hurting so much if I accept it. I will practice the basics of gratitude and acceptance in my life, and for all my present circumstances.

Healthy Sexuality   November 23

Many areas of our life need healing.

One important part of our life is our sexuality. Our feelings and beliefs about our sexuality, our ability to nurture, cherish, and enjoy our sexuality, our ability to respect ourselves sexually, our ability to let go of sexual shame and confusion, may all be impaired or confused by our codependency.

Our sexual energy may be blocked. Or for some of us, sex may be the only way we learned to connect with people. Our sexuality may not be connected to the rest of us; sex may not be connected to love — for ourselves or others.

Some of us were sexually abused as children. Some of us may have gotten involved in sexuality addictive behaviors —

compulsive sexual behaviors that got out of control and produced shame.

Some of us may have gotten involved in sexual codependency: not paying attention to what we wanted, or didn't want, sexually; allowing ourselves to get involved sexually because it was what the other person wanted; shutting off our sexuality along with our other feelings; denying ourselves healthy enjoyment of ourselves as sexual beings.

Our sexuality is a part of ourselves that deserves healing attention and energy. It is a part of us that we can allow to become connected to the whole of us; it is a part of us that we can stop being ashamed of.

It is okay and healthy to allow our sexual energy to open up and become healed. It is connected to our creativity and to our heart. We do not have to allow our sexual energy to control us or our relationships. We can establish and maintain healthy, appropriate boundaries around our sexuality. We can discover what that means in our life.

We can enjoy the gift of being human beings who have been given the gift of sexual energy, without abusing or discounting that gift.

Today, I will begin to integrate my sexuality into the rest of my personality. God, help me let go of my fears and shame around my sexuality. Show me the issues I need to face concerning my sexuality. Help me open myself to healing in that area of my life.

Surrender   November 24

Surrender means saying, "Okay, God. I'll do whatever You want." Faith in the God of our recovery means we trust that, eventually, we'll like doing that.

Today, I will surrender to my Higher Power. I'll trust that God's plan for me will be good, even if it is different than I hoped for or expected.

339

When we first become aware of a problem, a situation, or a feeling, we may react with anxiety or fear. There is no need to fear awareness. No need.

Awareness is the first step toward positive change and growth. It's the first step toward solving the problem, or getting the need met, the first step toward the future. It's how we focus on the next lesson.

Awareness is how life, the Universe, and our Higher Power get our attention and prepare us for change. The process of *becoming changed* begins with awareness. Awareness, acceptance, and change — that's the cycle. We can accept the temporary discomfort from awareness because that's how we're moved to a better place. We can accept the temporary discomfort because we can trust God, and ourselves.

Today, I will be grateful for any awareness I encounter. I will display gratitude, peace, and dignity when life gets my attention. I will remember that it's okay to accept the temporary discomfort from awareness because I can trust that it's my Higher Power moving me forward.

Letting Go of Self-Criticism November 26

Look how far we've come!

It's good to focus on the task ahead, on what remains to be done. It's important to stop and feel pleased about what we've accomplished too.

Yes, it may seem that the change has been slow. At times, change is grueling. Yes, we've taken steps backward. But we're right where we're supposed to be. We're right where we need to be.

And we have come so far.

Sometimes by leaps, sometimes with tiny steps, sometimes kicking and screaming all the while, sometimes with sleeves rolled up and white knuckles, we've learned. Grown. Changed.

Look how far we've come.

Today, I will appreciate my progress. I will let myself feel good about what has been accomplished.

We Can Trust Ourselves   November 27

For many of us, the issue is not whether we can trust another person again; it's whether we can trust our own judgment again.

"The last mistake I made almost cost me my sanity," said one recovering woman who married a sex addict. "I can't afford to make another mistake like that."

Many of us have trusted people who went on to deceive, abuse, manipulate, or otherwise exploit us because we trusted them. We may have found these people charming, kind, decent. There may have been a small voice that said, "No — something's wrong." Or we may have been comfortable with trusting that person and shocked when we found our instincts were wrong.

The issue may then reverberate through our life for years. Our trust in others may have been shaken, but our trust in ourselves may have been shattered worse.

How could something feel so right, flow so good, and be such a total mistake? We may wonder. How can I ever trust my selection process again, when it showed itself to be so faulty?

We may never have the answers. I believe I needed to make certain "mistakes" to learn critical lessons I'm not certain I would have otherwise learned. We cannot let our past interfere with our ability to trust ourselves. We cannot afford to function with fear.

If we are always making the wrong decision in business or in love, we may need to learn why we insist on defeating ourselves.

But most of us do improve. We learn. We grow from our mistakes. Slowly, in increments, our relationships improve. Our business choices improve. Our decisions about how to handle situations with friends or children improve. We benefit from our mistakes. We benefit from our past. And if we have made mistakes, we needed to make them in order to learn along the way.

Today, I will let go of my fears about trusting myself because I have made mistakes in the past. I understand that these fears only serve to impair my judgment today. I will give my past, even my mistakes, validity by accepting and being grateful for it all. I will strive to see what I've gained from my mistakes. I will try to look at all my good decisions too. I will keep a watchful eye for improvement, for overall progress, in my life.

Back to the Steps   November 28

Go back to the Steps. Go back to a Step.

When we don't know what to do next, when we feel confused, upset, distraught, at the end of our rope, overwhelmed, full of self-will, rage, or despair, go back to the Steps.

No matter what situation we are facing, working a Step will help. Focus on one, trust your instincts, and work it.

What does it mean to work a Step? Think about it. Meditate on it. Instead of focusing on the confusion, the problems, or the situation causing our despair or rage, focus on the Step.

Think about how that Step might apply. Hold on to it. Hang on as tightly as we hang on to our confusion or the problem.

The Steps are a solution. They work. We can trust them to work.

We can trust where the Steps will lead us.

When we don't know what step to take next, take one of the Twelve.

Today, I will concentrate on using the Twelve Steps to solve problems and keep me in balance and harmony. I will work a Step to the best of my ability. I will learn to trust the Steps, and rely on them instead of on my protective, codependent behaviors.

Step Twelve   November 29

The Twelfth Step says that having had a spiritual awakening, we try to carry this message to others. Our message is one of hope, love, comfort, health — a better way of life, one that works.

How do we carry it? Not by rescuing. Not by controlling. Not by obsessing. Not by becoming evangelists for the recovery cause.

We carry the message in many small, subtle, but powerful ways. We do our own recovery work and become a living demonstration of hope, self-love, comfort, and health. These quiet behaviors can be a powerful message.

Inviting (not ordering or demanding) someone to go to a meeting is a powerful way to carry the message.

Going to our meetings and sharing how recovery works for us is a powerful way to carry the message.

Being who we are and allowing our Higher Power to guide our actions are powerful ways to carry the message. Often, we find ourselves carrying the message more effectively than we do when we set out to reform, convince, or coerce someone into recovery.

Caretaking and controlling are not ways to carry the message. All those behaviors carry is codependency.

Still, the most powerful form of helping others comes down to helping ourselves. When we do our own work and are honest and open about it, we impact others more than by our most well-intentioned "helping" gesture. We cannot change others, but when we change ourselves, we may end up changing the world.

Today, I will strive to carry the message in ways that work. I will let go of my need to "help" people. Instead, I will concentrate on helping and changing myself. If an opportunity comes up to share my recovery with someone, I will do so quietly. God, help me show others comfort, empowerment, and hope. I can be a channel to help others when I am ready. I do not have to force this; it will happen naturally.

Detachment   November 30

One day, my son brought a gerbil home to live with us. We put it in a cage. Some time later, the gerbil escaped. For the next six months, the animal ran frightened and wild through the house. So did we — chasing it.

"There it is. Get it!" we'd scream, each time someone spotted the gerbil. I, or my son, would throw down whatever we were working on, race across the house, and lunge at the animal hoping to catch it.

I worried about it, even when we didn't see it. "This isn't right," I'd think. "I can't have a gerbil running loose in the house. We've got to catch it. We've got to do *something*."

A small animal, the size of a mouse had the entire household in a tizzy.

One day, while sitting in the living room, I watched the animal scurry across the hallway. In a frenzy, I started to lunge at it, as I usually did, then I stopped myself.

No, I said. I'm all done. If that animal wants to live in the nooks and crannies of this house, I'm going to let it. I'm done worrying about it. I'm done chasing it. It's an irregular circumstance, but that's just the way it's going to have to be.

I let the gerbil run past without reacting. I felt slightly uncomfortable with my new reaction — not reacting — but I stuck to it anyway.

I got more comfortable with my new reaction — not reacting. Before long, I became downright peaceful with the situation. I had stopped fighting the gerbil. One afternoon, only weeks after I started practicing my new attitude, the gerbil ran by me, as it had so many times, and I barely glanced at it. The animal stopped in its tracks, turned around, and looked at me. I started to lunge at it. It started to run away. I relaxed.

"Fine," I said. "Do what you want." And I meant it.

One hour later, the gerbil came and stood by me, and waited. I gently picked it up and placed it in its cage, where it has lived happily ever since. The moral of the story? *Don't lunge at the gerbil.* He's already frightened, and chasing him just scares him more and makes us crazy.

Detachment works.

Today, I will be comfortable with my new reaction — not reacting. I will feel at peace.

December

Letting People Be There for Us

Sometimes, we need nurturing. Sometimes, we need people to support us.

Many of us have been deprived of support and nurturing for so long we may not realize it's something we want and need. Many of us have learned to block or stop ourselves from getting what we want and need.

We may not reach out to have our needs met. We may be in relationships with people who cannot or will not be available to meet our needs. Or we may be in relationships with people who would be happy to respond to a direct request from us.

We may have to give up something to do this. We may have to let go of our martyr or victim role. If we ask for what we want and need, and get those needs met, we will not be able to punish people, or push them away later on, for disappointing us.

We may have to let go of our fears enough to experience the intimacy that will occur when we allow someone to love and support us. We may even have to learn, one day at a time, how to be happy and content.

Learn to let others be there for us.

Today, I will be open to identifying what I need from people, and I will ask for what I want directly. I will let others be there for me.

Putting Our Life on Hold

We cannot afford to put our needs on hold, waiting for another person to fulfill us, make our life better, or come around and be who and what we want that person to be. That will create resentment, hostility, an unhealthy dependency, and a mess to deal with later on.

If we have decided we want a particular relationship or want to wait about making a decision in a particular relationship, then we must go on with our own life in the interim.

That can be hard. It can feel natural to put our life on hold. That is when we get caught up in the codependent beliefs: That person can make me happy. . . . I need that particular person to do a particular thing in order to be happy. . . .

That's a circumstance that can hook our low self-esteem, our self-doubt, and our tendency to neglect ourselves.

We can get into this situation in a number of ways. We can do this waiting for a letter, waiting for a job, waiting for a person, waiting for an event.

We do not have to put our life on hold. There will be repercussions from doing this. Go on with your life. Take life a day at a time.

What is something I could be doing now to take care of myself, make myself feel better, get my needs met in an appropriate, healthy way?

How can I own my power to take care of myself, despite what the other person is or isn't doing?

What will happen if I break the system and begin taking care of myself?

Sometimes, we get the answer we want immediately. Sometimes, we wait for a while. Sometimes, things don't work out exactly the way we hoped. But they always work out for good, and often better than we expected.

And in the meantime, we have manifested love for ourselves by living our own life and taking the control away from others. That always comes back to us tenfold, because when we actually manifest love for ourselves, we give our Higher Power, other people, and the Universe permission to send us the love we want and need.

Stopping living our life to make a thing happen doesn't work. All it does is make us miserable, because we have stopped living our life.

Today, I will force myself, if necessary, to live my own life. I will act in my own best interest, in a way that reflects self-love. If I have given power or control of my life to someone other than myself, and someone besides a Power greater than myself, I will take it back. I will begin acting in my own best interests, even if it feels awkward to do that.

Developing Healthy Tolerance   December 3

Many of us are skilled at denying and discounting what hurts us. We may endure a particular situation, telling ourselves repeatedly it's not that bad; we shouldn't be so demanding; it'll change any day; we should be able to live with it; it doesn't annoy us; the other person didn't really mean it; it doesn't hurt; *maybe it's just us.*

We may fight and argue with ourselves about the reality and validity of our pain — our right to feel it and do something about it.

Often we will tolerate too much or so much that we become furious and refuse to tolerate any more.

We can learn to develop healthy tolerance.

We do that by setting healthy boundaries and trusting ourselves to own our power with people. We can lessen our pain and suffering by validating and paying attention to ourselves. We can work at shortening the time between identifying a need to set a boundary, and taking clear, direct action.

We aren't crazy. Some behaviors really do bug us. Some behaviors really are inappropriate, annoying, hurtful, or abusive.

We don't have to feel guilty about taking care of ourselves once we identify a boundary that needs to be set. Look at the experience as an experiment in owning our power, in establishing new, healthy boundaries and limits for ourselves.

We don't have to feel guilty or apologize or explain ourselves after we've set a boundary. We can learn to accept the awkwardness and discomfort of setting boundaries with people. We can establish our rights to have these limits. We can give the other person room to have and explore his or her feelings; we can give ourselves room to have our feelings — as we struggle to own our power and create good, working relationships.

Once we can trust our ability to take care of ourselves, we will develop healthy reasonable tolerance of others.

God, help me begin striving for healthy boundaries and healthy tolerance for myself and others.

Letting Go   December 4

"How much do we need to let go of?" a friend asked one day.

"I'm not certain," I replied, "but maybe *everything*.''

Letting go is a spiritual, emotional, mental, and physical process, a sometimes *mysterious metaphysical process* of releasing to God and the Universe that which we are clinging to so tightly.

We let go of our grasp on people, outcomes, ideas, feelings, wants, needs, desires — everything. We let go of trying to control our progress in recovery. Yes, it's important to acknowledge and accept what we want and what we want to happen. But it's equally important to follow through by letting go.

Letting go is the action part of faith. It is a behavior that gives God and the Universe permission to send us what we're meant to have.

Letting go means we acknowledge that hanging on so tightly isn't helping to solve the problem, change the person, or get the outcome we desire. It isn't helping *us*. In fact, we learn that hanging on often blocks us from getting what we want and need.

Who are we to say that things aren't happening exactly as they need to happen?

There is magic in letting go. Sometimes we get what we want soon after we let go. Sometimes it takes longer. Sometimes the specific outcome we desire doesn't happen. Something better does.

Letting go sets us free and connects us to our Source.

Letting go creates the optimum environment for the best possible outcomes and solutions.

Today, I will relax. I will let go of that which is upsetting me the most. I will trust that by letting go, I have started the wheels in motion for things to work out in the best possible way.

Difficult People   December 5

Few things can make us feel crazier than expecting something from someone who has nothing to give. Few things can frustrate us more than trying to make a person someone he or she isn't; we feel crazy when we try to pretend that person is someone he or she is not. We may have spent years negotiating with reality concerning particular people from our past and our present. We may have spent years trying to get someone to love us in a certain way, when that person cannot or will not.

It is time to let it go. It is time to let him or her go. That doesn't mean we can't love that person anymore. It means that we will feel the immense relief that comes when we stop denying reality and begin accepting. We release that person to be who he or she actually is. We stop trying to make that person be someone he or she is not. We deal with our feelings and walk away from the destructive system.

We learn to love and care differently in a way that takes reality into account.

We enter into a relationship with that person on new terms — taking ourselves and our needs into account. If a person is addicted to alcohol, other drugs, misery, or other people, we let go of his or her addiction; we take our hands off it. We give his or her life back. And we, in the process, are given our life and freedom in return.

We stop letting what we are not getting from that person control us. We take responsibility for our life. We go ahead with the process of loving and taking care of ourselves.

We decide how we want to interact with that person, taking reality and our own best interests into account. We get angry, we feel hurt, but we land in a place of forgiveness. We set him or her free, and we become set free from bondage.

This is the heart of detaching in love.

Today, I will work at detaching in love from troublesome people in my life. I will strive to accept reality in my relationships. I will give myself permission to take care of myself in my relationships, with emotional, physical, mental, and spiritual freedom for both people as my goal.

Letting Go of Shame   December 6

Many of us were victimized, sometimes more than once. We may have been physically abused, sexually abused, or exploited by the addictions of another.

Understand that if another person has abused us, it is not cause for us to feel shame. The guilt for the act of abuse belongs to the perpetrator, not the victim.

Even if in recovery we fall prey to being victimized, that is not cause for shame.

The goal of recovery is learning self-care, learning to free ourselves from victimization, and not to blame ourselves for past experiences. The goal is to arm ourselves so we do not continue to be victimized due to the shame and unresolved feelings from the original victimization.

We each have our own work, our issues, our recovery tasks. One of those tasks is to stop pointing our finger at the perpetrator, because it distracts us. Although we hold each person responsible and accountable for his or her behavior, we learn compassion for the perpetrator. We understand that many forces have come into play in that person's life. At the same time, we do not hold on to shame.

We learn to understand the role we played in our victimization, how we fell into that role and did not rescue ourselves. But that is information to arm us so that it need not happen again.

Let go of victim shame. We have issues and tasks, but our issue is not to feel guilty and wrong because we have been victimized.

Today, I will set myself free from any victim shame I may be harboring or hanging on to.

When the Time Is Right December 7

There are times when we simply do not know what to do, or where to go, next. Sometimes these periods are brief, sometimes lingering.

We can get through these times. We can rely on our program and the disciplines of recovery. We can cope by using our faith, other people, and our resources.

Accept uncertainty. We do not always *have to* know what to do or where to go next. We do not always have clear direction. Refusing to accept the inaction and limbo makes things worse.

It is okay to temporarily be without direction. Say "I don't know," and be comfortable with that. We do not have to try to force wisdom, knowledge, or clarity when there is none.

While waiting for direction, we do not have to put our life on hold. Let go of anxiety and enjoy life. Relax. Do something fun. Enjoy the love and beauty in your life. Accomplish small tasks. They may have nothing to do with solving the problem, or finding direction, but this is what we can do in the interim.

Clarity will come. The next step will present itself. Indecision, inactivity, and lack of direction will not last forever.

Today, I will accept my circumstances even if I lack direction and insight. I will remember to do things that make myself and others feel good during those times. I will trust that clarity will come of its own accord.

Valuing Our Needs   December 8

When we don't ask for what we want and need, we discount ourselves. We deserve better.

Maybe others taught us it wasn't polite or appropriate to speak up for ourselves. The truth is, if we don't, our unmet wants and needs may ultimately come back to haunt our relationships. We may end up feeling angry or resentful, or we may begin to punish someone else for not guessing what we need. We may end the relationship because it doesn't meet our needs.

Intimacy and closeness are only possible in a relationship when both people can say what they want and need. Sustained intimacy demands this.

Sometimes, we may even have to *demand* what we want. That's called setting a boundary. We do this not to control another person, but to gain control of our life.

Our attitude toward our needs is important too. We must value them and take them seriously if we expect others to take us seriously. When we begin to place value and importance on our needs, we'll see a remarkable change. Our wants and needs will begin to get met.

Today, I will respect the wants and needs of myself and others. I will tell myself, others, and my Higher Power what I want and need. I will listen to what they want and need too.

Asking for Help   December 9

It's okay to ask for help.

One of the most absurd things we do to ourselves is not asking for the help we need from a friend, a family member, our Higher Power, or the appropriate resource.

We don't have to struggle through feelings and problems alone. We can ask for help from our Higher Power and for support and encouragement from our friends.

Whether what we need is information, encouragement, a hand, a word, a hug, someone who will listen, or a ride, we can ask. We can ask people for what we need from them. We can ask God for what we need from God.

It is self-defeating to not ask for the help we need. It keeps us stuck. If we ask long and hard enough, if we direct our request to the right source, we'll get the help we need.

There is a difference between asking someone to rescue us and asking someone in a direct manner for the help we need from him or her. We can be straightforward and let others choose whether to help us or not. If the answer is no, we can deal with that.

It is self-defeating to hint, whine, manipulate, or coerce help out of people. It is annoying to go to people as a victim and expect them to rescue us. It is healthy to ask for help when help is what we need.

"My problem is shame," said one woman. "I wanted to ask for help in dealing with it, but I was too ashamed. Isn't that crazy?"

We who are eager to help others can learn to allow ourselves to receive help. We can learn to make clean contracts about asking for and receiving the help we want and need.

Today, I will ask for help if I need it — from people and my Higher Power. I will not be a victim, helplessly waiting to be rescued. I will make my request for help specific, to the point, and I will leave room for the person to choose whether or not to help me. I will not be a martyr any longer by refusing to get the help I deserve in life — the help that makes life simpler. God, help me let go of my need to do everything alone. Help me use the vast Universe or resources available to me.

Empowerment   December 10

You can think. You can make good decisions. You can make choices that are right for you.

Yes, we all make mistakes from time to time. But we are not mistakes.

We can make a new decision that takes new information into account.

We can change our mind from time to time. That's our right too.

We don't have to be intellectuals to make good choices. In recovery, we have a gift and a goal available to each of us. The gift is called *wisdom*.

Other people can think too. And that means we no longer have to feel responsible for other people's decisions.

That also means we are responsible for our choices.

We can reach out to others for feedback. We can ask for information. We can take opinions into account. But it is our task to make our own decisions. It is our pleasure and right to have our own opinions.

We are each free to embrace and enjoy the treasure of our own mind, intellect, and wisdom.

Today, I will treasure the gift of my mind. I will do my own thinking, make my own choices, and value my opinions. I will be open to what others think, but I will take responsibility for myself. I will ask for and trust that I am being guided by Divine Wisdom.

Affirmations   December 11

One of our choices in recovery is choosing what we want to think — using our mental energy positively.

Positive mental energy, positive thinking, does not mean we think unrealistically or revert to denial. If we don't like something, we respect our own opinion. If we spot a problem, we're honest about it. If something isn't working out, we accept reality. But we don't dwell on the negative parts of our experience.

Whatever we give energy to, we empower.

There is magic in empowering the good, because whatever we empower grows bigger. One way to empower the good is through affirmations: simple positive statements we make to ourselves: *I love myself. . . . I'm good enough. . . . My life is good. . . . I'm glad I'm alive today. . . . What I want and need is coming to me. . . . I can. . . .*

Our choice in recovery is not whether to use affirmations. We've been affirming thoughts and beliefs since we were old enough to speak. The choice in recovery is *what we want to affirm.*

Today, I will empower the good in myself, others, and life. I'm willing to release, or let go of, negative thought patterns and replace them with positive ones. I will choose what I want to affirm, and I will make it good.

God's Will   December 12

Each day, ask God what God wants us to do today; then ask God to help. A simple request, but so profound and far-reaching it can take us anywhere we need to go.

Listen: all that we want, all that we need, all the answers, all the help, all the good, all the love, all the healing, all the wisdom, all the fulfillment of desire is embodied in this simple request. We need say no more than *Thank You.*

This Plan that has been made for us is not one of deprivation. It is one of fullness, joy, and abundance. Walk into it.

See for yourself.

Today, I will ask God to show me what God wants me to do for this day, and then ask for help to do that. I will trust that is sufficient to take me into light and joy.

Giving   December 13

Don't be afraid of giving.

For a while, we may need to back off from giving as we learn to discern the difference between healthy giving and caretaking, which leaves us feeling victimized and others feeling resentful.

This is a temporary spot.

To be healthy, to do our part in this spiritual way of life, to be part of the endless cycle of the Universe, guided by our Creator, we need to give and receive.

Both parts are important.

What is healthy giving?

This is a fine-lined behavior each of us must seek to understand for ourselves. It is giving that feels good and does not leave us feeling victimized.

It is giving that holds the giver and the receiver in high esteem.

It is giving based on a desire to do it rather than from a sense of guilt, pity, shame, or obligation.

It is giving with no strings attached. Or it is giving based on a clean, direct contract.

Whether it is giving of our time, efforts, energy, comfort, nurturing, money, or ourselves, it is giving that we can afford.

Giving is part of the chain of giving and receiving. We can learn to give in healthy ways; we can learn to give in love. We need to keep an eye on our giving, to make sure it has not crossed the line into caretaking. But we need to learn to give in ways that work for us and others.

Today, God, guide me in my giving. Help me give to others in healthy ways. Help me give what feels right, what feels good, what feels clean, and what I can afford.

Clear Thinking   December 14

Strive for clear thinking. Many of us have had our thinking clouded by denial. Some of us have even lost faith in ourselves because we've spent a degree of time in denial. But losing faith in our thinking isn't going to help us. What we need to lose faith in is denial.

We didn't resort to denial — either of someone else's problem or our own — because we were deficient. Denial, the shock-absorber for the soul, protects us until we are equipped to cope with reality.

Clear thinking and recovery don't mean we will never resort to denial. Denial is the first step toward acceptance, and for most of our life, we will be striving to accept something.

Clear thinking means we don't allow ourselves to become immersed in negativity or unrealistic expectations. We stay connected to other recovering people. We go to our meetings, where peace of mind and realistic support are available. We work the Steps, pray, and meditate.

We keep our thinking on track by asking our Higher Power to help us think clearly — not by expecting Him, or someone else, to do our thinking for us.

Today, I will strive for balanced, clear thought in all areas of my life.

Feelings   **December 15**

It's okay to have and feel our feelings — all of them.

Years into recovery, we may still be battling with ourselves about this issue. Of all the prohibitions we've lived with, this one is potentially the most damaging and the most long-lived.

Many of us needed to shut down the emotional part of ourselves to survive certain situations. We shut down the part of us that feels anger, sadness, fear, joy, and love. We may have turned off our sexual or sensual feelings too. Many of us lived in systems with people who refused to tolerate our emotions. We were shamed or reprimanded for expressing feelings, usually by people who were taught to repress their own.

But times have changed. It is okay now for us to acknowledge and accept our emotions. We don't need to allow our emotions to control us; neither do we need to rigidly repress our feelings. Our emotional center is a valuable part of us. It's connected to our physical well-being, our thinking, and our spirituality.

Our feelings are also connected to that great gift, instinct. They enable us to give and receive love.

We are neither weak nor deficient for indulging in our feelings. It means we're becoming healthy and whole.

Today, I will allow myself to recognize and accept whatever feelings pass through me. Without shame, I will tune in to the emotional part of myself.

Taking Care Of Ourselves Emotionally   December 16

What does it mean to take care of myself emotionally? I recognize when I'm feeling angry, and I accept that feeling without shame or blame.

I recognize when I'm feeling hurt, and I accept those feelings without attempting to punish the source of my pain. I recognize and feel fear when that emotion presents itself.

I allow myself to feel happiness, joy, and love when those emotions are available. Taking care of myself means I've made a decision that it's okay to feel.

Taking care of my emotions means I allow myself to stay with the feeling until it's time to release it and go on to the next one.

I recognize that sometimes my feelings can help point me toward reality, but sometimes my feelings are deceptive. They are important, but I do not have to let them control me. I can feel, and think too.

I talk to people about my feelings when that's appropriate and safe.

I reach out for help or guidance if I get stuck in a particular emotion.

I'm open to the lessons my emotions may be trying to teach me. After I feel, accept, and release the feeling, I ask myself what it is I want or need to do to take care of myself.

Taking care of myself emotionally means I value, treasure, explore, and cherish the emotional part of myself.

Today, I will take care of myself emotionally. I will be open to, and accepting of, the emotional part of myself and other people. I will strive for balance by combining emotions with reason, but I will not allow intellect to push the emotional part of myself away.

Nurturing Ourselves   December 17

Many of us have been so deprived of nurturing that we think it's silly or self-indulgent. Nurturing is neither silly nor self-indulgent; it's how we show love for ourselves. That's what we're striving for in recovery — a loving relationship with ourselves that works, so we can have loving relationships with others that work.

When we hurt, we ask ourselves what we need to help us feel better. When we feel alone, we reach out to someone safe. Without feeling that we are a burden, we allow that person to be there for us.

We rest when we're tired; eat when we're hungry; have fun or relax when our spirits need a lift. Nurturing means giving ourselves gifts — a trip to the beauty salon or barber shop, a massage, a book, a new jacket, or a new suit or dress. It means a long, hot bath to forget about our problems and the world for a few moments when that would feel good.

We learn to be gentle with ourselves and to open up to the nurturing that others have to offer us.

As part of nurturing ourselves, we allow ourselves to give and receive positive touch — touch that feels appropriate to us, touch that is safe. We reject touch that doesn't feel good or safe and is not positive.

We learn to give ourselves what we need in a gentle, loving, compassionate way. We do this with the understanding it will not make us lazy, spoiled, self-centered, or narcissistic. Nurtured people are effective in their work and in their relationships.

We will learn to feel loved by ourselves so much that we can truly love others and let them love us.

Today, I will nurture myself. I will also be open to the nurturing that I can give to others and receive from them.

Staying Open to Our Feelings   December 18

Many of us have gotten so good at following the "don't feel" rule that we can try to talk ourselves out of having feelings, even in recovery.

"If I was really working a good program, I wouldn't feel angry."

"I don't get angry. I'm a Christian. I forgive and forget."

"I'm not angry. I'm affirming that I'm happy."

These are all statements, some of them quite clever, that indicate we're operating under the "don't feel" rule again.

Part of working a good program means acknowledging and dealing with our feelings. We strive to accept and deal with our anger so it doesn't harden into resentments. We don't use recovery as an excuse to shut down our emotions.

Yes, we are striving for forgiveness, but we still want to feel, listen to, and stay with our feelings until it is time to release them appropriately. Our Higher Power created the emotional part of ourselves. God is not telling us to not feel; it's our dysfunctional systems.

We also need to be careful how we use affirmations; discounting our emotions won't make feelings go away. If we're angry, it's okay to have that feeling. That's part of how we get and stay healthy.

Today, I will refuse to accept shame from others or myself for feeling my feelings.

How easy it is to dive into roles at work. How easy it is to place other people in roles. Sometimes, this is necessary, appropriate, and expedient.

But we can also let our self shine through our role.

There is joy in giving our gift of skill at work, at giving ourselves to the task at hand so thoroughly that we experience an intimate relationship with our work. There is joy when we create or accomplish a task and can say, "Well done!"

There is also joy when we are our self at work, and when we discover and appreciate those around us.

The most unpleasant, mundane task can be breezed through when we stop thinking of ourselves as a robot and allow ourselves to be a person.

Those around us will respond warmly when we treat them as individuals and not job-defined roles.

This does not mean we need to become inappropriately entangled with others. It means that, whether we are an employer or an employee, when people are allowed to be people who perform tasks instead of task performers, we are happier and more content people.

Today, I will let myself shine through my task at work. I will try to see others and let them shine through too — instead of looking only at their tasks. God, help me be open to the beauty of myself and others at work. Help me maintain healthy relationships with people at work.

Expectations of Others December 20

It is our job to identify our needs, and then determine a balanced way of getting those needs met. We ultimately expect our Higher Power and the Universe — not one particular person — to be our source.

It is unreasonable to expect anyone to be able or willing to meet our every request. We are responsible for asking for what we want and need. It's the other person's responsibility to freely choose whether or not to respond to our request. If we try to coerce or force another to be there for us, that's controlling.

There's a difference between asking and demanding. We want love that is freely given.

It is unreasonable and unhealthy to expect one person to be the source for meeting all our needs. Ultimately, we will become angry and resentful, maybe even punishing, toward that person for not supporting us as we expected.

It is reasonable to have certain and well-defined expectations of our spouse, children, and friends.

If a person cannot or will not be there for us, then we need to take responsibility for ourselves in that relationship. We may need to set a boundary, alter our expectations, or change the limits of the relationship to accommodate that person's unavailability. We do this for ourselves.

It is reasonable to sprinkle our wants and needs around and to be realistic about how much we ask or expect of any particular person. We can trust ourselves to know what's reasonable.

The issue of expectations goes back to knowing that we are responsible for identifying our needs, believing they deserve to get met, and discover an appropriate, satisfactory way to do that in our life.

Today, I will strive for reasonable expectations about getting my needs met in relationships.

Balance   December 21

Strive for balanced expectations of others. Strive for healthy tolerance.

In the past, we may have tolerated too much or too little. We may have expected too much or too little.

We may swing from tolerating abuse, mistreatment, and deception to refusing to tolerate normal, human, imperfect behaviors from people. Although it's preferable not to remain in either extreme too long, that is how people change — real people who struggle imperfectly toward better lives, improved relationships, and more effective relationship behaviors.

But if we are open to ourselves and to the recovery process, we will, at some time, begin another transition: it becomes time to move away from extremes, toward balance.

We can trust ourselves and the recovery process to bring us to a balanced place of tolerance, giving, understanding, and expectations — of ourselves and others.

We can each find our own path to balance as we begin and continue recovery.

Today, I will practice acceptance with myself and others for the way we change. If I have had to swing to the other extreme of a behavior, I will accept that as appropriate, for a time. But I will make my goal one of balanced tolerance and expectations of myself and others.

Good Things Coming   December 22

Do not worry about how the good that has been planned for you will come.

It will come.

Do not worry, obsess, think you have to control it, go out hunting for it, or tangle your mind trying to figure out how and when it will find you.

It will find you.

Surrender to your Higher Power each day. Trust your Higher Power. Then, stay peaceful. Trust and listen to yourself. That is how the good you want will come to you.

Your healing. Your joy. Your relationships. Your solutions. That job. That desired change. That opportunity. It will come to you — naturally, with ease, and in a host of ways.

That answer will come. The direction will come. The money. The idea. The energy. The creativity. The path will open itself to you. Trust that, for it has already been planned.

It is futile, a waste and drain of energy, to worry about how it will come. It is already there. You have it already. It is in place. You just cannot see it!

You will be brought to it, or it will be brought to you.

Today, I will relax and trust that the good I need will find me. Either through my leadings, or the leadings of others, all I want and need will come to me when the time is right.

Holiday Triggers   **December 23**

One year, when I was a child, my father got drunk and violent at Christmas. I had just unwrapped a present, a bottle of hand lotion, when he exploded in an alcoholic rage. Our Christmas was disrupted. It was terrible. It was frightening for the whole family. Now, thirty-five years later, whenever I smell hand lotion, I immediately feel all the feelings I did that Christmas: the fear, the disappointment, the heartache, the helplessness, and an instinctive desire to control.
— Anonymous

There are many positive triggers that remind us of Christmas: snow, decorations, "Silent Night," "Jingle Bells," wrapped packages, a nativity scene, stockings hung on a fireplace. These "triggers" can evoke in us the warm, nostalgic feelings of the Christmas celebration.

There are other kinds of triggers, though, that may be less apparent and evoke different feelings and memories.

Our mind is like a powerful computer. It links sight, sound, smell, touch, and taste with feelings, thoughts, and memories. It links our senses — and we remember.

Sometimes the smallest, most innocuous incident can trigger memories. Not all our memories are pleasant, especially if we grew up in an alcoholic, dysfunctional setting.

We may not understand why we suddenly feel afraid, depressed, anxious. We may not understand what has triggered our codependent coping behaviors — the low self-worth, the need to control, the need to neglect ourselves. When that happens, we need to understand that some innocuous event may be triggering memories recorded deep within us.

If something, even something we don't understand, triggers painful memories, we can pull ourselves back into the present by self-care: acknowledging our feelings, detaching, working the Steps, and affirming ourselves. We can take action to feel good. We can help ourselves feel better each Christmas. No matter what the past held, we can put it in perspective, and create a more pleasant holiday today.

Today, I will gently work through my memories of this holiday season. I will accept my feelings, even if I consider them different than what others are feeling this holiday. God, help me let go, heal from, and release the painful memories surrounding the holidays. Help me finish my business from the past, so I can create the holiday of my choice.

Getting Through the Holidays   December 24

For some, the sights, signs, and smells of the holidays bring joy and a warm feeling. But, while others are joyously diving into the season, some of us are dipping into conflict, guilt, and a sense of loss.

369

We read articles on how to enjoy the holidays, we read about the Christmas blues, but many of us still can't figure out how to get through the holiday season. We may not know what a joyous holiday would look and feel like.

Many of us are torn between what we *want* to do on the holiday, and what we feel we *have* to do. We may feel guilty because we don't want to be with our families. We may feel a sense of loss because we don't have the kind of family to be with that we want. Many of us, year after year, walk into the same dining room on the same holiday, expecting this year to be different. Then we leave, year after year, feeling let down, disappointed, and confused by it all.

Many of us have old, painful memories triggered by the holidays.

Many of us feel a great deal of relief when the holiday is ended.

One of the greatest gifts of recovery is learning that we are not alone. There are probably as many of us in conflict during the holidays than there are those who feel at peace. We're learning, through trial and error, how to take care of ourselves a little better each holiday season.

Our first recovery task during the holidays is to accept ourselves, our situation, and our feelings about our situation. We accept our guilt, anger, and sense of loss. It's all okay.

There is no right or perfect way to handle the holidays. Our strength can be found in doing the best we can, one year at a time.

This holiday season, I will give myself permission to take care of myself.

The Holidays   December 25

Sometimes, the nolidays are filled with the joy we associate with that time of year. The season flows. Magic is in the air.

Sometimes, the holidays can be difficult and lonely.

Here are some ideas I've learned through personal experience, and practice, to help us get through difficult holidays:

Deal with feelings, but try not to dwell unduly on them. Put the holidays in perspective: A holiday is one day out of 365. We can get through any 24-hour period

Get through the day, but be aware that there may be a post-holiday backlash. Sometimes, if we use our survival behaviors to get through the day, the feelings will catch up to us the next day. Deal with them too. Get back on track as quickly as possible.

Find and cherish the love that's available, even if it's not exactly what we want. Is there someone we can give love to and receive love from? Recovering friends? Is there a family who would enjoy sharing their holiday with us? Don't be a martyr; go. There may be those who would appreciate our offer to share our day with them.

We are not in the minority if we find ourselves experiencing a less-than-ideal holiday. How easy, but untrue, to tell ourselves the rest of the world is experiencing the perfect holiday, and we're alone in conflict.

We can create our own holiday agenda. Buy yourself a present. Find someone to whom you can give. Unleash your loving, nurturing self and give in to the holiday spirit.

Maybe past holidays haven't been terrific. Maybe this year wasn't terrific. But next year can be better, and the next a little better. Work toward a better life — one that meets your needs. Before long, you'll have it.

God, help me enjoy and cherish this holiday. If my situation is less than ideal, help me take what's good and let go of the rest.

Just as when we were children and grew out of favorite toys and clothes, we sometimes grow out of things as adults — people, jobs, homes. This can be confusing. We may wonder why someone or something that was so special and important to us last year doesn't fit the same way in our life today. We may wonder why our feelings have changed.

When we were children, we may have tried to fit into an outgrown article of clothing on to our body. Now, as adults, we may go through a time of trying to force-fit attitudes that we have outgrown. We may need to do this to give ourselves time to realize the truth. What worked last year, what was so important and special to us in times past, doesn't work anymore because we've changed. We've grown.

We can accept this as a valid and important part of recovery. We can let ourselves go through experimentation and grief as we struggle to make something fit, trying to figure out if indeed it no longer fits, and why. We can explore our feelings and thoughts around what has happened.

Then, we can put last year's toys away and make room for the new.

Today, I will let last year's toys be what they were: last year's toys. I will remember them with fondness for the part they played in my life. Then, I will put them away and make room for the new.

Near the Top   December 27

I know you're tired. I know you feel overwhelmed. You may feel as though this crisis, this problem, this hard time will last forever.

It won't. You are almost through.

You don't just *think* it has been hard; it has been hard. You have been tested, tried, and retested on what you have learned.

Your beliefs and your faith have been tried in fire. You have believed, then doubted, then worked at believing some more. You have had to have faith even when you could not see or imagine what you were asked to believe. Others around you may have tried to convince you not to believe in what you were hoping you could believe.

You have had opposition. You have not gotten to this place with total support and joy. You have had to work hard, in spite of what was happening around you. Sometimes, what motivated you was anger; sometimes fear.

Things went wrong — more problems occurred than you anticipated. There were obstacles, frustrations, and annoyances en route. You did not plan on this being the way it would evolve. Much of this has been a surprise; some of it has not been at all what you desired.

Yet, it has been good. Part of you, the deepest part that knows truth, has sensed this all along, even when your head told you that things were out of whack and crazy, that there was no plan or purpose, that God had forgotten you.

So much has happened, and each incident — the most painful, the most troubling, the most surprising — has a connection. You are beginning to see and sense that.

You never dreamt things would happen this way, did you? But they did. Now you are learning the secret — they were meant to happen this way, and this way is good, better than what you expected.

You didn't believe it would take this long, either — did you? But it did. You have learned patience.

You never thought you could have it, but now you know you do.

You have been led. Many were the moments when you thought you were forgotten, when you were convinced you had been abandoned. Now you know you have been guided.

Now things are coming into place. You are almost at the end of this phase, this difficult portion of the journey. The lesson is almost complete. You know — the lesson you fought, resisted, and insisted you could not learn. Yes, that one. You have almost mastered it.

You have been changed from the inside out. You have been moved to a different level, a higher level, a better level.

You have been climbing a mountain. It has not been easy, but mountain climbing is never easy. Now, you are near the top. A moment longer, and the victory shall be yours.

Steady your shoulders. Breathe deeply. Move forward in confidence and peace. The time is coming to relish and enjoy all which you have fought for. That time is drawing near, finally.

I know you have thought before that the time was drawing near, only to learn that it wasn't. But now, the reward *is* coming. You know that too. You can feel it.

Your struggle has not been in vain. For every struggle on this journey, there is a climax, a resolution.

Peace, joy, abundant blessings, and reward are yours here on earth. Enjoy.

There will be more mountains, but now you know how to climb them. And you have learned the secret of what is at the top.

Today, I will accept where I am and continue pushing forward. If I am in the midst of a learning experience, I will allow myself to continue on with the faith that the day of mastery and reward will come. Help me, God, understand that despite my best efforts to live in peaceful serenity, there are times of mountain climbing. Help me stop creating chaos and crisis, and help me meet the challenges that will move me upward and forward.

Don't panic!

If panic strikes, we do not have to allow it to control our behaviors. Behaviors controlled by panic tend to be self-defeating. No matter what the situation or circumstance, panic is usually not a good foundation. No matter what the situation or circumstance, we usually have at least a moment to breathe deeply and restore our serenity and peace.

We don't have to do more than we can reasonably do — ever! We don't have to do something we absolutely cannot do or cannot learn to do!

This program, this healthy way of life we are seeking, is built on a foundation of peace and quiet confidence — in ourselves, in our Higher Power, in the recovery *process.*

Do not panic. That takes us away from the path. Relax. Breathe deeply. Let peace flow through our body and mind. From this base, our Source shall supply the necessary resources.

Today, I will treat panic as a separate issue that needs immediate attention. I will refuse to allow panicky thoughts and feelings to motivate me. Instead, I will let peace and trust motivate my feelings, thoughts, and behaviors.

Moving On   **December 29**

Learn the art of acceptance. It's a lot of grief.
                              — Codependent No More

Sometimes, as part of taking care of ourselves, it becomes time to end certain relationships. Sometimes, it comes time to change the parameters of a particular relationship.

This is true in love, in friendships, with family, and on the job.

Endings and changes in relationships are not easy. But often, they are necessary.

Sometimes, we linger in relationships that are dead, out of fear of being alone or to postpone the inevitable grieving process that accompanies endings. Sometimes, we need to linger for a while, to prepare ourselves, to get strong and ready enough to handle the change.

If that is what we are doing, we can be gentle with ourselves. It is better to wait until that moment when it feels solid, clear, and consistent to act.

We will know. We *will* know. We can trust ourselves.

Knowing that a relationship is changing or is about to end is a difficult place to be in, especially when it is not yet time to act but we know the time is drawing near. It can be awkward and uncomfortable, as the lesson draws to a close. We may become impatient to put closure on it, but not yet feel empowered to do that. That's okay. The time is not yet right. Something important is still happening. When the time is right, we can trust that it will happen. We will receive the power and the ability to do what we need to do.

Ending relationships or changing the boundaries of a particular relationship is not easy. It requires courage and faith. It requires a willingness on our part to take care of ourselves and, sometimes, to stand alone for a while.

Let go of fear. Understand that change is an important part of recovery. Love yourself enough to do what you need to do to take care of yourself, and find enough confidence to believe that you will love again.

We are *never* starting over. In recovery, we are moving forward in a perfectly planned progression of lessons. We will find ourselves with certain people — in love, family, friendships, and work — when we need to be with them. When the lesson has been mastered, we will move on. We will find ourselves in a new place, learning new lessons, with new people.

No, the lessons are not all painful. We will arrive at that place where we can learn, not from pain, but from joy and love.

Our needs will get met.

Today, I will accept where I am in my relationships, even if that place is awkward and uncomfortable. If I am in the midst of endings, I will face and accept my grief. God, help me trust that the path I am on has been perfectly and lovingly planned for me. Help me believe that my relationships are teaching me important lessons. Help me accept and be grateful for middles, endings, and new beginnings.

Laying the Foundation   December 30

The groundwork has been laid.

Do you not see that?

Don't you understand that all you have gone through was for a purpose?

There was a reason, a good reason, for the waiting, the struggle, the pain, and finally the release.

You have been prepared. The same way a builder must first tear down and dig out the old to make way for the new, your Higher Power has been cleaning out the foundation in your life.

Have you ever watched a builder at construction? When he begins his work, it looks worse than before he began. What is old and decayed must be removed. What is insufficient or too weak to support the new structure must be removed, replaced, or reinforced. No builder who cares about his or her work would put a new surface over an insufficient support system. The foundation would give way. It would not last.

If the finished product is to be what is desired, the work must be done thoroughly from the bottom up. As the work progresses, it often appears to be an upheaval. Often, it does not seem to make sense. It may appear to be wasted time and effort, because we cannot see the final product yet.

But it is so important that the foundation be laid properly if the fun work, the finishing touches, is to be all that we want it to be.

This long, hard time in your life has been for laying of groundwork. It was not without purpose, although at times the purpose may not have been evident or apparent.

Now, the foundation has been laid. The structure is solid.

Now, it is time for the finishing touches, the completion.

It is time to move the furniture in and enjoy the fruits of the labor.

Congratulations. You have had the patience to endure the hard parts. You have trusted, surrendered, and allowed your Higher Power and the Universe to heal and prepare you.

Now, you shall enjoy the good that has been planned.

Now, you shall see the purpose.

Now, it shall all come together and make sense.

Enjoy.

Today, I will surrender to the laying of the foundation — the groundwork — in my life. If it is time to enjoy the placement of the finishing touches, I will surrender to that, and enjoy that too. I will remember to be grateful for a Higher Power that is a Master Builder and only has my best interests in mind, creating and constructing my life. I will be grateful for my Higher Power's care and attention to details in laying the foundation — even though I become impatient at times. I will stand in awe at the beauty of God's finished product.

*Fun becomes fun, love becomes love, life becomes worth liv-
ing. And we become grateful.*
                                        — Beyond Codependency

Wait, and expect good things — for yourself and your loved
ones.

When you wonder what is coming, tell yourself the best
is coming, the very best life and love have to offer, the best
God and His universe have to send. Then open your hands
to receive it. Claim it, and it is yours.

See the best in your mind; envision what it will look like,
what it will feel like. Focus, until you can see it clearly. Let
your whole being, body and soul, enter into and hold onto
the image for a moment.

Then, let it go. Come back into today, the present moment.
Do not obsess. Do not become fearful. Become excited. Live
today fully, expressing gratitude for all you have been, all
you are, and all you will become.

Wait, and expect good things.

*Today, when I think about the year ahead, I will focus on the good
that is coming.*

INDEX

A

Acceptance — Feb. 17, Apr. 3, Oct. 29
Accepting Change — Apr. 19, June 30
Accepting Help — Jan. 5
Accepting Imperfection — Feb. 25
Accepting Our Best — Aug. 30
Accepting Ourselves — Mar. 3
Acting As If — Jan. 17
Affirmations — Dec. 11
Affirming the Good — Dec. 31
After-burn — Mar. 27
Amends, Making — Aug. 26
Amends, Willing to Make — Aug. 25
Anger — Nov. 4
Anger at Family Members — Apr. 28
Anger, Accepting — Jan. 14
Anger, Letting Out — Nov. 14
Apologies — Sept. 19
Appreciating Our Past — Jan. 22
Appreciating Ourselves — Mar. 24
Asking for What We Need — Jan. 31, Aug. 9
Awareness — Nov. 25

B

Balance — Mar. 28, Apr. 30, Dec. 21
Balance, Finding — Jan. 12
Be Who You Are — Mar. 5, Oct. 1
Being Honest with Ourselves — Oct. 16
Being Is Enough — July 21
Being Right — Feb. 18
Beliefs About Money — Nov. 10

Boundaries — May 17
Boundaries, Flack from Setting — Mar. 23
Bring Any Request to God — July 11

C

Celebrate — July 4
Charity — June 3
Clarity — Oct. 26
Clarity and Direction — Mar. 13
Clear Thinking — Dec. 14
Clearing the Slate — Jan. 24
Commitment — May 30
Commitment, Considering — Mar. 21
Communication — Apr. 15
Compulsive Disorders, Freedom from — May 4
Conflict and Detachment — Sept. 11
Conflicts, Negotiating — Apr. 4
Control — Feb. 15, May 5
Controlling Versus Trust — Oct. 14
Coping with Stress — Apr. 22

D

Deadlines - Apr. 20
Denial — July 24, Aug. 31, Nov. 3
Detaching in Love — Apr. 5
Detaching in Relationships — Aug. 21
Detaching with Love — Oct. 20
Detaching with Love with Children — Sept. 2
Detachment — Feb. 16, June 24, Nov. 30
Detachment, Conflict and — Sept. 11
Difficult People — Dec. 5
Directness — June 1, July 3, Aug. 12
Discipline — Nov. 11
Divinely Led — Feb. 11

E

Empowerment — Mar. 17, Dec. 10
Enjoying Life — Nov. 6
Enjoying Recovery — Feb. 4
Enjoying the Good Days — May 10
Enjoyment — Apr. 13, May 23
Expectations of Others — Dec. 20
Experiment — Mar. 30

F

Facing Our Darker Side — Apr. 2
Faith and Money — Oct. 4
Families, Coping with — Oct. 2
Families, Living with — Mar. 10
Family Buttons — July 15
Family Issues, Separating from — Jan. 4
Family Members, Responsibility for — Aug. 22
Fear — Jan. 10, July 28
Feeling Good - May 6, June 16
Feelings — Dec. 15
Feelings, Accepting Our — Nov. 19
Feelings, Dealing with Painful — Jan. 7
Feelings, Good — Jan. 13
Feelings, Leaving Room for — Aug. 15
Feelings, On the Job — Mar. 2
Feelings, Recognizing — Feb. 24
Feelings, Staying Open to Our — Dec. 18
Feelings, Those Old-Time — Apr. 7
Finances — Mar. 31
Financial Fears — Nov. 21
Financial Goals — Apr. 11
Financial Responsibility — Feb. 5, Oct. 21
Finding Direction — Sept. 4
Foundation, Laying the — Dec. 30
Freedom — Apr. 18

Friends — Aug. 13
Fulfillment — Mar. 7
Fun — June 8
Fun, Have Some — July 29

G
Getting It All Out — July 7
Getting Needs Met — Mar. 29, May 21
Getting Through Discomfort — Oct. 3
Getting Through Hard Times — Sept. 15
Gifts, Not Burdens — Mar. 26
Giving — Apr. 9, Dec. 13
Giving Ourselves What We Deserve — May 8
God As We Understand God — July 13
God's Will — June 29, Dec. 12
Going Easy — Apr. 1
Going with the Flow — July 8
Good Feelings — June 21
Good Points, Our — Oct. 19
Good Things Coming — Dec. 22
Gossip — May 26
Gratitude — Jan. 18, Aug. 1
Gratitude and Acceptance, the Magic of — Nov. 22
Grief and Action — Nov. 17
Grief Process, The — Nov. 2, Dec. 6
Grief, Being Gentle with Ourselves During Times of —
    Oct. 12
Grief, Transformation Through — Nov. 1
Growth — Dec. 26

H
Harmony, Achieving — June 27
Healing — Aug. 11, Sept. 12
Healing Thoughts — Aug. 17
Healthy Limits — Jan. 2

384

Healthy Tolerance, Developing — Dec. 3
Help, Asking for — Dec. 9
Higher Power as a Source — Mar. 4
Higher Power, Our — May 2
Holding Your Own — Oct. 22
Holiday Triggers — Dec. 23
Holidays, Getting Through the — Dec. 24
Holidays, The — Dec. 25
Honesty — May 14
Honesty in Relationships — Aug. 20

I
In-Between — Aug. 2
Insisting on the Best — July 16
Intimacy — May 12
Into Orbit — June 7

J
Job, Taking Care of Ourselves on the — Aug. 28

K
Keep at It — July 25
Knowledge — Oct. 5

L
Learning New Behaviors — May 9
Learning to Trust Again — July 22
Learning to Wait — Oct. 8
Lessons on the Job — Apr. 24
Let's Make a Deal — Nov. 5
Letting Go — Jan. 4, July 27, Dec. 4
Letting Go in Love — Feb. 9
Letting Go of Anger — Mar. 1
Letting Go of Being a Victim — Mar. 22
Letting Go of Chaos — Oct. 15

Letting Go of Confusion — Mar. 11
Letting Go of Denial — Feb. 28
Letting Go of Fear — Apr. 12, May 7
Letting Go of Fear of Abandonment — July 12
Letting Go of Guilt — Jan. 11, Feb. 8
Letting Go of Naiveté — Oct. 7
Letting Go of Need to Control — Apr. 27
Letting Go of Old Beliefs — June 23
Letting Go of Perfection — Aug. 10
Letting Go of Resistance — July 20
Letting Go of Sadness — Feb. 10
Letting Go of Self-Criticism — Aug. 16, Nov. 26
Letting Go of Self-Doubt — May 28
Letting Go of Shame — Aug. 19, Dec. 6
Letting Go of the Past — Oct. 25
Letting Go of Those Not in Recovery — Feb. 12
Letting Go of Timing — June 14
Letting Go of Urgency — Sept. 21
Letting Go of What We Want — July 31
Letting Go of Worry — Mar. 25
Letting People Be There for Us — Dec. 1
Letting the Cycles Flow — May 24
Letting the Good Stuff Happen — Sept. 18
Letting Things Happen — Apr. 16
Life, Putting Ours on Hold — Dec. 2
Living in the Present — Feb. 21
Living Our Lives — May 18
Love, Accepting — Nov. 9
Love, in Words and Actions — July 17
Love, Opening Ourselves to — Apr. 23, Oct. 24
Loving Ourselves Unconditionally — May 25

M

Making It Happen — July 23
Making Life Easier — June 19

Martyrs, Competition Between — June 15
Meditation and Prayer — Oct. 28
Meetings, Going to — Jan. 29
Middle, Staying Out of the — Mar. 19
Money, Attitudes Toward — Aug. 5
Money, The Importance of — Sept. 29
Morning Cues — Oct. 23
Moving Forward — June 11
Moving On — Dec. 29

N
Near the Top — Dec. 27
Needing People — Jan. 27
Needs, All Our — Oct. 31
Needy, Allowing Ourselves to Be — Sept. 24
New Beginnings — Jan. 20
New Energy Coming — Jan. 23
New Relationship Behaviors — Sept. 17
New Year, The — Jan. 1
Nurtured, Allowing Ourselves to Be — Nov. 18
Nurturing Ourselves — Dec. 17
Nurturing Self-Care — Jan. 3

O
Off the Hook — Jan. 26
Our Path — Feb. 19
Overspending and Underspending — July 9
Owning Our Energy — Aug. 29

P
Pain, Stopping Our — Sept. 8
Pain, Using Others to Stop Our — Apr. 10
Panic — June 9, Dec. 28
Past, Peace with the — Sept. 25
Patience — Apr. 6, Sept. 1

Payoffs from Destructive Relationships — Oct. 10
Peace — Mar. 6
People-Pleasers — Feb. 27
Perfection — May 11
Perfection, Letting Go of — Aug. 10
Perfectionism — Apr. 14
Perspective — Sept. 9
Positive Energy — Mar. 16
Power, Owning Our — Jan. 19, Feb. 7, June 2, July 26, Aug. 14
Power, Owning in Relationships — Aug. 3
Powerless over Others — Sept. 7
Powerlessness, Accepting — July 30
Powerlessness and Unmanageability — May 29
Prayer — Jan. 16, Sept. 28
Procrastination - Aug. 27
Property Lines — May 13
Protected, Feeling — Sept. 26
Proving It to Ourselves — July 19

R
Readiness, The Gift of — June 6
Receiving — July 1
Recognizing Choices — May 27
Recovery — Oct. 11
Recovery, Benefits of — Nov. 15
Recovery, Enjoying — Feb. 4
Recovery Prayer — May 1
Relationship Martyrs — June 20
Relationships — Jan. 6, Nov. 7
Relationships, Detaching in — Aug. 21
Relationships, Ending — July 10
Relationships, Hanging on to Old — June 13
Relationships, Honesty in — Aug. 20
Relationships, Initiating — Apr. 29
Releasing — Mar. 20

Religious Freedom — Jan. 30
Removing the Victim — Mar. 15
Reprogramming, Times of — May 22, Sept. 13
Rescuing Ourselves — Aug. 16
Resisting Negativity — Apr. 26
Responsibility — June 10
Responsibility for Ourselves — Jan. 9
Revenge — Sept. 16
Risks, Take — May 15

S

Sadness — May 20
Safety — Mar. 18
Saying No — Aug. 7
Saying Yes — Aug. 8
Self-Approval — Sept. 10
Self-Care — Apr. 8, Aug. 23
Self-Disclosure — Oct. 9
Self-Love — May 16
Self-Seeking, Freedom from — May 3
Self-Value — Oct. 30
Setbacks, Temporary — Sept. 27
Setting Our Own Course — Feb. 20
Sexuality, Healthy — Nov. 23
Shame, Combating — June 5
Shame, Rejecting — Feb. 3
Solving Problems — Feb. 22, May 19, Aug. 6
Spontaneity — Sept. 20
Spontaneity and Fun — June 12
Standing Up for Ourselves — Jan. 15
Staying in the Present Moment — Jan. 28
Step Eight — Aug. 24
Step Eleven — Oct. 27
Step One — Jan. 25
Step Seven — July 6

Step Ten — Sept. 5
Step Ten, The Good in — Sept. 6
Step Twelve — Nov. 29
Step Two — Feb. 1
Steps, Back to the — Nov. 28
Strength — Feb. 23
Substance over Form — Oct. 13
Surrender — Mar. 8, June 17, Nov. 24
Surrender, Feelings and — Oct. 17
Surviving Slumps — June 26
Survivor Guilt — July 5

T
Taking Care of Ourselves — Mar. 9, Apr. 17, Oct. 6, Nov. 13
Taking Care of Ourselves Emotionally — Dec. 16
Throwing Out the Rule Book — Oct. 18
Time to Get Angry — July 18
Time, When It's Right — Dec. 7
Timing — Mar. 12, Nov. 12
Tolerance — Sept. 23, Dec. 3
True to Ourselves — Nov. 8
Trusting God — June 4
Trusting Our Higher Power — Feb. 2
Trusting Ourselves — Feb. 13, Mar. 14, Sept. 22, Nov. 27
Truth, Finding Our Own — Apr. 25
Twelve Step Programs — Feb. 26

V
Valentine's Day — Feb. 14
Valuing Our Needs — Dec. 8
Valuing this Moment — Aug. 18
Victim, Not a — Sept. 30
Victim Trap, The — Nov. 16

Victimization, Stopping — Feb. 6
Vulnerability — Jan. 8, Aug. 4
Vulnerable — June 18

W
Waiting — Apr. 21
Wants and Needs — Jan. 21, Nov. 20
Warning Signs — July 30
We Are Lovable — July 14
What If? — May 31
What We Want, Coming to Terms with — July 10
What's Good for Me? — Sept. 14
When Things Don't Work — June 28
Who Knows Best? — July 2
Withholding — June 25
Word Power — Sept. 3
Work Histories — June 22
Work Roles — Dec. 19

Y
You Are Lovable — Feb. 29

THE TWELVE STEPS
OF ALCOHOLICS ANONYMOUS*

1. We admitted we were powerless over alcohol — that our lives had become unmanageable.
2. Came to believe that a Power greater than ourselves could restore us to sanity.
3. Made a decision to turn our will and our lives over to the care of God *as we understood Him.*
4. Made a searching and fearless moral inventory of ourselves.
5. Admitted to God, to ourselves, and to another human being the exact nature of our wrongs.
6. Were entirely ready to have God remove all these defects of character.
7. Humbly asked Him to remove our shortcomings.
8. Made a list of all persons we had harmed, and became willing to make amends to them all.
9. Made direct amends to such people wherever possible, except when to do so would injure them or others.
10. Continued to take personal inventory and when we were wrong promptly admitted it.
11. Sought through prayer and meditation to improve our conscious contact with God *as we understood Him,* praying only for knowledge of His will for us and the power to carry that out.
12. Having had a spiritual awakening as the result of these steps, we tried to carry this message to alcoholics, and to practice these principles in all our affairs.

---

*The Twelve Steps of A.A. are taken from *Alcoholics Anonymous*, 3rd ed., published by A.A. World Services, Inc., New York, N.Y., 59-60. Reprinted with permission of A.A. World Services, Inc.

THE TWELVE STEPS OF AL-ANON*

1. We admitted we were powerless over alcohol — that our lives had become unmanageable.
2. Came to believe that a Power greater than ourselves could restore us to sanity.
3. Made a decision to turn our will and our lives over to the care of God *as we understood Him.*
4. Made a searching and fearless moral inventory of ourselves.
5. Admitted to God, to ourselves, and to another human being the exact nature of our wrongs.
6. Were entirely ready to have God remove all these defects of character.
7. Humbly asked Him to remove our shortcomings.
8. Made a list of all persons we had harmed, and became willing to make amends to them all.
9. Made direct amends to such people wherever possible, except when to do so would injure them or others.
10. Continued to take personal inventory and when we were wrong promptly admitted it.
11. Sought through prayer and meditation to improve our conscious contact with God *as we understood Him*, praying only for knowledge of His will for us and the power to carry that out.
12. Having had a spiritual awakening as the result of these steps, we tried to carry this message to others, and to practice these principles in all our affairs.

---

*The Twelve Steps of Al-Anon are taken from *Al-Anon Faces Alcoholism,* 2nd ed., published by Al-Anon Family Group Headquarters, Inc., New York, N.Y., 236-37. The Twelve Steps of Al-Anon are copyrighted by Al-Anon Family Group Headquarters, Inc. They are reprinted here with the permission of Al-Anon Family Group Headquarters, Inc., and A.A. World Services, Inc.